GREED, FRAUD
& CORRUPTION

Samuel A. Malone

2000

First published in 2008 by Management Books 2000 Ltd
Forge House, Limes Road
Kemble, Cirencester
Gloucestershire, GL7 6AD, UK
Tel: 0044 (0) 1285 771441
Fax: 0044 (0) 1285 771055
Email: info@mb2000.com
Web: www.mb2000.com

British Library Cataloguing in Publication Data is available

ISBN 9781852525774

Printed and bound by:
Digital Book Print Ltd
www.digitalbookprint.com

Contents

Preface

This book is aimed at those who have the responsibility for ensuring that good ethics are established and maintained within their organisation.

Large organisations may have a specialist ethics manager position but in most organisations this responsibility is likely to fall on the HRM manager.

Trainers will find it a useful source of ideas for designing training programmes in business ethics.

Senior management teams will find the book a useful reminder of their corporate ethical responsibility. After all, they are ultimately accountable for the ethics practised in a company.

Board members will find the chapter on Corporate Governance a useful guide.

More employees are now involved in decision-making because of empowerment and decentralisation. This book will remind employees of their ethical responsibilities. Indeed surveys show that lapses in ethical standards are prevalent in all functions and ranks within a company including managers, supervisors and employees.

Most business degree programmes including MBAs and diplomas have an ethics component. Professionals and students studying business ethics will find that this book will give them a good practical insight into the business world, how ethical lapses occur and what can be done to counteract them.

Other professionals such as accountants and auditors will find that the book is a timely reminder of the type of unethical practices that may happen in organisations and their responsibility to ensure that they adhere to good ethics.

Consumer and environmental protection groups will find the book a source of information on the unethical practices of companies affecting customers and the environment.

Companies will find the ethics audit checklist at the end of the book particularly useful to determine if they are ethically compliant.

It is sad but true that greed, fraud, lies, bribery and corruption are part of business and organisational life. In the recent past, many prominent people have fallen from grace. This virus of corruption has affected all areas of modern life including business, politics, religion, medicine, and the judiciary. It is no longer remarkable or exceptional. Low standards in

high places are becoming the norm. Surveys consistently show that ethical standards in business and politics are low. It means that we should be eternally vigilant about the possibility of unethical behaviour and know about what can be done to counteract the problem.

The antidote to the virus of corruption is the practice of good ethics in business and public life. Ethics are moral principles, ideals, values or rules of conduct that guide people to deal fairly with others. They are about the universal principles of justice, honesty, sincerity, integrity, truth, fairness, compassion, respect for people and property, the right to privacy, concern for the environment and for people's health and safety. If a decision violates any of these principles then it probably is unethical.

A brief overview of the philosophies underlining ethics is covered in the early sections of the book. These provide managers with a useful framework when making decisions. Kohlberg's theory is a six-stage model of moral development suggesting a hierarchy of ethics. The stakeholder theory maintains that business has a responsibility to all its stakeholders. These include not only shareholders but all people affected by the business as well including employees, customers, suppliers and the community.

Good ethics are good for business. It leads to repeat sales, high morale, lower employee turnover, good reputation and consistent behaviour. It may prevent financial fraud, corporate collapse and discourage the practice of creative accounting. On the other hand, poor ethics can cause irreparable damage to the image of the company and result in lost sales, profitability and ultimate demise.

Corporate social responsibility (CSR) is a business philosophy which requires firms to behave as good corporate citizens. They do this by obeying the law, behaving ethically, providing good employment, and supplying goods and services that enhance the health and wellbeing of their customers without polluting the environment. The spectrum of CSR goes from those organisations that are models of social responsibility to those unfortunately who are socially irresponsible.

One way of implementing ethics is through a code of business ethics. Common areas covered by codes include conflicts of interest, gifts, confidentiality, insider dealing, health and safety, executive remuneration, the environment and equal opportunities. The main advantage of a code is that it demonstrates that a business takes ethics seriously. However, having a code is no guarantee of ethical behaviour in the workplace. Comprehensive and continuous training and publicity must support the code. When all else fails employees may be forced to blow the whistle on the company. Whistleblowers have brought major instances of corporate

scandal to public attention. Research shows that competition may compromise ethical standards and that the example of senior executives is essential to good business ethics.

Ethical issues of particular concern to senior management include tax avoidance, conflicts of interest, corporate manslaughter, insider dealing, and excessive remuneration packages. Others include misappropriation of company assets, cost-cutting, downsizing and accounting fraud. Some senior executives behave as if corporate assets are their own private property to be used as they wish for personal aggrandisement.

Ethical issues inside the company which concern employees include white-collar crime and receiving excessive gifts and entertainment. Surveys of white-collar crime show how serious the problems of employee fraud are. E-commerce and the Internet have given rise to cyber-crime. The computer has helped prevent and at the same time facilitate crime.

Ethical issues outside the company concern customers, suppliers, other organisations and the government. Those relating to customers include price-fixing, price exploitation, bait and switch, loss-leaders, sale of defective and dangerous products, misleading advertising and bribery. Those relating to suppliers include paying on time and subcontracting. Those relating to other organisations include exploitation of labour, outsourcing, industrial espionage, bribery and take-overs and mergers. Those relating to government include political contributions, bribery and corruption and human rights. In local government we have seen the exploitation of planning laws for personal gain both in business and politics.

From an environmental point of view, we know that the resources of the earth are finite and should be protected. In the past many companies have exploited and abused the environment to enhance corporate profits. They have depleted natural resources, marred scenic views, destroyed landscapes and polluted the sea, rivers and the air. Public pressure means that this corporate behaviour is no longer acceptable and that companies need sound environmental policies in place.

The HRM manager has a special role to play in ensuring that ethical standards are maintained throughout a company. Fair dealing with employees and customers is the best way to restore confidence in business morality. Those guilty of unethical behaviour should be subject to disciplinary measures. Nobody should be compelled to carry out unethical acts to achieve business results. In business all are responsible for the practice and maintenance of good ethics including the chief executive, directors, senior managers, middle managers, first line managers,

supervisors and employees. The chief executive and the senior management team will set the tone for the ethical climate in the company.

Good corporate governance – the regulation and control of the way a business is managed – is essential. This covers not only the way in which boards of directors oversee the running of a company by its managers, but also the way in which board members in turn are accountable to the shareholders of the company. Best practices of corporate governance include control of stock options, design and publication of good corporate governance guidelines, and ensuring that a majority of board members are non-executive directors. The position of chairman and chief executive should be kept separate. Audit committees are expected to oversee corporate governance, financial reporting, internal controls, internal audit function, and external audit services.

The book concludes with recommendations for creating an ethical workplace and a systematic problem solving approach for dealing with ethical dilemmas.

Each chapter in the book is supported by an ethics quotient quiz and a case study to test readers' ethical competence. The book is interspersed with inspirational quotations relating to ethical and integrity issues. A detailed ethics audit is provided at the end of the book to test ethical compliance.

When quoting published sources I have used the academic convention of citing author and year of publication rather than the full title of the work concerned – the quoted text can then be looked up in the section "References and Bibliography" at the end of the book. Thus, for example, "De George (1990)" refers to the book *Business Ethics* by Richard de George, published in 1990 by Macmillan Publishing Company, New York.

1. Theory of Business Ethics

♦ How do ethics evolve?
♦ What are ethics?
♦ What is the Greek perspective?
♦ What are the religious influences?
♦ What are the basic philosophies of ethics?
♦ What is the stakeholder theory?

"I have always recognised that the object of business is to make money in an honourable manner. I have endeavoured to remember that the object of life is to do good."

Peter Cooper

Ethics have evolved over many centuries. What is acceptable today may become unethical to-morrow. Ethics are moral principles or rules of conduct that guide people to deal fairly with others. Philosophy and religion have had a major influence on business ethics. Kohlberg's theory is a six-stage model of moral development. This theory may help managers and employees in their moral thinking. The stakeholder theory is widely accepted in business as a way in which managers should view ethical issues in business.

Evolution of ethics

Ethics evolve. Cooper (1989) points out that ethical principles develop over time:

"Ethical principles themselves are built into the enlightened conscience of human beings, refined through generations of experience, and put into context by philosophy and religion. We regard them as fundamental and essential. But human experience changes and develops, and the question of how to apply eternal principles to new phenomena needs working on. Applied philosophy, like creation, is a continuing process."

Just because an action is legal does not mean that it is fair, right and ethical. Slavery and racial discrimination were, until comparatively recently, legal in the USA but they certainly were not right. During the Second World War some Germany companies were involved in the deployment of Jewish slave factory labour and their deportation to extermination camps when they were too weak to work. They knew this was wrong but they turned a blind eye to the issue. Just over a hundred years ago women were not allowed to vote in elections. It was the suffragettes who fought and won women's right to vote in the early part of the 20th century.

> "Laws, religions, creeds, and systems of ethics, instead of making society better than its best unit, make it worse than its average unit, because they are never up to date."
>
> George Bernard Shaw

The issue of equal economic rights for women is still unresolved in many parts of the developed world. Sectarianism and discrimination is still rife in Northern Ireland in employment and job selection. The death penalty is still acceptable in some states in the USA whereas in Europe it is outlawed. Things that were once considered unacceptable such as divorce and single-parent families are now widely accepted. Women priests are accepted in many protestant denominations. Even same-gender marriages are now legal in some countries.

Girls and young women were excluded from education in Afghanistan. Even today women in many Islamic countries do not enjoy the same freedoms as men. Democracy is something we enjoy in the west. It is but an aspiration in most Muslim countries. In many developing countries there is rampant bribery and corruption in business and government. Child labour is still the norm and environmental protection legislation is practically non-existent. Multinationals who move to these countries and operate within these norms are not breaking the law but certainly are not being ethical. In the developed world major accounting fraud has come to light in prominent companies. Some of these have been due to pure greed, absence of personal values and abuse of power. Some of the practices involved were legal but were found to be unethical.

Definition of ethics

Ethics are moral principles: ideals, values or rules of conduct that guide people to deal fairly with others. Ethics deal with what is right or wrong or with moral duties and obligations. Business ethics are about the universal

principles of justice, honesty, sincerity, integrity, truth, fairness, compassion, respect for people and property, the right to privacy, concern for the environment and for people's health and safety. If a business decision violates one of these principles then it probably is unethical.

> "Fundamentally, the force that rules the world is conduct, whether it be moral or immoral. If it is moral, at least there may be hope for the world. If immoral, there is not only no hope, but no prospect of anything but destruction of all that has been accomplished during the last 5,000 years."
>
> Nicholas Murray Butler

There are five basic sources of values influencing businessmen: religious, philosophical, cultural, legal, and professional. The cultural, legal and professional aspects of ethics are dealt with in other chapters. The religious and philosophical aspects are dealt with in this chapter.

De George (1990) defines ethics as follows:

> "Ethics in general can be defined as a systematic attempt to make sense of our individual and social moral experience, in such a way as to determine the rules that ought to govern human conduct, the values worth pursuing, and the character traits deserving development in life."

Therefore, ethics determine the rules, codes, values, beliefs, and standards which *ought* to be adopted for morally right behaviour, integrity and truthfulness in human situations. Ethical systems, even in different cultures, virtually all accept that any action injurious to another person is wrong.

The Greek perspective

The Greek root of the word ethics comes from ethos meaning the character and sentiment of the community. This seems to suggest that ethics has a wider context than just the dealings between two people. Ethics have been studied and written about since the time of the Greek philosophers. The ancient Greeks maintained that the classic virtues of a good person were fortitude, temperance, prudence and justice.

Fortitude is the courage to persevere in the face of adversity. Temperance is self-restraint in the face of temptation. Prudence is practical wisdom and the ability to make wise choices. Justice is fairness, honesty, integrity and lawfulness in society. Thus ethical managers are

people of character. They tell the truth, keep their promises, follow through on their commitments, believe in the inherent self-worth of others, admit their mistakes, and create a climate for learning and development through trust and transparency.

> "Good character is that quality which makes one dependable whether being watched or not, which makes one truthful when it is to one's advantage to be a little less than truthful, which makes one courageous when faced with great obstacles, which endows one with the firmness of wise self-discipline."
>
> Arthur S. Adams

The Hippocratic oath

The Hippocratic oath, derived from the writing of the Greek physician Hippocrates, is a set of ethical principles followed by medical doctors. Hippocrates was an influential Greek physician who lived around the fifth century BC. The oath originally written by Hippocrates has been modified over the years, but its essence remains the same – a promise to treat all people fairly, to preserve life, and to do nothing which will harm the patient. To this day, graduates of most medical schools take some form of the Hippocratic oath before commencing medical practice.

Doctors have a special duty to adopt and practice values specific to patient care such as caring, compassion, competence, and respect for human dignity. Today dedicated doctors live by the four principles of medical ethics – beneficence, non-malfeasance, autonomy, and justice. The 16th-century French surgeon, Ambrose Pare, said that doctors should comfort always, alleviate often and cure sometimes. Apart from a few isolated cases the vast majority of doctors actively do good and have the welfare of their patients at heart.

Emiliani (2000) suggests that managers like doctors should take an oath of management similar to that of the Hippocratic oath. Managers like doctors have profound responsibilities in their dealings with people. They are also responsible for the welfare and safety of their employees and the decisions they take can have profound implications for the careers and lives of their employees and families. The oath would reinforce the perceived importance of the need for the practice of business ethics in all the actions that managers take.

Religious influence

The religious beliefs of Judaism, Christianity, Buddhism, and of Islam all agree that you should not hurt people, steal, cheat, or lie. These precepts form the basis for most legal systems. The Judeo-Christian tradition sums it up in the maxims "Love thy neighbour as thyself" and "It is more blessed to give than to receive". The same principles can also be applied in business. Indeed, it is basic marketing commonsense that to succeed in business one must identify and serve customer needs. Thus it is both profitable and ethical for a business enterprise to honestly serve and meet the needs of others.

Friedman (2004) reports that ethical principles derived from the Bible include the importance of caring for the stranger, the poor, employees, the environment and animals. In addition, a firm interested in following the values of the Bible will not give bad advice to others, will be extremely honest, will not attempt to hurt competitors, will be good employers and will behave in a fair manner. It also advises people to go beyond the requirements of the law. Thus certain actions may not be illegal but they certainly can be unethical.

Remember the old adages, "What goes around, comes around" and "Chickens come home to roost". A similar idea to the marketing concept of making people want to do business with you is the biblical saying, "As you sow, so shall you reap." Moral behaviour such as integrity, honesty and fair dealing builds trust. This attracts loyal customers, good employees, fair suppliers and creates goodwill. On the other hand, unethical behaviour discourages custom and creates badwill. It is very difficult to do business with an unethical company. If they make a commitment you won't be able to rely on it.

> "Aside from the strictly moral standpoint, honesty is not only the best policy, but the only possible policy from the standpoint of business relations. The fulfilment of the pledged word is of equal necessity to the conduct of all business. If we expect and demand virtue and honour in others, the flame of both must burn brightly within ourselves and shed their light to illuminate the erstwhile dark corners of distrust and dishonesty. The truthful answer rests for the most part within ourselves, for like begets like. Honesty begets honesty; trust, trust; and so on through the whole category of desirable practices that must govern and control the world's affairs."
>
> James F. Bell

Trust

All ethical behaviour and business is built on trust. A handshake seals a deal and a person's word is their bond. The basic business transaction involves a promise on one side to deliver goods in good condition and on the other side to pay the agreed price for the goods. The buyer trusts that the goods will be delivered and the seller trusts that he will receive payment in good time as agreed. Without trust the business transaction cannot take place. Ethics and trust are compatible because ethical behaviour leads to trust.

In management where there is no trust, a command and control style operates. Consequently, managers spend all their time watching and controlling others rather than carrying out their managerial tasks. A climate of suspicion is prevalent so that morale and performance suffers. On the other hand, high trust leads to high performance. An upward spiral is created leading to even greater trust. Similarly, team members who trust each other spend less energy worrying about what others are doing and more energy on getting the actual work done. Furthermore, such team members are more willing to look for assistance from others if they need to and allow others to do jobs that they have less expertise in.

John Akers, (1989) a former chairman of IBM, wrote:

> "No society anywhere will compete very long or successfully with people stabbing each other in the back; with people trying to steal from each other, with everything requiring notarised confirmation because you can't trust the other fellow; with every little squabble ending in litigation; and with government writing reams of regulatory legislation, tying business hand and foot to keep it honest . . . There is no escaping this fact; the greater the measure of mutual respect and confidence in the ethics of a society, the greater its economic strength."

Some ethical philosophies

There are a number of established ethical philosophies that have some practical use. These include relativism, utilitarianism, deontology, egoism, proportionality and equity theory. These philosophies offer some guidelines in certain situations. Some of them such as utilitarianism and proportionality are used in everyday management decision-making.

> **"If you take away ideology, you are left with a case by case ethics which in practise ends up as me first, me only, and in rampant greed."**
>
> Richard Neilson

Relativism

Ethical relativism suggests there may be situations in which an action could be considered morally right for one situation but not for another. This is summed up in the saying, "When in Rome, do as the Romans do." To be accepted and successful, multinationals must observe the laws, customs and moral codes of the host country in which they are guests. For example, when advertising ladies' clothes in Saudi Arabia it would not be appropriate to use scantily dressed women as this contravenes the strict moral codes of the Muslim religion. The indigenous people of Guatemala consider the taking of photos unacceptable as to them it is stealing their images.

However, some practices will always be unacceptable such as bribery and corruption. Though endemic in the cultures of some developing countries, this could never be accepted as normal practice by an ethical multinational. In some countries, unemployment levels are extremely high and consequently workers are so eager to get work that companies may be less discerning about local employment practices. This does not justify multinational engaging in exploiting local labour or turning a blind eye to the unethical practices of their suppliers. Ethical relativism also suggests that the prevailing values change from one time period to the next. What was considered ethical in the past may be unethical now.

Utilitarianism

Utilitarianism suggests that actions should be considered from the point of view of the greatest good for the greatest number. Morally good actions bring the best results for everyone they effect in terms of least cost, risk and harm. An executive using the utilitarian approach would make the decision benefiting the largest number of stakeholders using a cost-benefit approach. Indeed this is a common approach used in business decision-making. Generally, if a manager meets the requirements of customers, value will be created resulting in the greatest good for the greatest number of people.

An electricity company uses this approach when building transmission lines. Some farmers are going to be inconvenienced (even if they are compensated) by the erection of masts on their farmlands while the vast

majority of the public is going to benefit from access to electricity supplies. A similar situation arises with regard to road-building. Some people on the proposed route are going to be inconvenienced, and some farmers' properties may be split – but of course, the vast majority of people's lives will be improved by access to improved and new roads.

Take the example of a pharmaceutical company selling a drug that will cure 90 per cent of patients suffering from a particular disease but cause side effects resulting in the deaths of the other 10 per cent. The company using a utilitarian approach may argue that the drug should be sold as it benefits the majority of patients and will also make profits for the company. There are also flaws in the utilitarian philosophy as it would seem to support the concept of slavery provided the greatest happiness for the greatest number was achieved. Also under this approach the rights of minorities might not be given due consideration.

In 1990, Delta Airlines in Ireland received a telephone call from terrorists that one of its transatlantic flights would be bombed. It publicised the threat and gave passengers the option to transfer to other airlines without penalty. On the other hand, when Pan Am received a similar threat in 1988 it failed to notify the public. The subsequent loss of more than 200 lives in the terrorist bombing of Pan Am Flight 103 over Lockerbie damaged the reputation of the company. Delta had made the ethical choice while Pan Am had failed to do so.

Deontology

Deontology is the science of moral duty. The word deontology is derived from the Greek "duty". Deontologists base their ethical decisions on what is right in relation to principles such as truth, honesty, integrity, keeping promises, justice, compassion, privacy and respect for people and property. In Western thinking people have inalienable human rights such as the right to health and safety, the option to develop and realise one's potential, and the right to freedom, liberty, justice and the pursuit of happiness. People should not be used as a means to an end but should be seen as an end in themselves. In other words they should be respected because of their inherent human dignity. A manager operating within these principles recognises the rights of employees and treats them in a just and equitable manner. This in turn wins the respect and trust of employees. The difference between this approach and utilitarianism is that deontologists focus on doing what is right while a utilitarian's focus is on maximising the good of the greatest number.

Take the case of an auditor who knows that the financial statements presented to him do not tell the full story regarding the true financial position of the company. Taking a deontological approach the auditor would insist on telling the truth even though to do so is bound to result in the closure of the company and a loss of employment for the workers. Taking a utilitarian approach the auditor might decide to certify the financial statements on the basis that the employees will keep their jobs. This despite the fact that the benefit may only be short-term, as in the longer term the truth about the company's financial situation is bound to emerge.

Deontology does not solve the ethical dilemma of what to do when the rules are just not appropriate in certain circumstances. The debate about the abortion issue centres on the question of whether the rights of the mother or the foetus should take precedence. Also should you lie for your friend to save his life if you know that there is no other alternative?

Ethical absolutism is a deontological approach suggesting that there may be a universal standard or set of standards to judge the morality of an action. Thus murder, lying and stealing are condemned by all cultures. The golden rule "do unto others as you would have them do unto you" has universal application. However this maxim seems to support the idea of revenge killing which is anathema to the Christian tradition and, where practised, prolongs conflict, strife and misery by creating a vicious cycle of retaliation. This demonstrates that there are always exceptions to golden rules.

Ethical egoism

Ethical egoism suggests that every person should promote the greatest balance of good over evil for themselves. This promotes the idea of individual self-interest. If you don't love yourself you are unlikely to be able to love others. Realising our own potential means that we are in a better position to help others. According to Maslow (1970) self-actualising people have a deep feeling of identification, sympathy, and affection for human beings in general. They feel kinship and connection, as if all people were

members of a single family. Self-actualising people have a genuine desire to help the human race.

Egoism is the basis for our competitive society. It seems to be the driving force behind democracy and capitalism. "What's in it for me?" is the guiding principle. With the right checks and balances capitalism is probably the best system for running economies discovered so far and of course egoism is the foundation on which capitalism is built. The disintegration of the former Soviet Union would seem to support this viewpoint. Winston Churchill said that democracy is the worst kind of government ever conceived by the wit of man except that the alternative is even worse.

Principle of proportionality

The principle of proportionality states that one is responsible for whatever one does to achieve a particular end. If both the means and the end are good one may ethically risk the foreseen but unwilled side effects. However, there must be a proportionate reason for doing so. There is a proportionate reason if the good intended is equal to or greater than the evil risked. In line with the principle of proportionality, business people must seek to minimise the harmful impact of their activities. The end should justify the means. A good employer would not fire an employee if some lesser disciplinary action will produce the desired result. An employer will deduct a proportionate amount of wages for lateness in the hope that the employee will be reformed and come in on time in the future.

Honest business people use the principle of proportionality all the time. For example, the advertiser who has prepared copy carefully foresees that a few people may misread it. However, this is not the intention of the advertiser and the good service given to thousands of others outweighs the risk of harm. Of course, it would be quite different if the advertiser set out willingly to deceive people. An employer who installs a new machine and skimps on the safety measures to save costs is acting unethically since the potential harm may be greater than the increase in profits. The principle of proportionality suggests that a manager when making a decision should consider various alternatives and consider the one achieving the most good and least harm.

Equity theory

People believe that they should be treated fairly in relation to others. We naturally compare ourselves to others. We expect a fair recompense for our inputs. If we think we are doing the same job as others but getting less

pay we feel a sense of injustice. It is immaterial to the situation whether the sense of inequity is based on facts or just a perception.

Feelings of inequity cause tension and motivate a person to remove the source of the inequity. Some may request their union to negotiate with management to rectify the inequity. Others may reduce their efforts and commitment until the situation is solved to their satisfaction. Some may even resort to stealing to get even with the organisation – the rationalisation being that they are only taking what is justly due to them. Others may leave the organisation to get a job with better pay to redress the equity.

Kohlberg's model

Shea (1988) reports on the famous model developed by Kohlberg. Kohlberg projects six stages of moral development as follows:

Preconventional morality

1. Obey orders – to avoid punishment.
2. Marketplace morality – maximising pleasure, minimising pain.

Conventional morality

3. Conforming to group norms.
4. Focusing on law and order.

Postconventional morality

5. Principled morality – autonomous and responsible.
6. Universal morality.

This model suggests a hierarchy of ethics. It is somewhat similar to Abraham Maslow's "Hierarchy of Needs". Maslow talked about what motivates people, differentiating between a hierarchy of physical needs (at the bottom of the hierarchy), safety needs, relationships, esteem and self-actualisation needs (at the top). Some people progress up the hierarchy, while some others stop and even regress to earlier stages. People's ethical destiny depends on awareness, example, group norms, training, upbringing, experience and their own values.

According to Kohlberg's research fewer than 20 per cent of the population achieve principled thinking. It seems that most of us stop at stage five of Kohlberg's model and similarly few of us reach Maslow's stage of self-actualisation. Generally moral reasoning like wine improves

with age. It seems that in relation to ethics maturity does bring wisdom. Critics say that Kohlberg's model is more rigid than experience suggests but nevertheless it is accepted that stages of moral development do exist.

People do not develop in isolation. We develop through our dynamic relationships with the environment and others. Our ethics are influenced by the organisation in which we work. In turn we influence the organisation's ethics. An ethical business environment promotes ethical behaviour. Conversely an unethical business environment promotes unethical behaviour. Like a virus unethical behaviour can be caught. This was conclusively demonstrated in many recent business scandals. Just like people organisations can be at different stages of ethical development.

Preconventional morality

At the first two stages of this model, people's sense of right and wrong and good and bad are imposed from an external authority. Many of the accounting frauds seem to operate at the preconventional morality level. The culprits were motivated by self-interest and felt that the chances of being found out were very slim. Stage one people like to stick to rules to avoid physical punishment. People will do things to abide by the rules or if they feel they won't get caught. People will blindly obey the authority figure. In the case of children this is likely to be their parents. In the case of an employee it is likely to be the manager. The Nazi war criminals who pleaded that they were only following orders displayed typical stage one thinking. People aim to avoid punishment, maximise pleasure and minimise pain. For example an employee may refuse to accept a gift from a salesperson because it is against the policy of the company. Alternatively he may decide to accept the gift if he feels he won't get caught.

At stage two, people are more concerned with personal reward, satisfaction and looking after their own interests. There is a type of market reciprocity involved. People do things on the understanding they will be repaid in return. If somebody has been kind to you in the past you may consider returning the favour. If you took a work colleague out to lunch in the past you expect him to return the favour in the future.

Conventional morality

At the third and fourth stages, people are influenced by the need to conform to group expectations and win the approval of others. The standards of moral behaviour espoused by the group (which may be the company, the profession, or society as a whole) are the ones adopted. If the group norms are ethical, fine! However, if the group norms are

unethical you've got a problem. The trust and social support of the group is important. Dr Irving Janus developed the notion of "Group Think" to explain why highly cohesive business groups often make disastrous mistakes and unethical decisions. They suppress dissent and therefore fail to tap the resources of the group to come up with the best decision. Conforming to group norms is typical stage three behaviour.

Stage four behaviour broadens to include society. The person focuses on law and order and obeying rules that are for the common good. Compliance with authority, obeying the law and doing one's duty are the primary ethical concerns. People are also concerned with operating within the cultural norms and conventions of society. People are concerned about paying their bills, meeting their tax obligations, serving on juries, helping their friends, and supporting worthwhile causes. If an employee sees a safety infringement at work, they feel they have a duty to report it. A code of business ethics is a very good tool for people operating at the stage four level of moral reasoning.

> "Too many businessmen never stop to ponder what they are doing; they reject the need for self-discipline: they are satisfied to be clever, when they need to be wise."
>
> Louis Finkelstein

Postconventional morality

The fifth and six stages are sometimes called principled reasoning. Stage five is concerned with the social contract and individual rights. At stage five one realises that people hold a variety of values. The emphasis is still on rules and laws because these represent the social contract. However, one may also consider that the law is inadequate and needs to change to cover new situations. Sometimes an action is legal but the moral law would demand a more ethical approach. The fifth stage may require one to do more than what the law demands.

Stage six is concerned with universal ethical principles. At stage six the person can grasp complexity and realise that there are ethical dilemmas, which have no easy answers but nevertheless should be resolved in a logical and moral way in accordance with personal values, individual conscience and principles of justice. When laws violate principles then the person acts in accordance with their principles.

> "A disciplined conscience is a man's best friend. It may not be his most amiable, but it is his most faithful monitor."
>
> Henry Ward Beecher

Postconventional morality has inspired organisations like the International Red Cross, Amnesty International and numerous charities. The people who founded these organisations believed that suffering, injustice and cruel behaviour should not be tolerated. They set out to change the world and to a large extent succeeded in doing so. In particular, the work of Amnesty International has brought worldwide attention to bear on the pain and suffering inflicted by repressive regimes on their unfortunate citizens.

Training programmes can be used to help employees identify the level of ethical behaviour that they are at. They then can be guided through a process of analysis to proceed to higher levels of ethical thinking and behaviour. Kohlberg's model can be used to ascertain the ethical climate of a company and enhance the ethical environment if necessary. It is vital that managers are trained in ethical decision-making.

Ethical philosophies may offer some guidance in certain situations but all have shortcomings and are thus likely to be of only limited practical use to most managers.

The Irish philosopher William Berkeley said that at heart ethics consists in striking the right balance between two basic human feelings: concern for one's self and concern for others. Indeed, if we can empathise with other people we are unlikely to act unethically towards them. Ethics are good for you and also good for the people you come in contact with.

Stakeholder theory

There is a difference between shareholder and stakeholder theories. Shareholder theory suggests that the company is only responsible to the shareholders. Supporters of this theory argue that a manager who adopts a stakeholder viewpoint is acting inappropriately. The manager's duty is to meet the approval of and maximise the return to the shareholders.

Stakeholder theory suggests that we practise good ethics in our dealings with anyone who has a "stake" in the performance of business – customers, competitors, suppliers, lenders, shareholders, central and local government, employees, managers, the local community and trade unions. Companies with subsidiaries abroad have a responsibility to behave in an ethical manner in all their business dealings. They should contribute to human rights, education, welfare, and economic improvement of the countries in which they do business.

> "The decay of decency in the modern age, the rebellion against law and good faith, the treatment of human beings as things, as the mere instruments of power and ambition, is without a doubt the consequence of the decay of the belief in man as something more than an animal animated by highly conditioned reflexes and chemical reactions. For, unless man is something more than that, he has no rights that anyone is bound to respect, and there are no limitations upon his conduct which he is bound to obey."
>
> Walter Lippmann

Internal stakeholders

Employees expect security of employment, fair pay, safe and good working conditions, training and development opportunities, dignity, respect, equity of treatment, job satisfaction, and reasonable prospects. In fact Amnesty International has published human rights principles for business including one covering fair working conditions (www.web.amnesty.org). This states that companies should ensure just and favourable conditions of work, reasonable job security, and fair and adequate remuneration and benefits.

Employees expect employers to have good communication systems, to be honest in sharing information with them, limited only by legal and competitive constraints. They expect empowerment and participation in decision-making, particularly in issues directly affecting their jobs. (Too often, companies are operated like bureaucracies with command-and-control structures and lip service only paid to participation.) They expect freedom to organise or to join a trade union for representation and negotiation purposes. They expect their senior executives to manage the company in a fair and ethical manner having particular regard to the interests of the employees. Loyalty is a two-edged sword. Employees expect companies to be loyal to them in return for their loyalty. Contrary to the notion that employees are the company's most valued assets, too often they are treated like disposable human resources.

Managers expect security of employment, power, achievement, and career advancement. They expect their company to support them when making ethical business decisions. Like employees they expect the company to be loyal to them in return for their loyalty. Managers should have the interests of the company in mind rather than pursuing their own self-interest.

Unions expect recognition, right to collective bargaining and participation in decision-making for members. In some countries unions liaise with government and employers in setting national wage

agreements. In Ireland this has created the conditions for economic stability and prosperity.

External stakeholders

Customers expect fair dealing, value for money, quality, honest and truthful advertising and good after-sales service. In particular they expect companies to keep their promises. So if a company makes a commitment to deliver at a particular day and time customers expect them to keep it. They expect the products or services offered will not harm their health and safety and that the environment will not be harmed because of their production. There is a clear link between certain diseases and increased exposure to toxins in the environment.

> "Sincerity is to speak as we think, to do as we pretend and profess, to perform what we promise, and really to be we would seem and appear to be."
>
> John Tillotson

Suppliers expect continuous business, ethical dealing, fairness and to be paid on time in return for value, quality, competitiveness and reliability. On the other side, companies dealing with suppliers should expect them to adopt employment practices that respect human dignity. They should share information with suppliers and integrate them into their planning processes. Some businesses maintain their liquidity at the expense of suppliers by taking very long credit periods. This is morally wrong and unethical. Suppliers have often to get bank overdraft facilities incurring extra interest charges in order to maintain their own liquidity.

Lenders expect the repayment of loans and interest payments when due. Shareholders want to be kept informed about how the business is doing subject to legal requirements and competitive constraints. They expect to achieve capital growth for their investment, and dividend payment when due. They also expect directors to manage the company in an ethical and legal manner with the shareholder's interest in mind. They expect their requests, suggestions, complaints, and formal resolutions to be treated with respect.

Competitors expect honest dealing in an open market and that companies will not try to acquire sensitive commercial information by dishonest or unethical means, such as through industrial espionage. Companies have a responsibility to promote competitive behaviour that is socially and environmentally beneficial and shows mutual respect for competitors. They should not disparage the reputation of their competitors.

Companies should not engage in bribery or corrupt practices in order to achieve competitive advantage.

The central government expects businesses to obey the law, pay their taxes and provide employment opportunities. Local government demand compliance with bylaws and respect for the environment and the rights of local communities. They also expect local businesses to pay rates and other local charges.

The local community expects corporate responsibility, employment, and support for athletic, charity, educational, cultural and social activities. It expects companies to collaborate with statutory organisations dedicated to health, education, and workplace safety. It expects companies not to endanger local communities by environmental pollution such as fumes, toxic waste, emissions and noise and to uphold the human rights of the people in the communities in which they operate.

> "Throughout the 1980s, we did hear too much about individual gain and the ethos of selfishness and greed. We did not hear enough about how to be a good member of a community, to define the common good and to repair the social contract. And we also found that while prosperity does not trickle down from the most powerful to the rest of us, all too often indifference and even intolerance do."
>
> Hillary Rodham Clinton

Challenge of stakeholder management

The challenge of stakeholder management is to meet the objectives of each stakeholder group. Before making business decisions, managers must consider the impact of the decision on the various stakeholders. This is achieved by considering the economic, legal, social and ethical responsibilities that the firm has to all its stakeholders. This involves implementing appropriate strategies or actions to deal with the challenges and exploit the opportunities presented by each stakeholder group.

Ignoring the interests and demands of any stakeholder group can have negative repercussions for the company.

Essentially the opportunities are to build good working relationships with the stakeholders. The challenge is to do this effectively by meeting the needs of stakeholders as failure to do so could result in negative publicity and bad goodwill. Companies who ignore their stakeholders may find themselves the targets of litigation, consumer pressure and boycotts, and the activities of whistleblowers. This is especially so in relation to environmental matters.

Summary

Ethics are moral principles or rules of conduct that guide people in their dealings with others. Ethics have been studied since the time of the Greek philosophers and have been influenced and shaped by religious teachings and the ideas of philosophers. Ethics evolve over time. They are refined by generations of experience and put into context by philosophy and religion. Law and ethics are not the same. An action can be legal but unethical.

Some well-known theories of philosophy relevant to business ethics include relativism, utilitarianism, deontology, proportionality and equity. These offer some guidance in certain situations but are only likely to be of limited use to the modern manager. Kohlberg's theory gives us a six-stage model of moral development suggesting a hierarchy of ethics. Managers and employees can be taught to use the model to help them develop their sense of ethics.

The stakeholder theory is now widely accepted in business. In the past it was thought that a business had a responsibility only to its shareholders. They owned the company and it was the duty of the business to provide them with a fair return on their investment. It is now accepted that a business has wider responsibilities and should take the interests of its stakeholders into account including customers, competitors, suppliers, lenders, shareholders, central and local government, employees, managers, the local community, and trade unions. All of these groups have a vested interest in the prosperity and survival of the company.

Check Your Ethics Quotient

(circle the appropriate response)

1. Ethics have evolved over many centuries What is acceptable today may become unethical tomorrow.　　True　　False

2. Just because it is legal does not mean it is ethical.　　True　　False

3. Ethics are moral principles, ideals, values or rules of conduct that guide people to deal fairly with others.　　True　　False

4. The Hippocratic oath is a set of ethical principles followed by managers.　　True　　False

5. Ethical relativism suggests that there may be situations in which an action could be considered right for one situation but not for another.　　True　　False

6. Bribery and corruption may be acceptable in some situations.　　True　　False

7. Utilitarianism suggests that actions should be considered from the point of view of the greatest good for the greatest number.　　True　　False

8. Deontology is the science of moral duty.　　True　　False

9. Equity theory suggests that people believe they should be treated fairly in relation to others.　　True　　False

10. There is no difference between the shareholder and stakeholder theory.　　True　　False

Total the number of true and false responses and check Appendix 2 at the back of the book for the solution.

Case Study: A company without values, principles or ethics

Enron was created in 1985 when two utility companies merged. This deal created the first US nation-wide natural gas pipeline system. In 1990 about 80 per cent of Enron's revenue was from the regulated gas pipeline system. However, at the time of its collapse in December 2001, the company had diversified considerably and was listed as the seventh largest company in the US, with over $100 billion in gross revenues and more than 20,000 employees worldwide.

Arthur Andersen had a 12-year relationship with Enron. It did not want to put at risk its lucrative consulting work in addition to its audit fees. Thus together with bankers and lawyers it misrepresented the company's finances by establishing complicated partnership arrangements as off-balance-sheet finance to hide the true extent of Enron's debt. The Chief Financial Officer, Andrew Fastow, pocked $30 million in management fees for setting up the financial partnerships. This practice enabled Enron to borrow substantial sums of money without these liabilities appearing on the balance sheet. This meant that shareholders and financial analysts were unaware of the true extent of the company's financial exposure. During its time Enron made significant political donations to both the Democratic and Republican parties. It was also heavily involved in lobbying the government about business issues. No wonder that in the public mind lobbying conjures up pictures of bribery and corruption.

Some people likened Enron to the *Dallas* television show, which caricatured businessmen as amoral. Expense accounts, for example, were routinely approved without a thorough review and vetting system. The corporate culture of greed created the unscrupulous employees, which eventually brought down the company. It rewarded economic performance without regard to business ethics. It was a Machiavellian philosophy of business. The absence of corporate morality was also reflected in the personal lives of its high-flying executives and employees. Office affairs were rampant and divorce among senior executives very common.

According to published reports, its employees were frequent visitors to a Houston strip club.

The senior executives used fraud, deception and dishonesty rather than visionary leadership to dupe the investing public into believing that the company was doing well when in fact it was in a poor financial state. At the same time they were lining their own pockets at the expense of shareholders. The CEO cashed in $100 million stock options just before the scandal came into the public domain. The President of Enron, Jeffrey Skilling hired his girlfriend, later his wife, as corporate secretary on an annual salary of $600,000.

Questions

♦ Why do employees follow the example set at the top?
♦ How would you describe the culture operating in Enron?
♦ What are the lessons to be learnt from the Enron affair?
♦ With the benefit of hindsight and a sense of values what should Enron have done differently?

2. Why Ethics in Business?

> ♦ Why should business adopt ethical practices?
> ♦ What perception has the general public about business ethics?
> ♦ How is creative accounting done?
> ♦ What is the Animal Rights Movement?
> ♦ What is consumerism?

"We demand that big business give people a square deal; in return we must insist that when any one engaged in big business honestly endeavours to do right, he shall himself be given a square deal".

Theodore Roosevelt

It makes sense for an organisation to practice good business ethics. Consumers, employees, environmentalists, investors and the general public demand ethical practices from business. Consumers are now more aware and are willing to punish a company for unethical behaviour. They have no hesitation in resorting to boycotts to right perceived wrongs and achieve accountability, transparency and ethical conduct.

Irreparable damage is done to the image of a business when unethical practices come to light. They say it takes years to build a good reputation and only seconds to destroy it.

Good ethics are good for business

The practice of good business ethics makes an important contribution to an organisation's success. It leads to repeat sales, high morale, lower employee turnover, enhanced reputation and consistent behaviour. It gives a company a competitive advantage. A company's good reputation and corporate image can be devastated by unethical behaviour. Ethical companies attract investors and have easy access to capital markets. As

ethical companies are more responsive to the needs of their stakeholders they are likely to be more efficient and profitable.

Ethics and people go together. Organisations have no conscience. People have a conscience, so that it is people working individually or in teams who determine the culture of a company and the ethical quality of business conduct. A company with good ethics is able to retain and attract top quality people into its ranks. **Research by Axiom Software into graduate recruitment identified that 75 per cent of graduates would not work for a company with a poor ethical record** (*Personnel Today*, 2002).

"It is truly enough said that a corporation has no conscience; but a corporation of conscientious men is a corporation with a conscience."

Henry David Thoreau

Pomeroy (2004) reports that in a recent online survey conducted by TheLadders.com, an executive job research service, 83 per cent of the survey's 1,020 respondents rated a company's record of business ethics as very important when deciding whether to accept a job offer. Only 2 per cent rated it as unimportant, and 15 per cent said it was important but not essential.

Unethical practices have destroyed personal reputations and brought down whole businesses. The chances of litigation being taken against a company are increased if its practices are unethical. Nothing is worse to the image of a company than a poor ethics record in relation to employees, customers, competitors, suppliers, shareholders and the general public. Nothing enhances the image of a company more than to be seen as a good corporate citizen. The standing of the company within the local community will be enhanced. Nothing increases the collaboration between all employees more than when they feel that they are treated with dignity, respect and consideration. Good ethics contribute to the success of a business. On a cost-benefit analysis basis, good ethics pay their way.

"Take from a man his reputation for probity, and the more shrewd and clever he is, the more hated and mistrusted he becomes."

Marcus Tullius Cicero

The general public is now better informed and better educated than ever before. Companies are now expected to be morally, socially and environmentally responsible. There is an expectation that companies should do more than just produce products or provide services, make profits, create jobs and obey the law. They are expected to be good corporate citizens as well. Consequently there is a greater probability that

a company will be punished for unethical conduct and rewarded for ethical behaviour.

Learn from surveys

Spooner (1992) mentions a study involving some 1,400 senior executives in 14 countries who were asked to rank the personal qualities of the ideal CEO in the year 2000. The highest ranking went to ethics. Unfortunately major corporate scandals since then would suggest that some CEOs lack this quality.

Poor ethics are prevalent in business. Hoffman et al (1986) refers to a 1984 Survey of Fortune 500 largest industrial corporations by the Centre for Policy Research. Roughly two-thirds had been involved in illegal behaviour over the previous ten years. The survey did not include unethical acts as judged by prevailing community standards. It focused exclusively on illegal acts. These included price-fixing, overcharging, breach of environmental laws, bribes, fraud, and infringement of patent and antitrust laws. It would have shown a worse outcome if unethical acts were included.

Webley (1988) refers to a survey conducted for the Market Research Society in England in January 1988, in which the question "How do you rate the standards of honesty among each of the following?" was asked of a representative sample of 1011 adults. The results were:

Figure 1

Market Research Society Survey				
		High %	Low %	No View %
1.	Doctors	83	2	15
2.	Police	62	7	31
3.	TV & Radio	47	10	43
4.	The City	22	24	54
5.	MPs	18	23	59
6.	Top Businessmen	17	29	54
7.	National Newspapers	12	41	47

This shows that business has a very poor ethical image compared to other professions. Businesspeople are not seen as honest and without honesty there can be no trust. This finding has been confirmed post 2000 with the major scandals in business.

> "A man is already of consequence in the world when it is known that we can implicitly rely upon him. Often I have known a man to be preferred in situations of honour and profit because he had this reputation: When he said he knew a thing, he knew it, and when he said he would do a thing, he did it."
>
> Edward Bulwer-Lytton

The *Gallup News Service* (7/12/04) reported that Gallup's annual survey on the honesty and ethical standards of various professions in the USA found nurses at the top of the list, stating that they had enjoyed this ranking every year bar one since they were first added to the poll in 1999. Generally, Americans tend to give their highest ratings to the public service professions, like the military, teachers, and members of the medical profession. The lowest rated professions tend to be those concerned with sales or big business, lawyers, politicians, and reporters. Surveys over the years just confirm the same old story as regards the low standing of business in relation to ethics.

Trevino et al (2004) reports that when the Ethics Resource Centre conducted its National Business Ethics Survey of 1,500 US employees, it found that more than one in eight employees feel pressure from their supervisors and managers to compromise ethical standards.

Fraud

A company with good ethics will deter fraud, prevent corporate collapse, fend off financial fraud, discourage creative accounting, and curb abuses of power.

Preventing corporate collapse

Unethical business practices have led to the collapse of many prominent companies. Everybody suffers. Investors are left with stocks and shares that are worthless. Employees lose their jobs and often their pensions. Suppliers are often left unpaid and lose a customer for their goods. Banks are left with huge debt write-offs. Customers are inconvenienced and often

lose deposits paid in advance for the delivery of goods. Unions lose trade union members and resultant revenue. Central and local government loses taxes. The local community loses a source of employment and a source of revenue for local businesses.

Preventing financial fraud

The financial services area has received a lot of unwelcome media attention. The issues receiving most attention include insider dealing, fraud and embezzlement, false accounting, improper use of company funds, forgery, executive remuneration and stock options, derivative trading, inadequate controls, bribery, concealing relevant facts, and breach of contract. The days when a person's word was their bond are long gone and have been replaced by greed, fraud, corruption and self-interest.

Accounting irregularities account for most of the financial fraud in companies. These typically involve under-reporting liabilities and over-reporting assets in the balance sheet, and under-reporting expenses and over-reporting revenues in the profit and loss account. Directors under pressure to meet financial targets, satisfy their own ambitions, please powerful shareholders or meet financial market expectations, often resort to creative accounting to boost profits and hide the real financial picture. In the short term these unethical practices are often camouflaged by rising share prices on the stock exchange. However, in the longer term when lower than expected financial results are ultimately reported, investigations will inevitably reveal the truth and the shaky foundations of sand on which the company's profitability is built.

> "A false balance is abomination to the Lord: but a just weight is his delight."
>
> The Bible. Proverb 11:1

Discouraging creative accounting

Creative accounting has played a major part in recent business scandals. Most people think that accounting is an exact science. In reality the bottom line result is influenced substantially by judgement. It may be used to create the false impression that the company is very profitable when in fact the opposite is true. Some senior executives have engaged in earnings management involving the manipulation of financial statements to achieve their own objectives. They have used various creative accounting techniques to hide losses including the following:

- Capitalising expenses and showing them as assets on the balance sheet. Leung et al (2003) reports that one Australian company, One.Tel, who went into liquidation, treated bonuses of A$14 million paid to the founders as deferred expenditure (to be accounted for in a subsequent period). This treatment, as well as other questionable accounting adjustments, had the effect of turning a loss into a profit. It was also claimed that the auditors supported these accounting practices.
- Off-balance-sheet items. Associated (non-subsidiary) companies are often formed to hide financial transactions and avoid disclosure. Some of these practices are legal but highly unethical. This practice enables a company to borrow substantial sums of money without these liabilities appearing on their balance sheet. Thus a company can maintain its high credit rating status with the banks, lending institutions and investment analysts.
- Making insufficient provisions for bad debts, stock write-offs, depreciation and potential legal liabilities. These increase profits and understate losses. Writing depreciation off over a longer number of years than justified increases profits.

> "Corporations cannot commit treason, nor be outlawed, nor excommunicated, for they have no souls."
>
> Sir Edward Coke

- Overvaluation of assets. This increases capital reserves in the balance sheet.
- Taking revenue into the profit and loss account before items are actually sold. This might include predated invoices and even invoices for fictitious sales. Global Crossing, a US company that was founded to build an undersea broadband network, was forced into bankruptcy in 2001 after fraudulently inflating revenues.
- Anticipating revenue to the profit and loss account from subsequent periods.
- Treating advertising expenses as capital expenditure rather than an operational expense on the logic that it has a long-term brand-building effect and is therefore beneficial for many years.
- Treating training costs as deferred expenditure and writing it off over a number of years instead of in one year. The justification for this is that the company will benefit from the training for many years.
- Treating the proceeds from the sales of fixed assets as profits from operations.

- Creative accounting for goodwill. There are many different ways of accounting for goodwill. Some companies may write it off in one instalment whereas others may spread it out over a number of years. The accounting treatment adopted may give scope for the manipulation of results.
- A parent company passes money to a subsidiary as a loan. The subsidiary then passes the money back to the parent company, which treats the money as profit. The profit is thereby overstated.

Preventing abuse of power

The 19th-century historian Lord Acton famously said that "power tends to corrupt, and absolute power corrupts absolutely". Many senior executives seem to have power without accountability. Some executives become so intoxicated with the feeling of power that they think they are omnipotent and abuse their privileged position. They act as if they are above the law. It is important that the executive does not abuse this power and that the organisation creates independent checks and balances to constrain such power and make executives accountable for their actions.

> "An honest private man often grows cruel and abandoned when converted into an absolute prince. Give a man power of doing what he pleases with impunity, you extinguish his fear, and consequently overturn in him one of the great pillars of morality."
>
> Joseph Addison

Consider the following scenario highlighting how people blindly follow the dictates of authority. Badaracco (1992) reports that in the early 1960s, a psychologist at Yale University carried out a famous experiment. Volunteers from all walks of life were asked to help a researcher learn about the effects of punishment on memory. The learner, who was actually the experimenter's colleague, was strapped to a chair. The volunteers were told to give electrical shocks to the learner, depending on whether or not his answers were correct. In actual fact, no shocks were given – the subject was just acting. About 60 per cent of the volunteers were obedient to authority: when the learner made mistakes, the volunteers followed the directions of the experimenter and administered the highest levels of shock. They did this even when the learner shouted, screamed, pleaded, and eventually fell silent.

This experiment demonstrated that some people tend to follow authority blindly. It is no excuse to say that you were just following orders. You must take responsibility for your own actions. Adolph Eichmann's

excuse that he was just following Hitler's orders was not accepted. He was held personally responsible for the murder of thousands of Jews in the concentration camps during World War 2 and executed for his crimes by the state of Israel.

The psychological phenomenon called groupthink indicates that people will often behave differently in a group than individually. In mass hysteria people will often follow the actions of the crowd and behave out of character. There is a tendency for various members of a group to try and achieve consensus. The need for agreement takes priority over the need to get sufficient information to make good decisions. This is often the reason why some groups make disastrous and often unethical decisions.

> **"Rather fail with honour than succeed with fraud."**
>
> Sophocles

Watchdog bodies

Watchdog bodies such as the media, environmental and consumer groups monitor the activities of companies and bring unethical practices to the public's attention. These put pressure on organisations to behave ethically. No company wants bad press through a mountain of complaints about its products or services. TV, radio and the national press are only too eager to expose and highlight unethical business conduct. Companies today are exposed to unprecedented scrutiny through the Internet and 24-hour news TV channels such as Sky.

Information is truly global and bad publicity travels faster than ever. The media in general are more interested in scandal and controversy than good news. Thus companies do not want to be portrayed in a bad light by the media. Corporate critics including former disgruntled employees and dissatisfied customers can now use e-mails, bulletin boards, chat rooms and rogue web sites to damage the reputations of companies if they want to. The practice of good business ethics is now seen as good public relations and more important than ever.

Environmental groups

The green movement is a powerful political lobby campaigning against pollution of our environment. Most member states of the EU now have a Green Party with parliamentary representation. In addition, movements such as Green Peace, Earthwatch and Friends of the Earth act as watchdogs by monitoring the potential damage that businesses can do to

ecological systems and the environment. Despite this, some manufacturing and major oil companies continue to cause major environmental damage.

Responding to customer needs

On a more positive note, many companies are responding to environmentalism and media attention by adopting green issues in marketing. Some have even made it a "unique selling point". For example, in response to the "lead in petrol issue" all car manufactures now offer catalytic converters as standard car features. In the UK, the Body Shop is committed to ecological issues and human and animal rights.

Supermarkets now stock organic vegetables and foodstuffs. McDonalds have discontinued the use of CFCs in fast food cartons. In 2003 a group of American teenagers took a case against McDonalds claiming that its food was addictive and made them obese. They lost the case on the grounds that it was not the purpose of the law to protect people from their own excesses. Nevertheless it did show McDonalds the type of lawsuit that it was exposed to. McDonalds management must be aware and concerned about the way lawsuits eventually went against the tobacco industry. So in response to the obesity issue they have varied the McDonalds menu and introduced healthy choices such as salads.

Animal rights issues

The animal rights movement promotes the rights of animals. Supporters seek to end all unnecessary cruelty and suffering inflicted by humans on animals (especially in scientific experimentation, drug safety, product testing, cosmetics and in food production). They believe that testing on animals is unethical because it harms, hurts and even kills the animals and deprives them of their rights. They advocate vegetarianism and alternative more humane methods of research and experimentation.

On the other hand, researchers defend the practice of testing on animals by pointing out the great benefits created for society such as safe drugs, prevention of disease and safer cosmetics. Nevertheless, some companies have discontinued the practice of testing products on animals.

> "With animal rights, in contrast to human rights, (1) the oppressed can never by themselves exert leverage; and (2) the outsiders who work on their behalf, belonging as they do to a different species, must be exquisitely, imaginatively and compassionate in order to be drawn to the cause. To judge by history, this is not a recipe for success."
>
> Robert Wright

Currently, in the UK, animal rights campaigners have succeeded in getting the UK government to outlaw fox-hunting. Although normally peaceful, using such methods as boycotting and lobbying, some elements of the animal rights movement have resorted to violence from time to time. In the past they have succeeded in getting department stores to withdraw stocks of fur coats. In Spain the practice of bullfighting with its inherent cruelty to animals is distressing to some and in the future will probably become unacceptable in a civilised society. In business generally there are many ethical dilemmas regarding the treatment of animals presently facing the meat, fur and hide industries.

Factory farming methods

The meat and animal products industries rely on factory farming techniques, which many consider cruel. For example, hens are often packed into crowded cages. They are unable to move and frequently suffer foot damage and other injuries. Birds are "debeaked" to prevent pecking injuries and cannibalism. Veal calves fare worse. To produce gourmet "milk-fed" veal, new-born calves are taken from their mothers. They are then chained in small crates. Here they spend their entire lives in total darkness. To increase weight and prevent muscle development, they are not allowed to exercise. Growth stimulators and antibiotics cause chronic diarrhoea.

Managers of these factory animal farms are not naturally cruel but are driven by profit rather than animal welfare or ethical considerations. The danger to humans from the ingestion of growth hormones and antibiotic residue should be a concern for the industry but is often ignored. What effects have these on our health? Obviously there are serious ethical issues such as the health and safety of consumers that managers should consider in addition to the profit motive.

Ethical Consumer (Feb/Mar 2002) reports that Bayer, the German pharmaceutical and pesticide multinational, was criticised by the US Food and Drug Administration for opposing cuts on the use of some antibiotics potentially dangerous to humans. These are used as growth-promoters for

battery poultry, and encourage the development of antibiotic-resistant "superbugs" in humans.

Consumerism

There has been a concerted movement over recent years to protect the interests of consumers by putting pressure on companies to behave in a more socially responsible manner. The movement developed because of the increasing technical complexity of products, the growing power of big business, the need of customers to be heard and the problems posed by environmental pollution. There are now consumer bodies in many countries such as the Consumer Association in the UK, which provide product-testing facilities and publish comparative information in their magazine *Which*.

Companies are being persuaded by investors, the general public and regulatory bodies to produce transparent financial reports, respect the environment, adhere to stringent employment laws, sell good quality products at a reasonable price and take a responsible approach to society in general.

Boycotts

Consumer boycotts are an effective way of bringing pressure to bear on companies whose ethical values are unacceptable. The media is quick to expose any business seen as immoral with some consumers refusing to buy the products of that business until it changes its behaviour. For example, Nestlé lost about €40 million as a result of a 7-year boycott launched in 1977 because of their sales of powdered baby milk to third-world mothers whom they were seen as exploiting. Powdered baby milk is just not the right product for third-world mothers who are often illiterate and haven't access to clean water supplies. In addition, it is generally accepted that breast-feeding is the natural and healthier choice for many mothers and there is no doubt that mothers after giving birth are very vulnerable and open to suggestion.

> "About morals, I know only that what is moral is what you feel good after and what is immoral is what you feel bad after."
>
> Ernest Hemingway

Products appropriate and acceptable in one culture may be inappropriate for another. The people who use the product and the environment in which

it is to be used should be considered. Companies have a continuing responsibility to their customers after the product is sold. They should monitor who is using the product and how. Products should not be sold to people who cannot safely use them. Marketing techniques may be inappropriate when they exploit people's vulnerabilities.

In early 1984, the boycott was lifted after Nestlé agreed to address such issues as product labelling, marketing in health facilities, gifts to medical personnel, and provision of free supplies to health institutions. The international image of Nestlé as a caring organisation was severely damaged as a result of the boycott and the morale of managers and staff significantly undermined. Similarly, Shell was confronted with a boycott of its petrol stations in 1995 when it sought to sink an oil platform, *The Brent Spar*, in the North Sea. Shell was demonstrating a very cavalier attitude to the environmental concerns raised by the public.

Boycotts have now become even more international. Consumer groups are now using the Internet to raise awareness of unethical organisations and to put pressure on them to behave responsibly. Protesters often send mass e-mails to disrupt corporate web sites and cause as much disruption as possible. Rogue web sites can be set up to blow the whistle and raise concerns about the conduct of companies. The *Irish Independent* (14/10/04) reported that students of University College Dublin have boycotted the sale of Coca-Cola because they accuse the company of anti-trade union activity in Colombia.

Car safety issues

Ferrell et al (2002) says that the modern consumer movement is generally considered to have begun in 1965 with the publication of Ralph Nader's book, *Unsafe at Any Speed*. This criticised the auto industry for putting profits and style before lives and safety. The General Motors car called *Corvair* was the main target of his criticism. His consumer protection organisation, popularly known as Nader's Raiders, fought successfully for legislation requiring car makers to equip them with safety belts, padded dashboards, stronger door latches, head restraints, shatterproof windshields, and collapsible steering columns. Today side impact bars and air bags for driver and passenger safety have been added to the list.

"Who can tell what goes into a car today? The consumer won't know and the dealers get angry if you ask them."

Ralph Nader

Trevino et al (2004) reported that General Motors claimed its side-saddle fuel tank design (placed outside the truck frame in order to carry more fuel) was safe and met all state regulations. However, a Georgia jury was not convinced that the company had met its ethical obligation to prevent harm. In the case of a 17-year-old who was killed when his pick-up truck's gas tank exploded, the jury found the company negligent and awarded the boy's parents over $100 million in punitive damages.

For years, Volvo pioneered and adopted safety in cars as its unique selling point. As far back as 1959 it had safety belts in its cars long before it became legally necessary. It has taken other car manufacturers much longer to adopt the safety culture. Eventually the lack of safety in cars became unacceptable to the general public.

Ford

Ford and Renault now emphasise the safety features of their cars. In 1999 Ford bought Volvo and has used the connection to raise its safety profile in the industry. Ford's concern for safety was not always the case. For years it actively campaigned against safety. In 1979, the Ford motor company became the first US corporation to be prosecuted for criminal homicide by the State of Indiana over its Pinto model which had a defect which could cause the gas tank to explode on impact from the rear. The Pinto had been introduced to the market in record time to meet competition and safety issues were not a prime consideration. In fact Ford knew about the safety problem with the gas tank before the car was launched but went ahead regardless. The old culture in Ford seemed to be that safety didn't sell.

The public were outraged when it came to light that Ford had done a cost-benefit analysis proving that causing death or injury was less costly than a recall and repair of the Pinto. Moral considerations were not factored into the equation. The cost of rectifying the gas tank problem would have been a mere $11 per vehicle. Ford decided to let hundreds of its customers die in situations that it could have prevented.

"The customer is an object to be manipulated, not a concrete person whose aims the businessman is interested to satisfy."

Erich Fromm

The senior executives in Ford would undoubtedly have felt different if the law had made them liable for the corporate murder of their customers. A life sentence in jail would have given them plenty of time to reflect on their unethical behaviour. In 1978, and under pressure from the media, Ford was eventually forced to recall all the Pintos built between 1970 and 1976.

This was only the first of several cases over the years damaging the public image of Ford. One of these involved a fatal accident where the driver's Ford Escort had no airbags. Ford had lobbied against government initiatives on this issue while at the same time installing airbags in more expensive models. This led to the perception that Ford valued its wealthier clients more highly.

Firestone

Gates (2004) reports that Firestone had to recall 6.5 million tyres that caused about 400 accidents, including 46 deaths. Firestone and Ford spent the first two weeks after the tyre story broke arguing about who was to blame. Meanwhile, people were dying and families were losing loved ones. The public was not interested in the politics of the situation and just wanted quick remedial action to be taken. The critical time lost dealt a severe blow to the credibility of both companies.

In each of the above cases early warning signs had been ignored with no preventative or corrective action taken. However, times have changed. Like St Paul on the road to Damascus, Ford has undergone a conversion. Since its take-over of Volvo, Ford has pushed the safety features in their cars and has become more ethically responsible.

Ethical investors

There is now a growing segment of ethical consumers who will only invest in companies whose business they consider to be ethical. In the investment market some investors will only invest in companies with a social conscience. Unions and churches prefer to invest ethically. For example, they will not invest in companies involved in the arms or tobacco industries.

> "Whence do I get my rules of conduct? I find them in my heart. Whatever I feel to be good is good. Whatever I feel to be evil is evil. Conscience is the best of casuists."
>
> Jean-Jacques Rousseau

Many investors choose not to invest in companies which test their products on animals. The demand for ethical investment funds is growing. These funds try to combine profit making with an ethical orientation. Although growing, ethical investment funds are tiny in comparison to total investment. It seems the average investor is more interested in getting a good return on investment rather than worrying about ethical considerations.

Summary

Good ethics are good for business. They lead to repeat sales, high morale, lower employee turnover, good reputation and consistent behaviour. They may prevent financial fraud, corporate collapse and discourage the practice of creative accounting. Poor ethics can cause irreparable damage to the image of a company and result in lost sales and profitability.

Surveys consistently show that ethical standards in business are low. Businessmen also rank poorly in relation to other professions. Customers prefer to buy from and employees prefer to work for ethical companies.

Pressure from the media, consumers, environmentalists and the investing public often persuade companies to behave in an ethical manner. The animal rights campaigners have made organisations more conscious of their ethical responsibilities towards animals. Similarly, consumerism has made organisations more conscious of their ethical responsibilities towards people. Boycotts often succeed in making companies more aware of issues so that they live up to their ethical responsibilities. The safety features in cars are largely as a result of public dismay and outrage at the number of preventable deaths on the road.

Check Your Ethics Quotient

(circle the appropriate response)

1. The practice of good ethics makes little contribution to an organisation's success   True   False

2. Unethical practices have brought down whole businesses.   True   False

3. In surveys of ethics senior executives have come out on top.   True   False

4. Many employees feel pressure from managers to compromise ethical standards.   True   False

5. Creative accounting is illegal.   True   False

6. Group think suggests that people may follow the majority rather than their own conscience.   True   False

7. Environmental awareness is not an important aspect of business.   True   False

8. Consumerism is an organised movement to protect the interests of consumers by putting pressure on companies to behave in a more ethically responsible manner.   True   False

9. Some companies have adopted green issues as a unique selling proposition in marketing.   True   False

10. Some people tend to follow authority blindly.   True   False

Total the number of true and false responses and check Appendix 2 at the back of the book for the solution.

Case study: Creative accounting

John, who recently qualified as an accountant has just started a new job in the financial accounting department of a large company. After a few weeks in the department he notices that the company writes off personal computer expenditure as a revenue expense. This is not in line with what he was taught during his professional studies, as the purchase of personal computers should be considered capital expenditure. This means they should be capitalised and shown in the balance sheet as a fixed asset and depreciated over, say four years, with the depreciation charge shown in the profit and loss account.

John brings this matter to the attention of his boss, Michael who is a senior financial accountant in the company. Michael explains that this has been the traditional way of dealing with expenditure on personal computers in the company. He maintains that the amounts involved were not material in relation to the total expenditure in the company. Personal computers were just like stationery items and therefore it was in order to write them off as operational expenses. John didn't pursue the point with Michael as he was just new in the company and didn't want to be rattling any cages. However, he was not convinced with Michael's justification for the method of dealing with the expenditure on personal expenditure.

However, John found that his conscience was not satisfied with Michael's reply. He decided to research and investigate the matter further. During lunchtime when other staff were away he looked through records of previous years and found that on average over the previous four years, €100,000 per annum was being spent on personal computers in the company. This was far from an insignificant amount. The implication of this was that the accumulated profits of the company were being understated by about €200,000 (€87,500 for equipment purchased in the most recent financial year, €62,500 for equipment purchased in the previous year, €37,500 for equipment purchased three years ago and €12,500 for equipment purchased four years ago). John is aware of the various financial scandals that came into the public

domain and how creative accounting was often a significant issue involved.

Again John approached Michael about the problem but was told on this occasion to keep his nose out of issues that did not concern him. John is not happy about the situation.

Questions

♦ What are the ethical issues in this case?
♦ Assume you are John and discuss the options and consequences available to him?
♦ Discuss any further information you need before you make a decision?

3. Corporate Social Responsibility

> ◆ What is corporate social responsibility?
> ◆ What motivates a company to be socially responsible?
> ◆ What is the case against corporate social responsibility?
> ◆ How are companies socially irresponsible?
> ◆ What is the case against sponsorship of certain products?
> ◆ How is corporate social responsibility implemented?

"Business and organisations have a privilege denied to ordinary mortals – they don't have to die. This makes them especially responsible."

Charles Handy

A company should do no harm and should endeavour to achieve some good. Companies now realise that it pays to be socially responsible. This approach has been called "enlightened self-interest". The world has become a smaller place and is now like a global village so that the actions of socially irresponsible multinationals abroad have often returned to haunt them at home.

Definition

Corporate social responsibility (CSR) is a business philosophy which requires firms to behave as good corporate citizens. They do this by having inspirational leaders, obeying the law, following ethical principles, producing reliable financial statements, providing good conditions of employment, helping local community groups, and supplying goods and services that enhance the health and welfare of its customers without polluting the environment. Companies are expected to respect human

rights. Workplaces should be free from employee abuse, and mental or physical coercion.

The case for CSR

Some companies want to be socially responsible because their managers believe it is the right thing to do and also because of a concern for its public image and pressure from government, environmentalists, consumer groups, the media, and unions. There is a general public perception and expectation that it is only fair that companies should reinvest a certain proportion of profits back into the communities that they earned them in. This creates a win-win situation for all.

The Corporate Reputation Watch, in cooperation with the Economist Intelligence Unit, conducted a survey of 175 executives globally in July 2004 from companies with an average revenue of $5 billion. The most common CSR strategies included:

♦   hiring a more diverse workforce (46%),
♦   giving money and time to charities (41%),
♦   improved environmental practices (37%),
♦   imposed socially responsible criteria on key suppliers (23%) and
♦   publishing a CSR report (22%).

It is surprising then to see that only 11 per cent thought it necessary to appoint an executive in charge of CSR. Only 12 per cent of executives said that they weren't concerned about CSR.

"The behaviour of the community is largely dominated by the business mind. A great society is a society in which its men of business think greatly of their functions. Low thoughts mean low behaviour, and after a brief orgy of exploitation, low behaviour means a descending standard of life."

A.N. Whitehead

CSR is not a new thing. Rowntree's founder, Joseph Rowntree provided housing and education to the poor around his chocolate factories. Guinness in its early days showed a similar concern for its employees. Company law mostly protects the interests of shareholders. It ignores the interests of customers, competitors, suppliers, employees and society at large. This gap in the legal framework has seen the rise of environmental protection legislation, employee protection legislation, equality legislation, consumer protection legislation and health and safety law. Companies that don't behave responsibly will often be forced to do so. The law always lags

behind social and technological change. However, as far as business ethics are concerned it pays a company to be proactive rather than reactive.

The UN and CSR

As Blair (2004) reports, the United Nations has got involved in the promotion of CSR. In 2000 it launched the Global Compact (GC), a voluntary association that requests corporate participants to uphold ten principles relating to human rights, labour, the environment, and non-corrupt business conduct. The GC has since published guidelines on CSR. Furthermore it has created a network that companies, non-governmental organisations, labour groups, and UN agencies can use to share ideas about becoming better corporate citizens. Many businesses in the developing world participate to show their concern about health, safety, and environmental codes. This helps them get supplier contracts from multinationals. Companies in the developed world focus on human rights by finding and eliminating possible areas of discrimination such as the exploitation of labour.

Gates (2004) reports that in 2002, PriceWaterhouseCoopers (PwC) surveyed 140 large, US based companies to see how they responded to the challenge of increasing long-term sustainability. PwC found that, in general, the respondents thought the public holds them more accountable now than ever before for the effects of environmental, social and economic activities. They also found that less than 30 per cent of respondents had programmes to systematically identify and evaluate these sustainability risks.

Research shows that socially responsible behaviour pays off in the long-term even if in the short-term there is a fall off in profits. CSR may protect a company from costly lawsuits, reduced access to capital, a fall in its share price and the bad public relations of being linked to human rights abuses, slave labour or environmental disasters. There is also the shame of the fall from grace and the possibility of jail sentences for senior executives.

The case against CSR

Some economists are opposed to the basic premise of CSR and feel that the sole responsibility of business is profit maximisation. The primary goal of a business is to get a fair return for its shareholders. To remain

competitive managers sometimes are forced to take unpopular decisions such as relocating production facilities overseas to take advantage of cheap labour or a more favourable tax environment. These decisions are seen by many as socially irresponsible. However, some managers see them as necessary to stay in business, while others feel that management is not trained to solve society's social problems and that this job should be left to sociologists and others with the expertise to do so. It is up to the government through legislation, and non-governmental organisations to ensure that the interests of society at large are catered for.

Social responsibility

Radin (2004) reports that an increasing number of firms are providing working conditions and benefits that are not merely adequate, but actually excel. Chiquita and Levi Strauss are two examples. Both companies have distinguished themselves through their responsible labour practices and provide numerous lessons for others.

> "Business only contributes fully to society if it is efficient, successful, profitable and socially responsible."
>
> Lord Sieff

Chiquita subscribes to values-based management, and its operations reflect its core values of integrity, respect, opportunity, and responsibility. Most of its operations are company owned. They have a corporate vice president serving as an official corporate responsibility officer. The company monitors the effectiveness of its CSR measures internally and externally. It maintains transparency through its annual corporate responsibility reports. It tries to sustain good relationships with its stakeholders including the local community and government.

Levi Strauss (LS) operates through local suppliers and contractors. Nevertheless its objective remains to only do business with those who maintain good labour practices and abide by good business ethics. The company has its own "Terms of Engagement" for supplier compliance. As with Chiquita, CSR is promoted throughout the organisation. Part of the company's goal is to raise the labour standards for all employees, not just their own. LS prefer to encourage contractors to change their behaviour before it deteriorates. It will only rescind a contract if the local contractor is unwilling to change its ways or is perceived as untrustworthy. LS contractors are encouraged to conduct ethical climate surveys to ensure they continue to operate the desired values. In Guatemala, LS lobbied the

government to increase labour standards for more widespread protection for workers.

Gunther (2004) reports that General Electric (GE) has now become more aware of its obligations towards society. In the past it was more concerned with profitability than meeting the concerns of its wider constituents. GE now audits its suppliers in the development world to make sure they comply with labour, environmental, health, and safety standards. In the autumn of 2004 GE was admitted to the Dow Jones sustainability index, a collection of 300 best of class firms that meet detailed criteria for environmental, social, and financial sustainability. The company now accounts for the cost of stock options. Since 2001, GE has diversified into water purification, solar and wind energy businesses. It has formed a partnership with Ghana's public health service, committing $20 million over five years.

Marks & Spencer is another CSR company. The *Guardian* (02/06/2004) reports that its attention to ethical standards in choosing its overseas suppliers is an example to the rest of corporate Britain. Its suppliers in Morocco offer literacy training to all their workers, an important achievement in a country where only half the adult female population can read. Some retailers turn a blind eye to the inequitable labour practices of their overseas suppliers.

> "A good man will extend his munificence to the industrious poor of all persuasions reduced by age, infirmity, or accident; to those who labour under incurable maladies; and to the youth of either sex, who are capable of beginning the world with advantage, but have not the means."
>
> Samuel Richardson

Shell

Frankental (2001) reports that Shell has become more socially responsible due to the threat to its public image following its clash with Greenpeace in 1995. Greenpeace foiled it when it tried to dispose of the *Brent Spar* oil platform filled with toxic waste at sea. It was then criticised internationally for its oil operations in Nigeria and its cosy relations with the military junta. Shell has been forced to rethink its strategy on CSR and has spent a lot of money to address the concerns of non-governmental organisations. Shell was one of the first major UK corporations to produce a social report illustrating its impact on society across a range of dimensions. Unlike financial reporting, social reporting is not yet legally mandatory.

Macalister (2004) reports that US shareholders launched a legal case against Shell alleging it had deliberately violated accounting rules by overstating its proven oil and gas reserves. Shell told a briefing of analysts on January 9th 2004 that it had undertaken an extensive review of its reserve base worldwide and needed to downgrade assets in Australia and Nigeria to meet Securities and Exchange Commission (SEC) requirements. Shares in the company immediately fell 7 per cent.

Model corporate citizens

Dennis et al (1998) reported that Body Shop International (BSI), founded by Anita Roddick, was a business with ethics. The company promotes its products as natural and not tested on animals. From its foundation Roddick, who died in 2007, established her company as a model of CSR and she has been referred to as "the Mother Theresa of capitalism". In 1994, the company sold 3.5 million shares to organisations that support child abuse prevention, women's issues and an art museum. Also, the company donated 3 per cent of pre-tax profits to charity in 1994. In 1995, BSI initiated a campaign against domestic violence. Furthermore, the company developed the Trade not Aid programme. This was intended to support developing countries by trading with them, instead of simply giving them money. They also treat factory waste on site in an ecological friendly fashion.

Dennis et al (1998) reported that Ben & Jerry Inc the ice cream business was a CSR company. The company's mission states one of its goals as "initiating innovative ways to improve the quality of life of the broad-based community at a – local, national and international level". Ben & Jerry donate 7.5 per cent of pre-tax profits to charity, compared to the average US company donation of 1 per cent. Some of the organisations that receive this money include environmental groups, AIDS projects, a centre for immigrant rights, American Indians, and the homeless. It has very good conditions of employment for its employees.

There is no doubt that even the best of companies have shortcomings. For example, critics of the Body Shop allege that the claim that its products are not tested on animals is not completely true. In the case of Ben & Jerry it sells a product that is high in sugar and saturated fat and may contribute to obesity. As we know in life nobody is perfect and everybody has some faults. Nevertheless there is no doubt that these companies are doing a lot to become more socially responsible.

Social irresponsibility

In the past the tobacco industry has come in for a lot of criticism. The shipping, chemical and food industries also demonstrate socially irresponsible attitudes towards their customers from time to time.

> "The percentage of student activists who regard business as overly concerned with profits as against social responsibility has increased sharply in just one year."
>
> John D. Rockefeller

The tobacco industry

For years the tobacco industry denied that its products were addictive and injurious to people's health. It took years of consistent irrefutable scientific research, adverse publicity and even a legal case before they admitted that smoking was addictive and caused lung cancer. The industry engaged in systematic misrepresentation, deception, denials, half-truths and lies to obscure the evidence of the cancers, heart disease and addiction that its product causes. It intentionally targeted young people and people in developing countries to get them hooked on tobacco so that they would have lifetime customers.

The *Guardian* (08/06/2001) reported that Philip Morris, the world's largest cigarette manufacturer, was found guilty of fraud, negligence and selling a defective product. Mr Boeken, a terminal cancer patient, was awarded $3billion in damages. Thousands of more cases are pending.

> "Lies save trouble now, but may return in thunder and lightning."
>
> Mason Cooley

The unethical behaviour of tobacco companies does not end with just the side effects of smoking. Macalister (2003) reports that the British government has called on British American Tobacco (BAT) the world's number two cigarette group to withdraw from Burma. There is widespread condemnation of BAT and other western investors from UK politicians angry at the brutal crackdown of the main opposition party, the National League for Democracy. The leader of the party has been arrested and up to 100 of her supporters allegedly killed. The Burma Campaign, an organisation championing the cause of human rights, praised the government's stand against BAT. It also pointed out that BAT had shown no loyalty to British and other international workers when 1,300 redundancies were announced in June 2003.

The chemical industry

In multinationals, ethical standards should be applied consistently throughout the world in subsidiaries (whilst having due regard to local cultural and other differences). Sometimes this is not done.

We rightly expect companies to protect the health, safety and welfare of its employees and those of the local community. Corporate standards on health and safety should be uniform worldwide and never compromised. There is now a significant loss of public confidence in the chemical industry because of concerns about its safety record. The general public and workers in particular have a right to be informed about the potential hazards of chemical manufacturing when they plan to locate in a particular area.

The shipping industry

In 1987 we had the capsize of the P&O ferry *Herald of Free Enterprise* at Zeebrugge as reported in *Corporate Watch News* (14/1/2003). The coroner found that 192 passengers had been unlawfully killed. The ferry had put to sea with its bow doors open. The Sheet inquiry found that human safety concerns were subjugated to the need to minimise the turnaround time at port, to maximise crossings and increase profit margins. Some critics feel that in cases like this the senior executives responsible should be charged with corporate murder.

> "Business is religion, and religion is business. The man who does not make a business of his religion has a religious life of no force, and the man who does not make a religion of his business has a business of no character."
>
> Maltbie Babcock

The food industry

The food industry is coming under fire because of the amount of sugar, salt, and additives it is putting into its products. Sugar is high in calories and low in nutrients. It is a major cause of tooth decay and also contributes to obesity. Salt is necessary as part of a healthy diet but it is estimated that we are consuming as much as four times the amount that we need. High levels of salt in a diet have been linked to high blood pressure, heart problems, kidney disease and stroke. Some products also contain additives such as colouring and flavourings. It is known that these can adversely affect children's moods and behaviours and cause

hyperactivity. The food industry has a moral duty to take a more responsible attitude to additives in food products.

Using advertisements to link crisps with famous football stars in the minds of children is unethical. Sports stars should seriously consider the ethics of doing such work. Crisps are contributing to obesity and the excessive salt intake of children. Soft drinks because of their high sugar content cause dental cavities and other associated health problems. The acids in soft drinks also cause tooth decay and the erosion of the hard enamel on the surface of the tooth. Caffeine found in many fizzy drinks is a highly addictive drug causing hyperactivity in some children. Many cereals made to appeal to children are packed full of sugar, high in salt and low in fibre. Fast food contributes to obesity. Children are being targeted through aggressive advertising and toy promotions. Fast food restaurants project themselves as benevolent friends of children when in fact the bottom line is profit.

A lot of these problems could be solved by the food industry in the morning if they had the will to do so and had the health interests of their customers at heart. Food companies should actively promote healthier products and cut their fat, salt and sugar content. They should also remove the colourings and preservatives, which cause hyperactivity. In the long term, adherence to good ethical principles will increase sales and profits. Parents have a primary duty to ensure that their children eat a balanced healthy diet.

Sponsorship

Sport sponsorship by producers of potentially unhealthy products like alcohol and tobacco has now become unacceptable. It is immoral to promote products that cause disability and death. Many people die prematurely from tobacco- related diseases. It is wrong to engage in deception by linking cigarette smoking with healthy pursuits such as sport, sexual prowess or attractiveness. In some countries laws regulating the use and advertising of these products have been passed. Warning labels such as "Smoking kills" have been put on cigarette packages.

> "Temperance is a mean with regard to pleasure."
>
> Aristotle

The cost of alcohol abuse and smoking to society in terms of health and hospital care has now become a major source of debate in many countries. In response to criticism some of the major brewers have taken out advertisements advising younger drinkers to take a more responsible

attitude to drink. Many countries have banned or limited smoking in offices and public spaces. In 2004 Ireland was the first country to institute a total smoking ban in pubic spaces. Many other countries around the world, including the UK, have since followed suit.

Multinational dilemmas

Multinationals are often faced with ethical issues when local practices differ from home. The dilemmas faced differ from location to location. What should they do when officials expect bribes to secure contracts, or when confronted with the exploitation of child and female labour in the third world? In developing countries standards of literacy may be low. To what extent should a multinational get involved in upgrading the literacy standards of their employees and indeed of the local community? Infrastructure is poor in many developing countries. To what extent should multinationals get involved in improving roads and services?

In developing countries health and dental facilities may be poor or non-existent. To what extent should the company get involved in providing healthcare for their workers and indeed for their families? Should they be concerned about the lower regulatory standards in some of these countries? Should they lobby government to improve these standards? For example laws protecting the safety and welfare of employees at work are often poor or non-existent. Even when they exist they are often ignored or not enforced. Should multinationals lobby government to improve the protection of employees at work? The traditional response – "When in Rome, do as the Romans do"– is no longer appropriate. Some multinationals are in fact facing up to their responsibilities and dealing proactively with some or all of these issues. Many multinationals have developed codes of conduct to help them solve some of these dilemmas.

> "Respect is not fear and awe; it is the ability to see a person as he is, to be aware of his unique individuality. Respect, thus, implies the absence of exploitation. I want the loved person to grow and unfold for his own sake, and in his own ways, and not for the purpose of serving me."
>
> Eric Fromm

Arnold et al (2003) makes the valid point that the intentional violation of the legal rights of workers in the interest of economic efficiency is fundamentally incompatible with the duty of multinationals to respect workers. When it suits them multinationals use laws to ensure that their contracts are fulfilled, their property is secure, and their patents are

protected. When violations occur, multinationals protest vociferously. Therefore, it is inconsistent for multinationals to permit the violation of the legal rights of workers while at the same time demanding that its own rights be protected.

Implementing CSR

A company can do this by:

- Communicating clearly with its stakeholders. It can use its annual report to highlight areas showing its contribution to CSR issues. The costs and benefits of such initiatives should be detailed.
- Identifying social trends and reacting before it becomes legally mandatory to do so. For example, in Ireland some pubs and restaurants provided smoke-free areas on their premises before it became legally mandatory to do so.
- Investing time and money in providing good employment conditions. The company benefits from improved employee morale, reduced labour turnover and by being seen generally as a good employer.
- Treating its customers with respect. It is easier to retain existing customers than find new ones.

> "We'll be known as the helpful store. The friendly store, the store with a heart. The store that places public service ahead of profit. And, consequently, we'll make more profits than ever before."
>
> George Seaton

- Refusing to do business with oppressive regimes. Companies may suffer loss of reputation through association.
- Ensuring that suppliers or subcontractors in its supply chain are socially responsible, and setting appropriate minimum ethical standards for approved suppliers and contractors.
- Avoiding being linked to suppliers with low pay, dangerous working conditions and anti-union policies.
- Supporting the local community by supporting social, charitable, educational and sporting activities in the area. The payback includes the custom of local shoppers and the recruitment of local loyal employees who see the company as a potentially good employer.
- Sponsoring worthy causes. When the Special Olympics were held in Ireland many companies provided sponsorship, enhancing their image as caring and family friendly organisations.

◆ Philanthropy. Many companies support causes that relate to their mission. For example, a health company may support breast cancer awareness campaigns. A food company may support healthy eating by providing educational material on diet and nutrition.
◆ Social reporting, in addition to financial reporting. This is now well established in many companies as a way of accounting for community, employee and supplier relationships. Although not legally required, social reporting is a way of showing that the company takes CSR seriously. It is wrong to assume that environmental damage is free. The wider community ultimately carries the cost of such behaviour.

Summary

CSR is a business philosophy, requiring firms to behave as good corporate citizens. They do this by obeying the law, behaving ethically, providing good employment, and supplying goods and services that enhance the health and wellbeing of its customers without polluting the environment. Some economists are opposed to the basic premise of CSR and feel the sole responsibility of business is profit maximisation.

Some examples of CSR companies such as the Body Shop and Ben & Jerry were discussed. This shows that there are companies who take CSR very seriously. On the opposite side of the spectrum some examples of social irresponsibility were also discussed including the tobacco, chemical and shipping industries.

The sponsorship of sport in order to sell tobacco and alcohol is now viewed as unethical. Linking tobacco and alcohol to healthy sporting activities is wrong and unethical especially as this advertising is often aimed at the young and impressionable.

CSR is implemented through communication, supporting the local community, supporting local social and charitable causes, creating good employment conditions, philanthropy, and through environmental reporting.

Check Your Ethics Quotient

1. CSR requires firms to behave as good corporate citizens.　　True　　False

2. Companies are legally required to impose socially responsible criteria on key suppliers.　　True　　False

3. Company law mostly protects the interests of shareholders.
It ignores the interests of customers, competitors, suppliers, employees and society at large.　　True　　False

4. The UN has got involved in the promotion of CSR.　　True　　False

5. Economists believe the sole responsibility of business is profit maximisation.　　True　　False

6. Good companies audit their suppliers to ensure they comply with labour, environmental, health and safety standards.　　True　　False

7. Most companies are driven by ethics rather than cost considerations.　　True　　False

8. It is illegal to export dangerous products abroad.　　True　　False

9. It is illegal to sell products that cause disability and death.　　True　　False

10. Most companies do social reporting.　　True　　False

Total the number of true and false responses and check Appendix 2 at the back of the book for the solution.

Case study: Corporate irresponsibility

For decades up to the 1970s asbestos was used extensively as an insulator in buildings, ships and even in car brake pads. The dangers of inhaling even small amounts of asbestos fibre were not realised until the 1970s because the incubation period for the cancer caused was anywhere between ten and forty years. However, by the mid-1970s thousands of people began to suffer the fatal diseases that are considered characteristic of asbestos exposure.

Gellerman (1986) reports that Manville, a manufacturer of asbestos, was aware for 40 years that the inhalation of asbestos was a cause of asbestosis – a debilitating lung disease – but did nothing about it. It also causes lung cancer and mesothelioma, another type of fatal lung disease. Manville's managers suppressed the research. Moreover, as a matter of policy, they concealed the information from affected employees. The company's medical staff collaborated in the cover-up. It seems that many companies when confronted with ethical problems, indulge in a culture of secrecy and cover-up rather than deal with them.

A California court found that Manville had hidden the asbestos danger from its employees rather than looking for safer ways to handle it. It was less expensive to pay workers' compensation claims than to develop safer working conditions. Even more telling, a New Jersey court found that Manville had made a conscious, cold-blooded business decision to take no protective or remedial action, in flagrant disregard of the rights of others. It is impossible to know what rationalisations the managers of Manville made to justify such unethical conduct but it seemed to be sanctioned from the top.

Questions

- What are the lessons that can be learned from the actions of Manville?
- With the benefit of hindsight what policies should Manville put in place to make sure this problem does not arise in the future?

- ♦ Should companies put profits before the health and safety of its employees? Is a cost benefit analysis appropriate in such circumstances?

4. Implementing Ethics

> - Where are codes needed?
> - What are the guidelines for codes of business ethics?
> - What are the limitations of codes?
> - What training is needed to support ethics?
> - How can ethical dilemmas be resolved?
> - What is whistleblowing?

"The first step in the evolution of ethics is a sense of solidarity with other human beings".

Albert Schweitzer

The code of business ethics is primarily influenced by the corporate philosophy of the company. Ethical programmes must have the support of top management to succeed. Gandhi said that we must become the change we wish to see in the world. Senior executive must lead by example. A general code is needed for the whole business, and specific codes for each department.

Codes demonstrate that a business takes ethics seriously but on their own do not guarantee an ethical business. It is easy to inadvertently ignore or overlook them in the heat and pressures of everyday business. Continuous vigilance is needed to ensure that high ethical standards are pursued and maintained throughout the company. Continuous training ensures that codes are put into practice. In the final analysis concerned employees may be forced to blow the whistle on the company.

Corporate culture

Ethics should be linked to the culture, values and beliefs of the company, corporate policy, vision statement, corporate philosophy, strategic objectives and ultimately, its mission.

Values are an important aspect of a company's culture. Values are a company's essential and enduring beliefs. These should be adhered to and

should not be compromised for short-term expediency or gain. The core values of truth, trust, integrity, respect and fair dealing should form the cornerstone of a company's belief system. The beliefs are the character of the company and the foundation for its policies, practices and goals.

> "I'm not willing to look the other way when somebody is off base with regard to integrity on the grounds that they're making such a wonderful technical or professional contribution that we can't afford to live without them. To me it's an easy choice."
>
> Paul O'Neill, CEO of ALCOA

Each company needs to develop its own values to suit its own circumstances and belief systems. What suits one company needn't necessarily suit another. Visionary companies tend to have only a few core values. Humans have a limited memory span so that it is important that they concentrate on the few core values. These values will never change. Values sometimes reflect the personal character of the founder of the company. Johnson & Johnson has set out its values clearly in a document called "the credo". The credo is integrated into everyday decision-making and so became a living document for its employees rather than a mere aspiration.

> "Character is the foundation stone upon which one must build to win respect. Just as no worthy building can be erected on a weak foundation, so no lasting reputation worthy of respect can be built on a weak character. Without character, all effort to attain dignity is superficial, and results are sure to be disappointing."
>
> R.C. Samsel

The values of the company support the ethics programme. The programme should include a code of ethics, training, an ethics hotline or office, an ethics committee and a system for anonymous reporting of misconduct. Employees will follow for good or for bad the example and expectations of the top senior executive role models. In psychology, this is known as the Pygmalion effect, whereby people live up to the expectations that role models set for them. An unethical Pygmalion effect results if managers set unethical expectations and people adopt them. Recent scandals suggest that this principle operates in practice.

Senior management must communicate an uncompromised ethical message to all staff. Employees expect companies, with codes of business ethics, to lead by example and provide employee training and

communication about corporate ethical standards and they expect the company to implement them. It lowers employee morale if this is not done.

Ethics codes

Most people look outside themselves for guidance, hence the importance of a business code of ethics. **An ethics code is a set of rules for the company setting out what behaviours are acceptable and unacceptable.** We need to be more aware of ethical issues when making decisions. More employees are now involved in decision-making because of empowerment and decentralisation. This means that more employees need to be trained in ethical principles. Customers demand that organisations practice good business ethics in their dealings with them.

Codes vary in length, content and readability. The longer the code the fewer employees are likely to read it. On the other hand, if the code is too short it may be too broad and abstract to have any practical meaning. Obviously it would be impossible to have a code covering every possible ethical dilemma faced by employees. A useful code will focus on values, philosophy and broad principles and should guide employees in typical ethical situations. Some companies divide their code into sections. The first section might deal with the broad guiding principles. This is followed by sections providing detailed applications to common cases and answers to frequently asked questions.

Some organisations have specific codes for each functional department. Each department will have its own particular ethical challenges. Thus we should have codes for Marketing, HRM, Finance, Purchasing, Property, Public Relations, Information Technology and so on. Training should be a vital ingredient of any ethics programme.

> "Reading about ethics is about as likely to improve one's behaviour as reading about sports is to make one into an athlete."
>
> Mason Cooley

Guidelines

Moon (1989) recommends the following guidelines for introducing a code based on an Institute of Business Ethics survey in 1987:

♦ The code should have top management support and employees should be consulted.

- One person should have the responsibility for drafting the code. This person should consult the company secretary, human resource and public relations departments.
- The code should deal specifically with conflicts of interest, gifts, confidentiality of company information, inside dealing, health and safety, the environment and equal opportunities. The code should specify clearly what disciplinary action will be taken against those who break the code.
- Each employee should get a copy of the code as part of the contract of employment. The line manager should explain and discuss the significance of the code to the employee.

Advantages

- Having a code suggests that a business takes ethics seriously.
- It creates a positive public image for the company. Employees like to work for ethical companies and investors like to invest in them.
- The code will encourage employees to discuss and debate ethical issues and seek out just solutions to ethical dilemmas.
- Employees who work in an organisation with a code of ethics engage in less unethical behaviour. They are more like to seek advice about ethics and more likely to report ethical code violations.
- It informs managers and employee of what is expected of them.
- It gives guidance to managers and employees on how to handle typical ethical issues.
- It expresses the philosophy and values of the company.
- It will raise standards of ethical behaviour in the company. It lays down the principles under which the company operates and the standards by which it should be judged.
- Litigation is less likely against a company that implements and observes a code of business ethics.

> "I would like to learn, or remember, how to live. "
>
> Annie Dillard

In modern business there are all sorts of pressures on managers to adopt unethical practices. Managers engaged in organisational politics often resort to unethical practices such as lying, cheating and manipulating others to achieve their objectives and personal ambitions. Organisational politics is not necessarily bad provided it respects the rights of others and it is practised in a fair and equitable manner. A code of business ethics

helps to counteract the tendency of managers to play politics and assists in maintaining high standards of behaviour.

> **"Try not to become a man of success, but rather a man of values"**
> .Albert Einstein

Limitations

Some companies feel that codes are too general and too broad to be of any practical use. It is impossible to cover all possible ethical issues and eventualities that an employee might face in the work situation. Some codes are not publicised. The code should be given to shareholders, recruitment agencies and suppliers. The code should be available to all who request it, placed in a prominent place in company buildings, and serve as a daily reminder to managers and employees of their ethical responsibilities. Customers should also be told about the company code. Some companies print codes or "customer charters" on the backs of their invoices.

Thus codes are mere guidelines. They can't realistically cover everything. Some issues will require the discretion, judgement and problem-solving skills of managers. When in doubt, a manager should think about how it would look if it appeared on the television news or on the front page of the national newspaper. How would they feel if their family and friends were made aware of a poor ethical decision?

Common themes

While the areas covered in codes vary from one industry and company to another some common topics include:

◆ Honesty and legal compliance.
◆ Product safety and quality.
◆ Health and safety at work.
◆ Computer fraud.
◆ Employee Internet use.
◆ Conflicts of interest.
◆ Insider dealing.
◆ Outside employment.
◆ Executive remuneration.
◆ Employment practices such as fair recruitment, equal opportunities for training and work-family balance.
◆ Discrimination on the basis of age, sex, race or religion.

- Sexual harassment.
- Bullying.
- Outside employment.
- Marketing, selling and advertising.
- Financial reporting.
- Creative accounting.
- Supplier relationships such as procurement, negotiating contracts and payment on time.
- Pricing, invoicing and contracting.
- Bribery and gifts.
- Competitive tendering.
- Use of privileged information.
- Use of company assets.
- Respecting privacy and confidentiality.
- Environmental protection.
- Political contributions.
- Attitude towards whistleblowing.

When an ethics code is ignored

There is no guarantee that employees will follow the code. Enron had a very good code of ethics. The problem was that everybody from the top to the bottom ignored it. There is a universal law called the law of sowing and reaping. It means that you reap what you sow.

> "Each time you are honest and conduct yourself with honesty, a success force will drive you toward greater success. Each time you lie, even with a little white lie, there are strong forces pushing you toward failure."
>
> Joseph Sugarman

Enron sowed a culture of moral corruption in the company and eventually reaped corporate death and destruction. The following are a few actual excerpts from its code giving new meaning to the word hypocrisy:

- We want to be proud of our company and to know that it enjoys a reputation for fairness and honesty and that it is respected.
- Ruthlessness, callousness, and arrogance don't belong here.
- We work with customers and prospects openly, honestly and sincerely.
- We are dedicated to conducting business according to all applicable local and international laws and regulations....and with the highest professional and ethical standards.

Enron did the opposite of the ideals set out in its code of ethics. We now know that:

- The term "Enronitis" has crept into the English language signifying corrupt corporate behaviour.
- Its senior executive team behaved in a ruthless, callous and arrogant fashion by awarding themselves excessive compensation packages and selling their shares in the company before it collapsed while telling employees to do the opposite.
- Senior management did not exercise sufficient oversight or control and did not respond quickly to pressing issues. The board failed to get information that it needed and did not fully understand the implications of some of the information that it did receive.
- The audit committee only performed cursory reviews and did not realise the inadequacies of the company's internal controls.
- Some of their dealings with customers were dishonest and manipulative.
- Their code of ethics meant nothing and the professional conduct of its managers and auditors was abysmal.

To be effective a code must be implemented vigorously and disciplinary action taken against employees who break it.

Ten ethical commandments

Shea (1988) reports that Bertrand Russell, the mathematician, philosopher, and winner of the Nobel Prize in literature, came up with ten ethical commandments as guidelines to ethical decision-making:

1. Do not feel absolutely certain of anything.
2. Do not think it worthwhile to proceed by concealing evidence, for the evidence is sure to come to light.
3. Never try to discourage thinking, for you are sure to succeed.
4. When you meet with opposition, even if it should be from your wife, husband, or your children, endeavour to overcome it by argument and not by authority, for a victory dependent upon authority is unreal and illusory.
5. Have no respect for the authority of others, for there are always contrary authorities to be found.

6. Do not use power to suppress opinions you think pernicious, for if you do the opinion will suppress you.
7. Do not fear to be eccentric in opinion, for every opinion now accepted was once eccentric.
8. Find more pleasure in intelligent dissent than in passive agreement, for, if you value intelligence, as you should, the former implies a deeper agreement than the latter.
9. Be scrupulously truthful, even if the truth is inconvenient, for it is more inconvenient when you try to conceal it.
10. Do not feel envious of the happiness of those who live in a fool's paradise, for only a fool will think that it is happiness.

"The good I stand on is my truth and honesty."

William Shakespeare

Business code surveys

Verschoor (2004) reported that the Business Roundtable Institute for Corporate Ethics surveyed CEOs of large corporations and found that the five most important ethics issues in order of priority were:

1. Regaining the public trust.
2. Effective company management to meet the expectations of investors.
3. Ensuring the integrity of financial reporting.
4. Fairness of executive compensation.
5. Ethical role-modelling of senior management.

The study also revealed that 81 per cent of CEOs believe that standards for corporate ethics have improved despite the recent scandals. Furthermore, 74 per cent of companies have made changes in how ethics issues are handled or reported within the last two years.

A survey by *Fortune* magazine in 2000 showed that of 500 American companies in the manufacturing sector, and a further 500 in the service sector, 91 per cent had a written code of ethics. Almost 50 per cent had ethics training in place for all employees. Almost 90 per cent surveyed believed that the public is now much more aware of ethical issues in business than they were in the past.

Communication of code

Salierno (2004) reports that a survey conducted by Deloitte Touche Tohmatsu and *Corporate Board Member* magazine found that corporate

ethics receive considerable attention within US companies. The survey found that 83 per cent of companies surveyed have developed formal codes of ethics and that 98 per cent agree that an ethics and compliance programme is essential. Results are mixed, however, concerning other activities such as training, implementation and follow-up.

When asked about compliance with the code of ethics, about 25 per cent of companies with a code said that they do not check for adherence by employees. Furthermore, about 32 per cent do not provide training on the requirements and responsibilities of the ethics code, and 45 per cent said that their company does not have an ethics officer.

The research also cited communication weaknesses in ethics programmes. Just over half of those surveyed said that their senior management teams discussed ethics and compliance programmes only once or twice each year. About one fifth said that management discussed the programme three or four times a year. Furthermore, although 90 per cent of responding firms include shareholders, suppliers, customers, and others in their ethics codes, only about half distributed the code to these parties. Only 40 per cent said that they gave reports to the board of directors at least quarterly.

Most companies reported that their ethics programme was known throughout the company, with more than 95 per cent indicating that their code applied to every employee, including senior management and board members. Moreover, more than 90 per cent of multinational companies said their code covered domestic and foreign operations. Researchers concluded that there was a discrepancy between intentions and actions. Although the vast majority of companies said that an ethics programme was essential to corporate governance many are poor at implementation and checking for compliance.

> "The best laws cannot make a constitution work in spite of morals; morals can turn the worst laws to advantage. That is a commonplace truth, but one to which my studies are always bringing me back. It is the central point in my conception. I see it at the end of all my reflections."
>
> Alexis de Tocqueville

Training

Steiner (1971), in a survey of business ethics, concluded that a college education and ethics training do not guarantee better business ethics. Furthermore, Weber (1990) generally found that although students' ethical awareness and reasoning improve after taking business ethics courses,

the improvement is short-lived. The code of ethics, and case studies dealing with real life ethical issues in the company, should be included in induction programmes for new employees and refresher training provided thereafter. In fact, in-company business ethics programmes seem to work.

Clarke (2003) reports on a 2003 survey conducted by the Ethics Resource Centre. This survey found that employees in organisations with formal programmes are more likely to report employee misconduct. **Ethics programmes are made up of four elements: written standards of conduct, training, ethics advice lines/offices, and systems for anonymous reporting of misconduct.** The more of the elements in place the more likely employees were to report misconduct. They also found that top management that speaks and behaves ethically is a major factor in building an ethical culture.

Designing ethics training programmes

The training programme for managers should concentrate on decision-making, the challenge of balancing responsibilities towards stakeholders, and the need to comply with laws and important regulations. Ongoing management training should include updates on current ethical thinking. Business ethics specialists from outside the organisation should be invited in as guest speakers.

> "The grand principles of virtue and honour, however they may be distorted by arbitrary codes, are the same the world over: and where these principles are concerned, the right or wrong of any action appears the same to the uncultivated as to the enlightened mind."
>
> Herman Melville

Departments should run programmes relevant to their functions. DVDs should be produced on business ethics and installed in the learning centres as a learning resource. Employees should be encouraged to view these. Posters with the company code of ethics should be put on notice boards. Summarised versions of the code should be printed on wallet sized cards and issued to all employees for perusal, reference and constant reminding.

Periodic reinforcement is important, using such methods as follow-up training, self-study programmes in the learning centre and reminder statements from top management emphasising the importance of ethics. Business ethics can also be integrated into mentoring programmes. Mentors should act as role models for the practice of business ethics.

Training should be provided for all employees and should be more than just being made aware of the company's ethical rules. It is not sufficient to show employees what to do in specific circumstances. More importantly, they should be taught to handle situations which are not clear-cut and for which there are no rules. They need philosophies, values and guidelines rather than rules for such situations. They also need to be equipped with good problem solving skills to identify and resolve ethical issues.

Training must be interactive using role-play, case studies, check lists, critical incidents and discussion groups. Examples of calls that have come into the ethics office may be used as the basis of training. Such training should include discussion of current cases as reported in daily newspapers and magazines. This makes the training timely and relevant. Business ethics must be internalised to affect and improve conduct. Just telling people to be good, honest and truthful is no guarantee that they will be. A model for resolving ethical issues is discussed in Chapter 10.

Advantages of ethics training

Ethics training should also cover the wider aspects of ethics such as corporate governance and CSR. The advantages of ethics training include:

♦ It makes employees aware of the corporate values of the business and their importance.
♦ It will provide employees with the tools and techniques to solve common ethical problems.
♦ It will make employees aware of the support system in the company for ethics such as an ombudsman, ethics office or ethics hotline.
♦ It will show the disciplinary action that will be taken against employees who indulge in unethical behaviour.
♦ It will make employees aware of the legal and ethical implications of taking unethical action.
♦ It may reduce the possibility of litigation cases taken against the company for breaches of ethics as employees are made more aware of their ethical responsibilities.
♦ Actual real-life case studies, role-play, check lists and critical incidents can be discussed showing the ethical dilemmas one may face in practice and how these can be resolved.

> "It's a funny thing about life; if you refuse to accept anything but the best, you very often get it."
>
> Somerset Maugham

More and more colleges are now providing formal qualifications in business ethics. Most MBA programmes now have a module on business ethics. Most primary business degrees and diplomas also have a module on ethics. The demand for education in business ethics is as a direct response to all the recent financial scandals. Students are now very receptive to studying ethics because of its perceived relevance and importance in the business world.

Ethics management

Ethics can be managed and controlled through ethical committees and the ethics audit. It is important that workplace practices support and reinforce ethical conduct

Ethical committees

An ethical committee might be set up to raise and resolve ethical issues, and create or update the company's code of ethics. Ferrell et al (2002) reports that Motorola maintains a Business Ethics Compliance Committee. This committee interprets, classifies, communicates, and enforces the company's code and ethics initiatives. An ethics committee can gather information on functional areas of the business. These might include manufacturing, personnel, property, suppliers, accounting, marketing and sales to ensure that the company's practices are ethical and in line with best practice elsewhere.

Senior managers from different functional areas should form the ethical committee. It should formulate policies, develop standards and compare actual practices against standards for compliance. It must be seen to be impartial when dealing with the rest of the organisation. An ethics committee that is just an extension of the CEO will not work. It needs the authority and responsibility to independently pursue its own agenda. It should be in a position to impartially guide the CEO and senior management in making ethical decisions.

Ethics audit

Just as a financial audit is done to test the financial health of a company an ethics audit is done to test the ethical and moral health of a company. The ethics audit will help the company determine if it has complied with the law and established ethical standards (see Appendix 1 for an ethics audit checklist). It acts as an early warning system that systematically

evaluates business practices to identify and prevent ethical problems from arising in the future. These audits can be done on an in-house basis and include employee surveys and group meetings. All departments of the business should be examined. However, some feel that outsiders should carry out the audit in order to ensure impartiality.

> "When mores are sufficient, Laws are unnecessary. When mores are insufficient, laws are unenforceable."
>
> Emile Durkheim

An annual ethics audit is another way of letting employees know the positive effects of their efforts. Managers should be encouraged to review all ethical decisions with their staff, asking "What did we do right? What did we not do that we should have done? How can we learn from our mistakes? What should we do in future similar circumstances?" Each departmental manager should sign a statement each year certifying that staff is abiding by the code of business ethics. A statement should also be signed by staff to show that they are aware of and have discharged their ethical responsibilities.

Many companies now carry out an ethics audit on their suppliers. This is to guard against the possibility of adverse publicity where the supplier might be seen to be involved in unethical practices in relation to the exploitation of labour. In the eyes of the public a company can be guilty of unethical conduct by association.

Typical ethical dilemmas

Ethical dilemmas arise when two or more important values, rights, or obligations conflict with each other. To make a decision we have to choose between equally unpleasant alternatives.

> "The most powerful lessons about ethics and morality do not come from school discussions or classes in character building. They come from family life where people treat one another with respect, consideration and love."
>
> Neil Kurshan

Typical ethical dilemmas include:

♦ Should companies do business with countries or oppressive regimes whose policies are anathema to the majority of employees, shareholders and the general public? In the past some companies had

to confront this issue to decide whether or not to do business with the apartheid regime in South Africa.

♦ In some countries, bribery is a fact of life. To refuse to engage in it means that the company is operating at a competitive disadvantage. Should the organisation engage in bribery to secure contracts, which will provide sustained employment for its workforce? Alternatively should it refuse to compromise its standards and suffer the consequences?

♦ In some countries the giving and receiving of gifts is traditional and an essential part of civilised negotiation. To refuse a gift may be considered an insult to the host. In Japan, for example, gifts are seen as a way of building up a relationship. Managers operating in such a culture may feel obliged to adopt the local custom. To what extent should the company agree to such practices?

♦ Should the organisation adopt positive discrimination in relation to women or minority groups to get a fairer representation in management jobs or employment generally?

♦ A work colleague and friend of yours routinely claims expenses that he is not entitled to. Should you blow the whistle on him and lose a lifelong friend or take the easier option and turn a blind eye?

♦ Everybody in the office in which you work seem to take company stationery and use the photocopier for their own personal use, and also make personal phone calls at the expense of the company. You are not happy with this situation. What should you do?

♦ You are a plant manager. Your director has told you in strict confidence that there are going to be some redundancies in your plant over the next few months. The planned redundancies will not be released for another month. One of your staff who is also a personal friend has approached you and asked you to confirm or deny the rumours about possible redundancies currently going around the plant. He tells you that he is about to get married and has got a substantial mortgage on a new house so it is critical that he knows what the true situation is. You know that he is one of the staff that has been chosen for redundancy. What should you do?

♦ Is there such a thing as a fair price, or is it a question of what the market will bear?

> "There is but one rule of conduct for a man to do the right thing. The cost may be dear in money, in friends, in influence, in labour, in a prolonged and painful sacrifice, but the cost not to do right is far more dear: you pay in the integrity of your manhood, in your honour, in strength of character; and, for a timely gain, you barter the infinite."
>
> Archer G. Jones

Companies that give the code to all employees, that include it on induction programmes, that provide refresher training, that carry out an ethics audit and that require employees to read the code are sending the right signal that they mean business.

Whistleblowing

Many of the great financial scandals came to light as a result of a whistleblower. In Ireland, unlike the UK and US, there is no legal protection for whistleblowers. In the US, *Time* magazine selected three whistleblowers as their persons of the year for 2002: Cynthia Cooper of WorldCom, Coleen Rowley of the FBI, and Sharron Watkins of Enron. All three whistleblowers went to their chief executives first and when the information was leaked they then went to outside sources. In the meantime, directors, accountants, lawyers, investment bankers and analysts all buried their heads in the sand. Sometimes you've got to stand up for what you believe in and do the right thing. As Martin Luther King, said:

> "The ultimate measure of a man (or woman) is not where he or she stands in moments of comfort and convenience, but where he or she stands at times of challenge and controversy."

Peters et al (1972) defines whistleblowing as the act of disclosing any information that an employee reasonably believes is evidence of a violation of any law, rule or regulation, mismanagement, corruption, abuse of authority, or threat to public health and safety at work. The typical types of activities that employees blow the whistle on include stealing, false accounting, waste, mismanagement, safety issues, sexual harassment, and unfair discrimination.

The whistleblower usually discloses the wrongdoing to people in authority. These may be insiders such as supervisors or senior managers and outsiders such as the media or government regulatory authorities. Most who go to outsiders have first used insiders without success.

Whistleblowers are prepared to put their jobs at risk to reveal the truth. Martin Luther King said that our lives begin to end the day we become silent about things that matter.

Retaliation

The whistleblower's life is not an easy one. They will generally find themselves ostracised at best and lose their jobs at worst. They are more likely to suffer retaliation if they go outside. Whistleblowers even have difficulty getting alternative employment. Nobody wants a potential whistleblower on their payroll. In the professions the tradition has been to close ranks when allegations of wrongdoing or incompetence are made. Whistleblowers are seen as people who betray their company and colleagues.

> **"All professions are conspiracies against the laity."**
> George Bernard Shaw

Therefore, many organisations see whistleblowers as informers, question their motives and see them as untrustworthy and disloyal to the company. They are often seen as having a chip on their shoulder and only interested in getting revenge for some perceived wrongdoing. When Jeffrey Wigand, a research executive with Brown & Williamson Tobacco Company, blew the whistle on his company he was subjected to a vitriolic smear campaign. Wigand's decision to blow the whistle was dramatised in the film called *The Insider*. In the film, Russell Crowe plays Jeffrey Wigand, a real life scientist who blew the whistle on the tobacco industry in the US at great personal cost.

The whistleblower is often seen as the bearer of bad news and prompts the reaction of "shoot the messenger". The whole experience for the whistleblower can be very traumatic and at great personal cost.

Reward rather than punish

Whistleblowers who bring to light serious infringements of ethical standards are not only complying with the law in some counties but are also acting ethically. Employees should be rewarded for such behaviour rather than demonised and penalised. It is difficult to blow the whistle on colleagues so the process should be facilitated, encouraged and rewarded by employers. A formalised and confidential system for whistleblowing should be in place. Companies should prefer to know about problems before they come to the media's attention.

Hotlines should be set up, ethics committees established and ombudsmen appointed and employees encouraged to use the system. Hotlines offer support and enable employees to discuss ethical concerns with an impartial and sympathetic ear. The anonymity of the hotlines ensures that employees can be candid about their ethical concerns. They act as an early warning system highlighting poor management, discrimination, environmental concerns, fraud and personal grievances. **Ethics committees should be in place to implement solutions to ethical problems.** The system will lose credibility if no action is taken about the concerns of those who raise issues. In particular, whistleblowers should not be victimised for their good work.

> "Corruption is worse than prostitution. The latter might endanger the morals of an individual, the former invariably endangers the morals of the entire country."
>
> Karl Kraus

Whistleblowing surveys

The *Irish Times* (27/7/2004) reported on a US whistleblowing study. It found that

♦ 100 per cent of whistleblowers were fired, with most unable to find alternative employment.
♦ 17 per cent lost their homes,
♦ their fellow workers harassed 54 per cent.
♦ 15 per cent were subsequently divorced and
♦ 80 per cent suffered physical deterioration.
♦ Almost 90 per cent reported emotional stress, a sense of powerlessness, depression, isolation and anxiety,
♦ while 10 per cent attempted suicide.

Thus the consequences for the whistleblower are very serious and therefore should not be undertaken lightly. They should only take the action if it has a reasonable chance of correcting the wrong, that attempts to rectify the situation through the normal channels have failed and that the whistleblower is not motivated by personal gain or revenge considerations. The wrong should be significant enough to justify the possible negative repercussions for the whistleblower, and his family and friends. Thus the principle of proportionality discussed in Chapter one can be applied here.

Whistleblowing cases

The consequences of whistleblowing include being ostracised by fellow employees, verbal harassment and intimidation, defamation, demotion or denial of promotion, relocation, poor performance appraisal, suspension and even dismissal.

♦ The *Guardian* (10/11/2002) reported that Dr Stephen Bolsin was the consultant anaesthetist at Bristol Royal Infirmary who blew the whistle in 1995 when he became concerned that the death rates for children undergoing heart surgery were higher than elsewhere. Bolsin was unable to get a job in the UK after going public with his allegations. The medical profession are particularly harsh on their whistleblowers and are inclined to close ranks. He subsequently got work in Australia. In another case, Andy Millar, the research scientist who exposed the inflated expectations of the cancer drug Marimastat while at British Biotech, suffered relentless character assassination before being vindicated.

♦ The *Guardian* (8/3/2002) reported that Mr Roy Olofson, once a senior figure in Global Crossing's finance department, filed a lawsuit against the company's directors, alleging that he was dismissed for questioning the accounting methods. He claims that Global Crossing was fraudulently accounting for capacity swaps with other telecom companies. The lawsuit alleges that directors were inflating revenue to exaggerate profits and keep the share price up. It was claimed when he tried to honestly discuss his concerns with the directors, they tried to entice him to join the conspiracy. When that failed they fired him. All of the allegations of fraudulent accounting have since been proved to be true.

♦ Vinten (2004) reported that an oil rig welder, Vaughan Mitchell, highlighted safety violations by his drilling company on a North Sea oil rig. This was in line with the British Department of Employment's poster guaranteeing that anonymity and confidentiality would be respected. Despite these assurances Mitchell was dismissed for his efforts and was unemployed for six months. To survive he had to lease his flat and incur debts, which took years to pay off.

♦ Vinten (2000) reported on two famous cases of whistleblowing. One concerned Karen Silkwood on which the 1983 film *Silkwood* was based. The other concerned the Challenger launch, which took place on 28 January 1986. Karen was concerned about the level of plutonium contamination at the nuclear plant where she worked. She became actively involved in the union helping to educate workers about

plutonium, recruiting votes for the rectification of the plant to meet safety concerns, and recording cases of contamination. She was killed in a car crash in sinister circumstances after leaving one such meeting. She was on her way to meet a reporter for the *New York Times*. She had a folder of evidence documenting contamination, and also proof that the company was doctoring its quality control records and processing defective rods. The file was never recovered. Her father took an action against the company and won. He was awarded $500,000 for personal injuries, $5,000 for property damage, and punitive damages of $10 million. The Nuclear Regulatory Commission has estimated that a worse case accident at a nuclear plant could cause as many as 100,000 deaths within a year, and as much as $300 billion in damage.

> **"We have grasped the mystery of the atom and rejected the Sermon on the Mount...The world has achieved brilliance without wisdom, power without conscience. Ours is a world of nuclear giants and ethical infants".**
>
> Omar Bradley

- ♦ Defective rocket booster seals caused the Challenger disaster. In July 1985 an engineer warned that there could be catastrophic losses if improvements were not made. Pressures to keep on schedule prompted NASA to ignore the warnings. Safety was being compromised by the need to keep on target. When the engineer concerned blew the whistle he was sacked.
- ♦ Ferrell et al (2002) reports that Tampa television reporter Jane Akre was fired after refusing to run a false report about a controversial drug used to increase milk production. In the original report, Akre and two other reporters revealed the cancer risks of the drug. After threats from the drug company, the report was edited, resulting in distorted news. Akre pursued the matter in court under Florida's whistleblower law, and the jury awarded her $425,000.
- ♦ Near et al (2004) reports that although Sherron Watkins of Enron was voted person of the year in 2004 by *Time* magazine nevertheless she was demoted and her job assignments taken away from her. Eventually, she quit and signed a book contract to tell her story. She had delivered a memo to Kenneth Lay, Chairman of Enron, to warn him about potential problems with accounting practices. He is now under investigation for fraud.

Summary

Business ethics should be integrated into the culture of the company. Ethical programmes should have the backing of top management.

One way of implementing ethics is through a general code for the whole business, and specific codes for each department. The main advantage of a code is that it demonstrates that a business takes ethics seriously. A code of business ethics helps counteract the worst excesses of organisational politics by ensuring that it is conducted fairly. However, having a code is no guarantee that it will actually ensure ethical behaviour in the workplace. It is often the personal values and moral standards that influence individual behaviour the most. It is therefore incumbent on a manager to seek out an employer with values consistent with their own.

Common areas covered by codes of ethics include conflicts of interest, gifts, confidentiality, insider dealing, health and safety, executive remuneration, the environment and equal opportunities. Codes should be supported by appropriate publicity and training.

When all else fails employees may be forced to blow the whistle on the company. Whistleblowers have brought major corporate scandals to public attention often at major cost to themselves. Research shows that competition may compromise ethical standards and that the example of senior managers is essential to good business ethics.

Check Your Ethics Quotient

(circle the appropriate response)

1. The motivation for companies to implement an ethics policy should be compliance with its values.   True   False

2. Business ethics codes vary in length, content and readability.   True   False

3. Ethical companies lead by example.   True   False

4. According to the Business Roundtable Institute for Corporate Ethics the most important ethical issue is ensuring the integrity of financial reporting.   True   False

5. University education and ethics training guarantee better business ethics.   True   False

6. Companies are poor at implementing their code of ethics and checking for compliance.   True   False

7. Employees in organisations with formal ethics programmes are more likely to report employee misconduct.   True   False

8. Business ethics are ignored on business degree programmes.   True   False

9. Even if a company has an ethics code there is no guarantee that employees will follow it.   True   False

10. An ethics audit is done to test the financial health of a company.   True   False

Total the number of true and false responses and check Appendix 2 at the back of the book for the solution.

Case study: How those who blow the whistle suffer

The *Guardian* (21/11/2001) reported that the European Union imposed record fines against drug companies for colluding to fix vitamin prices and overcharge customers. Eight companies were fined including Hoffman-La Roche of Switzerland, who were fined a record €662 million, and BASF of Germany, who were fined €296 million. The EU maintained that the price-fixing collusion enabled the firms concerned to charge higher prices than if market forces were allowed to operate freely. It overcharged customers allowing the companies to make excessive and illicit profits.

Under EU law companies found guilty of antitrust practices can be fined up to 10 per cent of their total annual sales. Under EU rules, which came into force in February 2002, the first firm to confess to price-fixing will get total immunity from EU fines. This is the situation provided the information allows the commission to undertake a "dawn raid" – the first step in breaking up a cartel.

Mario Monti, the European Commission's competition director-general said that the cartel could be dubbed "Vitamin Inc" and was the most damaging case the commission had ever investigated, as it continued throughout the entire Nineties and involved substances vital for healthy living.

Stanley Adams, the 74 year old who blew the whistle on Roche nearly 30 years ago had heard it all before. He handed over documents to the EEC, as it was then, detailing how Roche kept the price of vitamins high with the explicit collusion of its competitors. Adams had been promised anonymity but the EEC bungled badly and allowed a Roche official to photocopy some of the incriminating documents. The documents had Adams's signature on them so that he was exposed as the whistleblower.

The Swiss authorities arrested Adams and accused him of being a spy. Adams's wife was told he faced a 20-year jail sentence for industrial espionage. She committed suicide. In the end, Adams's only served six months in a Swiss prison. But it took him another 10 years to get compensation from the EU through the courts. In 1985 the EU agreed to pay Adams compensation. Adams

now feels vindicated that the work he started in the Sixties has come to an end.

Adams maintains that most of the major drug companies have senior politicians on their payroll to serve their interests.

(Based on an article in the *Observer*, 25/11/2001.)

Questions

- ◆ Bearing in mind what happened to Adams would you be prepared to whistle blow on your company?
- ◆ What policies should companies put in place to nurture, protect and award whistleblowers?
- ◆ What legislation should be put in place to protect the rights of whistleblowers?

5. Ethical Issues: Senior Management

> ◆ What is insider dealing?
> ◆ How do conflicts of interest arise?
> ◆ What is corporate manslaughter?
> ◆ How does tax become an ethical issue?
> ◆ What are the ethical issues in research?

"Nothing is illegal if a hundred businessmen decide to do it".
Andrew Young

The good character and values of senior executives is just as important to the success of a company as their knowledge and skills. The way they deal with ethical issues is of great importance to the continuity and future success of the company.

Ethical issues inside the company concerning managers include management fraud, tax avoidance, corporate manslaughter, conflict of interest, insider dealing, stock options, excessive executive remuneration, downsizing, and accounting fraud.

Executive greed

Greed, stealing of company assets for their own use, and fraudulent practices are some of the manifestations of the low standards operating in management. Greed, arrogance and business scandals are not new. In 1637 the market for tulips in Amsterdam collapsed bringing financial ruin to thousands of businessmen. During the height of the speculative frenzy all sorts of assets were exchanged for bulbs. There was even a market in futures. The market was driven by motives to get rich quick but ended in disappointment and bankruptcy for many.

The basic assumptions we all have that most people are basically honest and trustworthy make us complacent and probably facilitate fraud. We assume that corporations are honest, that banks are trustworthy, and that the integrity of directors is beyond reproach. The facts of recent times paint a different picture. The following cases will illustrate the type of

unethical behaviour found in business. The range of ethical lapses range from fraud, embezzlement, false accounting, misleading investors, money-laundering, misappropriation of company assets and conflicts of interest.

> **"There are more fakers in business that in jail."**
>
> Malcolm Forbes

Excess

The *Observer* (29/12/2002) reported that the CEO of Tyco, Dennis Kozlowski, who turned Tyco into a company worth $100 million at its peak, would be infamously remembered for using company funds to buy $6,000 worth of shower curtains. In addition the company loaned him millions to buy everything from an apartment to a $15,000 umbrella stand. For his second wife's birthday he was reputed to have spent more than $827,000 for a party in Sardinia.

Ferrell et al (2002) states that Lars Bildman, a senior executive with the US company Astra, chartered yachts with high priced prostitutes, and took relatives and family on vacation – all financed out of company funds. He renovated his house and ski lodge with more than $2 million of Astra's money. Bildman's Boston suburban home was furnished with a sauna, pool, wine cellar, and a martial arts facility for his children – all paid out of company funds.

Former GE boss, Jack Welch, one of America's most respected businessmen, is alleged to have spent millions of shareholders money to fund his own retirement. Court documents leaked during Welch's divorce revealed that GE gave him the use of a plane and a Central Park apartment. In addition it paid for his food and wine bills, flowers and laundry and ensured he was never short of tickets for the ball game. Jack Welch has written best selling books on business management and was seen as a paragon of ethical values.

> **"Greed is a bottomless pit which exhausts the person in an endless effort to satisfy the need without ever reaching satisfaction. "**
>
> Erich Fromm

Hollinger

The *Irish Times* (1/9/2004) reported that a special committee of Hollinger's board has blamed the excessive lifestyle of Lord Conrad Black and his wife Lady Barbara Amiel Black for the alleged fraud at the media's

publishing group. The report details how the former Hollinger chairman and a long-term colleague, Mr David Radler, allegedly colluded to steal $400 million from the company. The allegations ranged from relatively minor examples of misuse of company funds such as charging Hollinger $42,070 for Lady Black's birthday party in New York to larger scale allegations of fraud and tax avoidance. It concluded that executives were wrongfully paid nearly $200 million in "unjustifiable" management fees, even as the business was underperforming against their media peers.

Clark (2008) reports that although Lord Black claims he is still innocent, the court has confirmed his sentence of six and a half years and fine of $125,000. Black failed in his duty to act in the interests of shareholders rather than in his own selfish interest. His personal fortune was once estimated at £136 million and at the height of his career he controlled more than 200 newspapers worldwide.

> "There is enough in the world for everyone's need, but not enough for everyone's greed."
>
> Frank Buchman

In response, Westhead (2004) reports that Hollinger revised its code of business ethics in December 2004 and strengthened the rules concerning conflicts of interest and related-party transactions. The company has set out specific protocols for reporting accounting complaints and any illegal or unethical behaviour. The rules also specify guidelines for accepting business gifts, saying that the "value of gifts should be nominal, both with respect to frequency and amount". The company maintains that even repetitive small gifts may be perceived as an attempt to create an obligation to the giver and are therefore not appropriate. It seems to be a case of locking the stable door after the horse has bolted!

Looting the pension fund

Vogel (1992) reports that in 1991, Robert Maxwell, a prominent British businessman who controlled the Mirror Group of newspapers, was implicated in a number of wide-ranging abuses, including the looting of a large pension fund and fraudulent bookkeeping designed to conceal the insolvency of various firms that he controlled. Maxwell died in mysterious circumstances at sea before the true scale of the scam became public.

It was subsequently found that he had plundered £450 million from various pension funds under his control. His legacy included wound up companies, employees without jobs and pensioners deprived of their benefits. He had borrowed from reputable banks in London and was hailed

a hero in the US for rescuing the *New York Daily News*. His leadership was autocratic and anybody who wrote an article criticising him was the subject of a libel action.

Employees of Enron found that their retirement funds were rendered worthless by the collapse of the company. Pension investment funds should be diversified and not be totally dependent on the shares of the parent company. Putting all your eggs in one basket is a recipe for financial disaster.

Global Crossing which collapsed in January 2002, bankrupted its employees who had pension money invested in the company's shares and were prevented from selling much of the shares for five years. The shares are now practically worthless.

Italy's greatest business scandal

The reasons underlying the collapse of Parmalat are proving to be one of Italy's greatest scandals. The *Irish Times* (7/2/2004) reported that Parmalat was Italy's eight largest industrial group, employing 36,400 people at 139 plants in more than 30 countries worldwide and with an estimated revenue of €7.6 billion. False accounting was used to hide the reckless expansion of the group. It had classified $300 million in loans as investments, instead of debt.

"Things gained through unjust fraud are never secure."

Sophocles

Senior executives have been arrested and charged with fraud, embezzlement, false accounting and misleading investors. Grant Thornton International, auditors to Parmalat, and a number of major banks have been accused of collusion in the fraud. The banks were more motivated by greed and collecting enormous fees than following the rules. Investment analyst rated the company's shares a "buy" right up to the end. The *Irish Times* (3/1/2004) reported that the fraud came to light in December 2003 when the Bank of America found that a document showing €3.9 billion in an account held by a Cayman Island's subsidiary of Parmalat was false. It no longer surprises anybody that another audit firm has been implicated in facilitating the fraudulent accounting in a company.

When executives land in prison

Employees fall from grace can be swift and severe and involve prison sentences. The *Irish Times* (9/8/2002) reported that Mario Conde, a

Spanish banker, was the epitome of Spain's 1980s get rich quick lifestyle. Conde was photographed smiling with King Juan Carlos 11 when he received an honorary doctorate. The Pope invited him to lecture in the Vatican on business ethics and young Spaniards voted Conde their favourite role model. Spain's opposition party wanted him to lead it back to power. At one stage he seemed to have the world at his feet. His life is now in disarray because of misappropriation of funds, falsification of documents and fraudulent accounting. He was sentenced to 20 years in prison.

> **"Take care! Be on your guard against all kinds of greed; for one's life does not consist in the abundance of possessions."**
>
> Bible: New Testament, Luke 12:15

Vogel (1992) reports that in 1988 the "junk-bond king" Michael Milken and his firm, Drexel Burnham Lambert, were indicted in the USA for violating federal securities laws and regulations. Both had to pay large fines and Milken was sentenced to prison for ten years, subsequently reduced to two. The penalty of $650 million imposed on Drexel helped force the company into bankruptcy. These two gentlemen are still very wealthy people, which make a mockery of the popular saying that "crime does not pay".

Vogel (1992) reports that in 1987, Ernest Saunders, the chief executive of Guinness, was accused of attempting to illegally prop up his company's share price to help support its bid for the Distillers beverage group. In 1990, Saunders was found guilty of having helped engineer the increase in the stock's price and was sentenced to five years in prison for false accounting, theft and conspiracy. His sentence was later cut to two and a half years on appeal. However, in reality he only served 10 months after he was diagnosed as suffering from pre-senile dementia. He seems to have made a remarkable recovery from the illness since his release.

The only people who gain from these corporate collapses are the lawyers and accountants who are employed to unravel the mess. Also, most executives seem to walk away from these disasters with their wealth intact. On the other hand, shareholders may see the value of their shares wiped out overnight. Creditors may get very little if anything of what is owed to them back. Employees lose their jobs, trade unions lose membership, and often the pension fund is bankrupted if the main source of investment was the defunct company's shares.

Gifts and entertainment

When does a gift become a bribe? Certainly one would not consider calendars, diaries, pens and such like to be bribes. Similarly being taken out to a rare business lunch would not be considered excessive. On the other hand receiving a Rolex watch, tickets for premium sporting events, or being taken away for a golfing weekend to an expensive hotel would be considered excessive and potentially compromising. Problems may arise in some cultures where to refuse a gift is considered an insult. Buyers in particular may be exposed to the temptation of bribery.

> "Keep your hands clean and pure from the infamous vice of corruption, a vice so infamous that it degrades even the other vices that may accompany it. Accept no present whatever; let your character in that respect be transparent and without the least speck, for as avarice is the vilest and dirtiest vice in private, corruption is so in public life."
>
> Philip Dormer Stanhope

Stealing company assets.

The polite term for this is misappropriation of company assets. Some executives behave as if the company they manage is their own personal property. An executive who uses company maintenance staff to paint his house is behaving unethically. An executive who uses company funds to pay for his personal expenses is also behaving unethically.

In fact, people have a remarkable capacity to rationalise or compartmentalise things. Consider the businessman who goes to church on Sunday, and fiddles his expenses on Monday. He has learnt to put business issues in one compartment and religion in another.

Fraud

Bottom-line results can be improved, by inflating sales, profits and assets and understating expenses, losses or liabilities. Sales returns may not be recorded or delayed, sales may be booked early, closing stock may be inflated and cash may be recorded in two bank accounts at the same time. There is an inherent incentive for executives to commit this type of fraud where reward packages are based on sales or profitability.

Gellerman (1986) reports that at General Electric when one of its missile projects ran up costs greater than the US Air Force had agreed to pay, middle managers surreptitiously shifted those costs to other projects

under budget. When this came to light GE's reputation suffered badly and it had to pay a fine of $1.04 million. One of the most troubling aspects of the GE case was its admission that those involved were thoroughly familiar with the company's ethical standards before the incident took place.

> "Reputation's an impression
> Others get with lines uncrossed;
> It's a personal possession
> Rarely noticed till it's lost."
>
> Anon

PwC European Economic Crime Survey 2001 found that

- 42.5 per cent of major European organisations reported suffering at least one serious fraud between 1999 and 2001. These cost on average €6.7 million.
- 50 per cent of these frauds were discovered by accident.
- Only one-in-five organisations have been able to recover more than 50 per cent of their losses.
- Over 70 per cent of organisations believe that future fraud risks will be the same or greater.

Insider dealing (trading) .

People who practice insider dealing are operating at the preconventional morality level (see Kohlberg's model in Chapter 1). They are primarily motivated by self-interest. **These are transactions in financial securities by persons with privileged confidential inside information not currently available to the general investing public, and who as a result may personally profit from such knowledge.**

Insider dealing is as old as the stock market itself. However, it wasn't until after the 1929 Wall Street crash that things came to a head. An investigation revealed the rampant unethical practices of brokers and bankers who manipulated share prices to their advantage. As a result the Securities and Exchange Commission (SEC) was set up in 1934 in the USA to stamp out such practices.

Executives found guilty of insider trading are publicly disgraced (and often imprisoned). Directors and officers of the company have a fiduciary relationship with their shareholders. Insider trading is seen as breaking that bond of trust.

> "The only reason to invest in the market is because you think you know something others don't."
>
> R. Foster Winans

The objections to insider dealing are that the possessors of the inside information are gaining at the expense of those who do not – in effect, a form of theft. Insider trading is a criminal and civil offence in many countries so that the aggrieved party may also sue for damages. The perpetrators have been given prison sentences in the USA. However in some countries like New Zealand insider trading is not illegal and many view it as not being particularly unethical.

Examples of insider dealing

Those with inside information can include directors, managers and employees of the company. It can include relatives or friends of these people who gain such information indirectly through their friendships or dealings. Outside the company it could include reporters, suppliers, stockbrokers and those who print the annual report and accounts.

An example of insider dealing inside the company could be that of the director who is aware of potential negative information about the company and who sells his shares before this information becomes public knowledge, after which the price of such shares usually declines. On the other hand, he may become aware of a proposed take over bid, major oil find or gold discovery likely to push up the share price and buys more shares before the information becomes public.

An example of insider dealing outside the company might be the employee of a merchant bank operating on behalf of a client who is privy to price sensitive information such as details about a prospective merger. The bank employee buys shares in the target company on the expectation that the price will go up when the deal goes through. Similarly an executive who spreads malicious rumours to depress the value of shares in order to buy them at a lower price is behaving unethically.

> "Artificial inflation of stocks must be considered a crime as serious as counterfeiting, which it closely resembles."
>
> Andrew Maurois

More indirect insider dealing also exists. Take the example of the director who shares confidential information with financial advisors that the company's profits have been overstated over the past few years. The financial advisor then advises his clients to sell the shares and when the

information becomes public the share price falls and so the clients gain. Another example might be the financial journalist who hears through contacts that a certain company is about to go into liquidation. He tells his friends before the story is published, giving them an opportunity to sell their shares in the company before the share price collapses.

Insider information

Leaking insider information is a breach of trust and may be both illegal and unethical. There are all sorts of confidential information and trade secrets a manager or employee will come across during the course of employment. This may include research and development projects, patents and copyrights. A company's inventions, unique products, processes, procedures, knowledge, and systems give it a competitive advantage. Revealing such information to outsiders for any reason is a very serious matter, while doing so for personal gain is unethical as well as illegal.

Reward package

Reward package includes remuneration, stock options, loans, pensions and golden handshakes. All of these have come under critical scrutiny by the media and public in recent times.

Remuneration

There is no doubt that CEOs and senior executives should be well paid. Very few people get to the top without decades of hard work, dedication and experience. It is generally acknowledged that senior management positions are stressful. So nobody begrudges them a decent remuneration package. What people question is the huge amount of money they are awarded in comparison to others. Remuneration of CEOs and directors is often hundreds of times the average wage. From an ethical perspective it is difficult to justify that one individual is worth multiples of another. Shareholders feel that CEOs and senior executives are enriching themselves at their expense.

While employee wages have increased modestly, the remuneration of CEOs and directors has reached astronomical levels. Whereas shareholders' dividends are relative to profits made, senior executives often get increased salaries irrespective of results. What really annoys the ordinary employee is that during times of cutbacks and redundancies the remuneration of senior executives often increases rather than decreases.

Ordinary employees are seen as disposable, while at the same time senior executives are perceived to profit on the backs of redundant employees. One would imagine that remuneration packages for senior executives should be strictly results-related. Senior executives should be held accountable for the bad decisions they make – decisions which may adversely affect the future viability of the company.

Omestad (2004) reports that Richard Perle, after becoming chairman and chief executive of Hollinger Digital, participated in a plan rewarding himself and other executives with up to 22 per cent of the profits on successful ventures. However, there was no financial penalty if investments turned to losses. From 2000 to 2003, Perle reaped more than $3 million from the deal, on top of an annual salary of $300,000 and board fees.

Stock options

Stock options link top executives pay to a company's share price. This may encourage irresponsible behaviour such as creative accounting to inflate profits and shove up share prices to boost their compensation package further. Moreover, stock options do not have to be shown on the company's balance sheet and profit and loss account. Consequently one of the key indicators for a company, the price-earning ratio is distorted. This is the market price of a share divided by the company's earnings per share. **Not showing the stock options as an expense in the profit and loss account exaggerates the profits and thus the price earnings ratio.**

The inclusion of stock options on the balance sheet and as an expense in the accounts would more accurately reflect the true financial position of the company. When stock options are cashed in, a company has either to issue more stock or repurchase it on the open market. This dilutes the value of existing shareholders' shares. Ultimately there is no such thing as a free lunch and somebody pays for stock options. Hence the case for treating stock options as an expense in the financial accounts. This has now become official EU policy.

Loans

Boards have granted loans of millions of dollars to directors on preferential terms while at the same time agreeing to make thousands of employees redundant. This is an unethical and surreptitious way of rewarding executives.

Chief executives have awarded themselves exorbitant pensions when retiring. Excessive golden handshakes seem to be the order of the day.

Tax issues

Senior executives and others have engaged in tax avoidance schemes by channelling funds into off shore accounts. Sometimes this is done to enhance the wealth of the company while at other times it is done to enhance the personal wealth of senior executives.

> "Tax avoidance means that you hire a $250,000 fee lawyer, and he changes the word 'evasion' into the word 'avoidance'."
>
> Franklin D. Roosevelt

Tax havens

Some senior managers have used tax havens in such places as Bermuda and the Cayman Islands to avoid paying tax. Even if legal, these schemes are unethical. The CEO of Tyco, Dennis Kozlowski was indicted for tax avoidance of $1 million on valuable paintings. He was also charged with falsifying records to give the impression that the paintings were shipped out of state. Kozlowski resigned from Tyco when the charges became known.

The *Observer* (3/2/2002) reported that during his time as CEO investors alleged that Tyco's income was artificially inflated by aggressive and improper accounting practices to meet optimistic earnings forecasts. He is said to have netted $170 million by selling shares five months before the company was subjected to a SEC inquiry in December 1999.

Financial engineering, transfer pricing and other financial tricks are used to avoid paying tax. Transfer pricing happens, where multinationals operating in low tax economies, import their raw materials from the parent company at greatly reduced prices and export the finished product at inflated ones. Because they are on a very low rate of corporation tax they pay as much tax as possible in the low tax economy in order to avoid paying the higher rate of tax in the parent company's country.

Offshore accounts

Most of us do not like paying tax but businesses and the rich are in a particularly strong position to avoid paying tax if they want to. They can employ the best of accountants and tax consultants to advise them about the best tax avoidance schemes available. They can set up offshore accounts to avoid paying tax.

According to Oxfam, the use of offshore havens by multinationals is depriving developing countries of $50 billion each year. It also means that

the rest of us pay more tax than we should and that the government has less money to spend on vital services such as health, education, social and infrastructure.

The *Guardian* (12/4/2002) reported that almost one-third of the world's gross domestic product passes through such tax havens as Belize, Guernsey, Bermuda, the Isle of Man, the Bahamas and the Cayman Islands. Places like Belize offer secrecy and do not recognise judgements and claims from other jurisdictions. They specialise in opaque corporate and financial structures, with no annual company reports or disclosures – the ideal places for tax avoiders to stash their cash.

> **"Secrecy is the badge of fraud."**
>
> Sir John Chadwick

Many major and well-known companies – including Virgin, Microsoft, General Motors, Kodak, and Boeing – use offshore accounts to avoid tax obligations in host countries. According to the Centre for Public Integrity (www.publicintegrity.org) US-based oil and gas companies have nearly 900 subsidiaries located in tax haven countries such as the Cayman Islands and Bermuda.

Tax evasion in Ireland

It wasn't until the late 1990s that the extent of tax evasion became known. Tribunals set up revealed that companies, and self-employed such as shopkeepers, farmers, publicans and professional people avoided the payment of income tax and aided and abetted by their banks hid away millions of pounds in bogus offshore accounts. This happened during the 1960s, 1970s, and 1980s and into the early 1990s.

The McCracken Tribunal found that some of the top Irish business people deposited money in offshore accounts between the early 1970s and 1997. This became known as the Ansbacher scandal. Ansbacher (Cayman) was an unlicensed bank that operated from Cement Roadstone Holdings (CRH) offices in Dublin. It allowed business people and politicians to deposit large sums of money offshore while retaining the convenience of easy access at home. Its most famous customer was the ex Irish Prime Minister, Mr Charles Haughey who was also found to have received £210,000 as a "gift" from the supermarket tycoon, Mr Ben Dunne. There is no doubt that there is a strong possibility that political favours were expected in return for such gifts.

McCaffrey (2004) reports that investigations by the tax authorities have yielded about €42 million in tax and penalties owed. The owners of

Ansbacher Cayman have made a €7.5 million settlement with the tax authorities, despite claiming that they had no tax liability.

Financial institutions

O'Toole (2004) reports that AIB has a history of unethical and illegal conduct. At the Beef Tribunal in 1992 it emerged that the bank had been routinely cashing bogus cheques for the Goodman organisation. In 1986 about €4.5 million was processed by AIB in a fraud designed to evade tax. Plant managers in Goodman made out cheques in the names of non-existent hauliers or suppliers. They went down to their local AIB branches every Friday and cashed the cheques. The bank turned a blind eye to facilitate this massive tax fraud.

> "To be really great in little things, to be truly noble and heroic in the inspired details of everyday life, is a virtue so rare as to be worthy of cannonization."
>
> Harriet Beecher Stowe

During the 1980s and 1990s AIB created thousands of bogus non-resident accounts for the sole purpose of facilitating their clients to evade tax. In Ireland in the 1960s it seems that only pay-as-your-earn (PAYE) employees paid tax. The country was awash with cash and many people operating in the black economy were paid in cash to avoid income tax – a characteristic of the economy at the time.

In 1998 it emerged that National Irish Bank (NIB) had marketed an unauthorised investment scheme to more than 400 account holders, many of whom used the scheme to evade tax. NIB opened bogus non-resident accounts throughout its network for its customers to avoid deposit interest retention tax (DIRT). The bank was also investigated for overcharging interest. In 1994 an internal audit report discovered that NIB could be facing a serious DIRT liability. However, senior management decided to ignore the situation and no action was taken.

The High Court and Supreme Courts found that a current member of the Irish Parliament Ms Beverly Flynn helped customers evade tax while she was employed as a manager with NIB. Her excuse that she was only following orders was not accepted.

> "The lawyer and the doctor and other professional men have often a touch of civilisation. The banker and the merchant seldom."
>
> Jim Tully

In early 2005 it came to light that the insurance industry in Ireland were also involved in tax evasion on insurance products. People with retirement lump sums were encouraged to invest their money in single-premium policies. These were an attractive investment for people who wanted to evade tax as the insurance company paid the tax on the profits from the policy and the investor had no further liability when the policy matured. To date millions of Euros have been collected in tax arrears.

Politicians

Mr Denis Foley, an Irish Member of Parliament for North Kerry and businessman, who was a member of the PAC appointed to investigate tax evasion, was himself found to have been involved in tax evasion. He had amassed a small fortune during the Irish showband era in the 1960s and 1970s when operating as a ballroom manager. Those who make the law should uphold it rather than break it. Legislators should be role models for ethical behaviour rather than hypocrites. They have a duty of trust to their constituents.

The PAC found that tens of thousands of ordinary Irish people had opened bogus offshore accounts under the name of an overseas relative and used them to hide money from the tax authorities. The PAC found that bank management, including AIB, had in some cases actively encouraged and facilitated the process. The banks paid over €220 million to settle their DIRT liabilities with the tax authorities. Subsequently a further €494 million of tax arrears was collected from customers individually pursued by the tax authorities.

A former Minister for Justice, Mr Ray Burke, was forced to resign in 1997 after bribery allegations, tax evasion, and planning corruption. The Flood Tribunal found that he had received corrupt payments of more than a quarter of a million pounds over three decades of public life. In January 2005 the former government minister was jailed for six months for failing to make tax returns on over £100,000 over a ten-year period between 1982 and 1991. He made history by becoming the first government minister in the Irish Republic to be jailed. Like Al Capone he was nailed on tax evasion rather than bribery and corruption charges.

> "The accomplice to the crime of corruption is frequently our own indifference."
>
> Bess Myerson

Offshore accounts and tax avoidance schemes were commonplace amongst politicians and businesspeople alike. The attitude seemed to be

prevalent in the country that it was only the little people who paid tax. The legislators thought they were exempt from the laws that they themselves were passing.

The average PAYE employee had no choice since tax was deducted at source from wages through the pay as you earn system. The rest of the country mainly self employed and professional people avoided tax through elaborate tax avoidance schemes aided and abetted by banks and accountants. Even the revenue authorities and the Central Bank turned a blind eye for a considerable time to what was happening.

Most of these scandals would not have come into the public domain without the work of the media. The NIB only came to light when RTE's Charlie Bird and George Lee broadcast the results of their own investigation. The media were also instrumental in exposing the DIRT scandal.

Conflicts of interest

A conflict of interest arises when a person must choose between their own interests, those of the company, or those of some other group. To avoid conflicts of interest employees must be able to separate their private interest from those of the company. Thus a director with an interest in a supplier company should declare that interest. Auditors employed as auditors and management consultants compromise their independence and integrity and create a conflict of interest.

Medical journals are often financed through advertising. The pharmaceutical companies advertise their products in these journals and frequently the advertising revenue is the main source of funding for such journals. Some of these journals are sent free to doctors. Consequently the content of articles featured in these journals may be compromised by the nature of the funding. This represents a conflict of interest as the editorial independence of such journals is in doubt. Pharmaceutical companies often make large donations to non-profit hospitals, which may compromise the hospital position in relation to the choice of medicines used.

"As people get their opinions so largely from the newspapers they read, the corruption of the schools would not matter so much if the Press were free. But the Press is not free. As it costs at least a quarter of a million of money to establish a daily newspaper in London, the newspapers are owned by rich men. And they depend on the advertisements of other rich men. Editors and journalists who express opinions in print that are opposed to the interests of the rich are dismissed and replaced by subservient ones."

George Bernard Shaw

The *Guardian* (July 9, 2003) reported that Nottingham University Business School was widely attacked because of the conflict of interest inherent in its decision to run the UK's first MBA in CSR with a £3.8 million endowment provided by British American Tobacco. The business school ignored criticism from organisations such as Friends of the Earth, who believe that the decision makes a mockery of the concept of social responsibility. Tobacco companies are not noted for their high sense of business ethics. Cancer researcher, Professor David Thurston, left in protest, taking his cancer research team and grant to London University's School of Pharmacy. Obviously he felt that being associated with Nottingham University would be seen as a conflict of interest and compromise his integrity as a scientist.

Downsizing

Cost-cutting leading to redundancies may sometimes be unethical. The stereotype of the top manager or CEO being too ready to cut jobs and focusing on short-term profits while at the same time making personal fortunes for themselves in reward packages and stock options is sometimes not far from the truth. It is a lot easier to implement cutbacks rather than come up with innovative business strategies to consolidate or expand operations to preserve jobs.

The *Guardian* (2/6/2004) reports that US businessman, "Chainsaw Ali" Dunlap used simple tactics to turn around companies in financial difficulties. He would sell off the more profitable parts and make widespread redundancies. Having improved the bottom line he would then sell the company off at a healthy profit. When he was made head of appliance-maker Sunbeam in 1997, he lived up to his reputation by cutting 11,000 staff – nearly half of the company's workforce. He eventually got his comeuppance after investors realised that his savage cuts were a mask for little more than financial engineering and accounting tricks.

Dunlap had been using a "bill and hold" strategy with retailers. This boosted revenue. The strategy involves selling products at large discounts to retailers and holding them in third-party warehouses to be delivered at a future date. By booking sales ahead of the actual shipment and billing, Sunbeam was able to exaggerate its sales. Basically, what the strategy achieved was transferring sales from future accounting periods to the current one. The end result of all this was dubious financial statements, which misled potential investors who use financial statements as the basis for buying shares in a company. Like Enron and WorldCom, Sunbeam's

auditors were Arthur Andersen. Anderson had to make a settlement of $110 million to Sunbeam's shareholders for inflating profits in 1998.

> "As a single leaf turns not yellow but with the silent knowledge of the whole tree, so the wrong-doer cannot do wrong without the hidden will of you all."
>
> Kahlil Gibran

Ethics of relocation

The ethics of relocating where a company is already successful, just to increase profits further is questionable. Some relocations are motivated by the possibility of exploiting cheap labour, lax regulatory standards or favourable tax situations in other countries. In other situations the company may have no alternative if it wants to stay in business but to seek out low cost economies. Relocation is ethical provided that it is based on genuine economic, survival and competitive considerations. The clothing and shoe industry in particular has been forced by competition and cost considerations to relocate to low wage economies. Many companies are now relocating by moving jobs into the cheap labour economies of China, India and the Far East.

Under a policy of downsizing, employees are made redundant and local communities devastated. Customers are left without proper service and may leave to join competitors. Suppliers lose business. Trade unions lose membership subscriptions. Costs may escalate instead of decreasing. These ethical considerations should persuade managers not to undertake such moves lightly. It may be difficult to estimate the hardship caused by plant relocation on a community but nevertheless it should not be disregarded as a minor consideration. The uncaring way in which some companies have handled layoffs and downsizing has lowered the level of general trust in management.

Deception

Doost (2003) reports that the top executives of Enron cashed in hundreds of millions of dollars worth of stock and received hefty bonuses of $350 million in February 2001 for the year 2000. At the same time, the executives wouldn't allow their employees to cash in their shares but instead assured them, in writing and orally, that the company finances were sound and that the firm would even perform better in the future. All of this happened when they must have known that the company was in

severe financial difficulties, camouflaged by fraudulent accounting practices.

> "In every survey we conducted, honesty was selected more often than any other leadership characteristic; it consistently emerged as the single most important ingredient in the leader-constituent relationship. It's clear that if we're to willingly follow someone – whether it be into battle or into the boardroom, into the classroom or into the back room, into the front office or to the front lines – we first want to assure ourselves that the person is worthy of our trust. We want to know that the person is being truthful, ethical, and principled. We want to be fully confident of the integrity of our leaders, whatever the context. That nearly 90 per cent of constituents want their leaders to be honest above all else is a message that all leaders must take to heart."
>
> James M. Kouzes & Barry Z. Posner,
> *The Leadership Challenge*, Jossey-Bass, San Francisco (1995)

Polly Peck collapsed in 1990. It employed 40,000 people worldwide. It was a conglomerate involved in different businesses such as electronics and fruit. The *Observer* (7/9/2003) reported that in September 1990 the Fraud Squad raided its offices. Polly Peck's shares were suspended and the company was put into administration amid accusations of false accounting, embezzlement, and share price manipulation. The founder, Nadir declared himself a bankrupt in 1991, and was charged with theft totalling £34 million. He fled Britain in May 1993 and settled in Cyprus. He has never returned.

Cheating

In universities and colleges, we have the future captains of industry cheating at exams, plagiarising assignments and dissertations and even paying others to take the tests for them. Students taking professional accountancy exams have even used the difference in time zones to fax exam papers to students in other centres throughout the world. This is the reason why students doing some professional exams are not allowed to take the exam paper with them when they finish the exam.

Access to the Internet has made it so easy to cut and paste and plagiarise other author's work without crediting sources that some students don't even realise that they are breaking copyright by doing so. This is in fact stealing another author's intellectual property and thus is both unethical and illegal. It is also dishonest to claim authorship of a work that is not substantially your own.

> "With proper attribution, to quote another's thoughts and words is appropriate; plagiarism, however, is cheating, and it may break copyright law as well."
>
> Kenneth G. Wilson

The *Irish Times* (January 10, 1997) reported about 50 US stockbrokers paid up to $5,000 to impostors to take licensing exams for them. They were subsequently indicted in the biggest securities test-cheating scheme ever uncovered in the US. There were 54 people in the scheme, including two who took the tests, middlemen who helped carry out the scheme and 50 brokers who paid impostors to take the tests. The charges included forgery and possession of forged securities. The two who sat the exams were able to escape detection by taking the tests at a variety of different locations in different states while using fake photo identification.

There are even colleges on the web offering fake degrees. For example, the *Guardian* (5/7/2004) reported that a British website was offering fake degrees, GCSEs and A levels that appear authentic. The forged qualifications costing £165 ranged from medical to law degrees to masters in English. This highlights the need for employers to check out carefully the claimed qualifications of applicants. In some cases this is never done.

In sport we have some athletes taking performance-enhancing drugs, boxers who throw fights and jockeys who throw races. This has become a major problem in the Olympic Games and elaborate drug-testing is now in place to try and prevent it. It seems that the spirit and high ethical standards of the original founders of the games have not survived.

Misrepresentation

Managers trying to reach production targets may cut corners and take actions that they know are unethical. Ferrell et al (2002) reports that in the airline industry planes are sometimes approved for flights even though all repairs haven't been adequately done. To offset flight delays, some airline maintenance managers cut corners on non-critical repairs. In addition, some airlines schedule arrival times fifteen to thirty minutes later than actually expected, so that more flights appear to arrive on time. Customers, however, assume that all airlines are completely safe for flight, and that their planes will arrive and depart on time.

Destroying evidence

Arthur Andersen shredded thousands of documents relating to its audit of Enron when they realised the game was up. The people who shredded the documents said they were operating to instructions while the senior executives have denied this. It is very difficult to establish the truth if executives resort to lies and deceit to save their skin.

> "Delusions, errors and lies are like huge, gaudy vessels, the rafters of which are rotten and worm-eaten, and those who embark in them are fated to be shipwrecked."
>
> Buddha

Ferrell et al (2002) reports that Johnson & Johnson shredded thousands of documents relating to a federal investigation into whether the company had illegally promoted its Retin-A acne drug as a wrinkle remover. Fines and court costs total about $7.5 million, and three senior executives were fired. Obviously companies would only destroy evidence if they have something to hide.

Corporate manslaughter

Under law a company is a legal entity separate from those who make it up. This principle protects the directors from financial liabilities and reduces their personal safety obligations and criminal accountability. In the past, directors have rarely been prosecuted for corporate manslaughter. For example, the *Observer* (2/2/2003) reported that 11 companies in the UK had been prosecuted so far for manslaughter and 4 convicted. The number of directors who had been jailed for such offences was only 2.

In Britain, a Law Commission report in the mid-90s recommended a new offence of corporate killing but so far it has not got on the statute books. This is despite the thousands of deaths in Britain each year due to work-related incidents. Some of these deaths show blatant disregard for health and safety legislation.

Clark (2008) reports that Lord Browne, former chief executive of BP, denied all knowledge of safety lapses when making an hour-long deposition to a US court in April. He was referring to an explosion at a BP refinery in Texas City three years ago which killed 15 people and injured more than 180.

The Texas City blast was America's worst industrial accident for a generation. Three of the employees involved had worked for more than a

month without a day off and many of the victims were in trailers situated dangerously close to volatile equipment. BP was fined a record of $21 million by US regulators. Browne said he never read a report into the tragedy's causes by the Chemical Safety Board.

During his 12 years as BP's chief executive, Lord Browne created a new brand for the oil company as an environmentally conscious organisation with a distinctive sunflower logo. He presided over a sustained period of expansion and became one of Britain's most influential business chiefs. But BP's reputation suffered in 2005 and 2006 from serious failings in the US including the explosion at its Texas Oil refinery in 2005, a leak that shut down part of BP's pipeline in Alaska and a propane markets trading scandal. Browne survived these setbacks. However, he resigned in May 2007 after it emerged that he had lied under oath in court to hide the fact that he met his former boyfriend through an escort agency called "Suited and Booted".

> "The work of the miner has its unavoidable incidents of discomfort and danger, and these should not be increased by the neglect of the owners to provide every practicable safety appliance. Economies which involve sacrifice of human life are intolerable."
>
> Benjamin Harrison

Forgery

Forgery has long been perpetrated in the business, academic art and literary worlds. Forgery is inherently unethical. Forgery has always been considered a crime, especially so if one forges a signature on a cheque or a legal document such as a contract or a will. Modern technology can be used to detect forgery but can also facilitate the forgery process.

Business

Photocopying technology is now being used to counterfeit banknotes, which can easily be passed during busy shopping moments. King (2004) reports that the number of forgeries of Euro banknotes and coins is growing dramatically, according to the European Central Bank (ECB) and the European Union's anti-fraud office. The forgers' favourite is the €50 note and next is the €20 note. Counterfeit Euro banknotes withdrawn from circulation in the second half of 2003 had a total value of about €15.75 million. Retailers have now become conscious of this threat to their business.

The *Irish Times* (9/1/2004) reported that a senior executive of Parmalat allegedly used a scanner, scissors and glue to fabricate a false Bank of America letter confirming the infamous but non-existent Cayman Island account of € 3.9 billion. The discovery of this fraud by Bank of America led to the collapse of the group.

The greatest forgeries of all time

Even publishers have been taken in by forgeries. Scally (2003) reported on one of the greatest forgeries of all time known as the "Hitler Diaries". In April 28, 1983 *Stern* magazine declared it the find of the 20th century. The magazine told the story of how the diaries had come to light in an East German barn after being lost for half a century. However, within two weeks the story went from scoop to swindle when the diaries were exposed as fake. It cost Stern €5 million, several top editors their jobs and Germany's largest selling newsmagazine its reputation.

Stern, the *Sunday Times* and *Newsweek* were taken in by a compulsive liar, forger and crook named Konrad Kujau. Konrad had a history of deception having created a nice living out of forged paintings which he claimed were Hitlers. When *Stern* magazine offered Kujau £2.5 million sterling for the diaries he couldn't resist. He had become too greedy for his own good leading ultimately to his downfall. He and Gerd Heidemann, the journalist from *Stern*, were sentenced to four years in jail for fraud. Kujau died in September 12, 2000 aged 62 years.

Skulduggery

It is amazing what people will do to achieve fame. Even some academics have falsified their research results or taken credit for other people's ideas. Dr Reville (1996) reported that the most elaborate and successful scientific hoax of the last century was known as the Piltdown man affair. In 1911 at Piltdown Common in East Sussex in England a supposedly great scientific discovery was made. The fossilised skull of a creature mid-way between ape and human was unearthed. It consisted of skull fragments and assorted bones. It was supposed to represent the vital link in the chain of evolution. The scientific community generally accepted the findings even though evidence to the contrary was known to exist elsewhere.

"No science is immune to the infection of politics and the corruption of power."

Jacob Bronowski

For 37 years the skull was considered to belong to the early Ice Age in line with the age of the bones that were found with it. An investigation in 1953 showed clearly that the whole affair was an elaborate hoax. The jaw was shown to be that of an orang-utan with the teeth artificially stained and filed to resemble human teeth. Many of the bones found at the time had been treated with chemicals to feign that they were from the same period as the skull fragments. All the evidence showed that the cranium and the jaw could not have belonged to each other, and that their presence together was a planted forgery.

The prospective career advancement and glory and fame motivated the scientists to commit the elaborate hoax. Human nature is weak so that there will always be the temptation for some to stoop to the lowest levels to get the recognition that they so ardently desire. Obviously the integrity of scientific research is essential to the future wellbeing of mankind so that any tampering of results should be treated as the most heinous crime. This is particularly so in medicine where our health or lives may be at stake.

Art scams

Reville (2003) reports that the art of forgery is very old. The ancient Egyptians made false gems out of glass. Workshops in ancient Rome trundled out copies of Greek sculptures and jewellery. By the 17th and 18th centuries, forgers were copying the great European painters including Rubens, Rembrandt and Vermeer. Even the famous Turin shroud has been proved to be a fraud. In the late 1970s Walter C McCrone, a chemical expert on art forgeries, examined samples from the shroud under a microscope. The stains did not contain blood, but contained two red pigments, red ochre and vermilion, readily available in the Middle Ages. He concluded that the shroud was painted around 1355. Later radiocarbon dating confirmed the tests. Despite this some people still believe that the shroud is genuine.

Great forgers

Connolly (1998) reports that probably the most successful art forger of the 20th century was a Hungarian named Elmyr de Hory. He began by faking Picassos and progressed to turning out drawings by Matisse and Renoir. Between 1961 and 1967, in conjunction with French/Greek conman Ferdinand Legros, about $60 million worth of de Hory oil paintings were sold, 32 alone to a Texan oilman named Algur H. Meadows. When Meadows became suspicious and invited experts to verify the authenticity

of his collection the scam was revealed. The discovery put an end to de Hory's painting career and he committed suicide in 1976.

> **"Who will not be deceived must have as many eyes as hairs on his head."**
> German proverb

Connolly also reports that in 1911 the forgers Yves Chaudron and Eduardo de Valfierno, sold forgeries of the Mona Lisa to six different Americans for a total of $1.6 million. They were aided by the fact that they had stolen the original Mona Lisa earlier in the year. Later in 1911 the scam was discovered when they tried to sell the original to a Florentine art dealer. Art forgeries can be so authentic looking that even museums can be conned into believing that they are the real objet d'art.

In the art world improving photocopying technology is making it easier to produce high quality fakes. The *Guardian* (August 24, 2004) reported that Finnish police were investigating a large-scale art fraud in which dozens of high quality photocopies of works by artists such as Salvador Dali were passed off as originals and sold for up to €10,000 each.

Summary

Ethical issues inside the company concerning management include tax avoidance, conflicts of interest, corporate manslaughter, insider dealing, excessive executive pay and stock options. Others include misappropriation of company assets, destroying evidence, cost-cutting, downsizing and accounting fraud. Some senior executives behave as if corporate assets are their own private property to be used as they wish for personal aggrandisement. The role of tax havens and offshore accounts and examples of insider dealing were discussed. Tax havens are used extensively by multinationals to minimise their tax liability.

The greed and excesses of some senior executives were highlighted and discussed. Excessive remuneration packages for some senior executives are hard to justify morally. Stock options are used as part of the compensation package. Forgery is a problem not only in the corporate world but also in the academic, art and literary worlds. Some famous cases of forgery were examined and discussed.

Check Your Ethics Quotient

(circle the appropriate response)

1. Using company property for your own personal use is unethical.   True   False

2. We can no longer trust the gatekeepers of the financial system such as auditors, bankers and investment analysts to protect our interests.   True   False

3. Misappropriation is the polite term for stealing company assets.   True   False

4. Insider dealing is unethical.   True   False

5. Stock options do not need to be shown on the company's financial statement.   True   False

6. Senior executives have engaged in tax avoidance schemes by channelling funds into offshore accounts.   True   False

7. Insurance policies have been used for tax evasion scams.   True   False

8. Conflicts of interest may arise when employees fail to differentiate their private interests from those of the company.   True   False

9. Forgery is illegal and unethical.   True   False

10. The prospect of career advancement and recognition has motivated scientists to fraudulently claim breakthroughs.   True   False

Total the number of true and false responses and check Appendix 2 at the back of the book for the solution.

Case study: Executive greed

The *Guardian* (9/7/2004) reported that John Rigas, founder of US cable company Adelphi Communications, had been convicted together with one of his sons, Timothy Rigas, on charges relating to the embezzlement of $1 billion from the business. The embezzlement was spent on building a $13 million golf course, using the company's private jet for personal trips and buying apartments for the extended family in New York, Colorodo and Mexico. Cash was also spent on the purchase of Adelphi shares, country club membership and holidays to Mexico. John Rigas even used $25 million of Adephi funds to buy the rights to forested land to preserve the view from his ranch. On one occasion he ordered two Christmas trees to be flown to his daughter in New York, at a cost of $6,000.

Dravesky (2004) reports that in June 2002, Adelphia declared bankruptcy. The new management started a turnaround effort to rebuild the company's reputation internally and make sure that the actions that brought down the company would never happen again. Part of the process was to adopt a new code of ethics and make sure that it was available to all employees of Adelphia. The initiatives included:

♦ Setting up a hotline for employees to call if they wanted to report ethical problems or ask questions about ethical concerns.
♦ Designing a poster, that highlighted the hotline number, reinforced the company's new business values and showed how the new values supported ethics.
♦ Producing train-the-trainer kits, which included an employee presentation that HR managers could give at staff meetings to strengthen the ethical messages contained in the folder, and to provide an opportunity for employees to ask questions.
♦ Frequently asked questions about ethical issues were prepared for HR and line managers to share with their employees.

Questions

- "Power tends to corrupt, and absolute power corrupts absolutely." Discuss.
- Why do some senior executives use company property as if it were their own?
- Was it a case of closing the stable door after the horse has bolted for Adelphi?

6. Ethical Issues: Employees

- ◆ What is white-collar fraud?
- ◆ When does a gift become a bribe?
- ◆ How does cyber-crime arise?
- ◆ What are sweatshops?
- ◆ What are the ethics of child labour?

"There is no twilight zone of honesty in business – a thing is right or it's wrong – it's black or it's white."

John F. Dodge

Surveys confirm that white-collar fraud is a major problem in business. Poor internal controls facilitate the process. E-commerce and the Internet have given rise to cyber-crime. The detection and prevention of computer crime is also a major issue in many organisations. Many of the Internet companies were built on a foundation of sand. Hence the collapse of the dotcoms.

White-collar crime

Poor cash and inventory control systems can provide the opportunities for employees to steal. The company should do everything possible to keep temptation out of the way of employees. Fraud is deliberate deception, or misrepresentation of a material fact in the books of account, company documentation or in financial statements.

"Crime is naught but misdirected energy. So long as every institution of today, economic, political, social, and moral, conspires to misdirect human energy into wrong channels; so long as most people are out of place doing the things they hate to do, living a life they loathe to live, crime will be inevitable."

Emma Goldman

White-collar fraud may be facilitated in many different ways. Employees may forge the signatures on cheques, change invoices, falsify documentation or manipulate the accounts to hide embezzlement, mistakes, incompetence and misappropriation of money.

Invoices may be fabricated for a non-existent supplier, with cheques drawn and the proceeds converted to the employee's own use. Debtors may be manipulated using team and lading procedures or issuing fake credit notes. Backhanders and kickbacks for awarding valuable contracts, placing "dummy" employees on a payroll and falsifying expenses and overtime claims are some other examples of fraud committed by employees. Underpaid employees may justify fraud on the basis that they are only taking what is due to them. Paying employees well will deprive them of this rationalisation for dishonesty.

Men commit most fraud

Men commit four out of five frauds. Trusted employees are often the ones who commit the fraud. Those who commit white-collar crime are rarely prosecuted and usually get off with a reprimand or dismissal. Many firms want to avoid the bad publicity involved if the case was brought to court. This sends the wrong message to staff who realise that they can commit fraud without fear of prosecution or the possibility of a jail sentence. Some companies have even given employees dismissed for fraud good references. Others may just transfer the culprits to other departments with less opportunity for stealing. Nevertheless, those tried and convicted of white-collar crime are now more likely to get prison sentences than ever before. Fraud is very costly and the cost of investigation and prevention is substantial.

> "Crime is a fact of the human species, a fact of that specie as alone, but it is above all the secret aspect, impenetrable and hidden. Crime hides, and by far the most terrifying things are those which elude us."
>
> George Bataille

In practice women rarely commit fraud. It seems to be the prerogative of men. However, the *Observer* (25/4/2004) reported on a fraud committed by a woman. Joyti De-Laurey, a secretary with Goldman Sachs, was convicted of stealing £4.4 million from her bosses' bank accounts. She forged chequebook signatures and arranged the transfer of moneys from the personal accounts of three wealthy bankers. Out of the money she financed a lifestyle of expensive jewellery, fast cars, powerboats and a villa in Cyprus. Her trial shone an unwanted light on the frenetic and privileged

lifestyle of bankers. They were so busy having a good time that they failed to notice that their accounts were being systematically robbed of millions of pounds. De-Laurey impressed her bosses and went from a temporary member of staff to a permanent position. She was deemed to be very trustworthy by her managers. Thorough pre-employment background checks had not been carried out. Let that be a lesson for future employers.

Stealing company assets

An employee who uses the company's photocopying machine for personal use or who uses the company's postal system to send out personal Christmas cards is also behaving in an unethical fashion. Some employees feel that taking the odd pencil or pen or piece of stationery is acceptable because everybody is doing it. A single piece of stationery costs very little but, cumulatively the total cost to a large company over a period of time can be very significant and is in fact stealing.

Some employees think nothing of taking sick leave when they are in fact well. This is a false appropriation of valuable company time. You are getting paid for time that you are not entitled to. Some doctors collude in the process by certifying sick leave where the case is dubious.

Abuse of expense accounts

This may arise when employees claim for expenses that they did not occur, exaggerate the actual cost of expenses incurred or otherwise falsify claims. Employees are only entitled to legitimate expenses actually spent on behalf of the company. Sound business practice suggests proper documentation, approval and audit of expense accounts. Some employers may agree to pay some of the wages due to their employees in the form of expenses so that the employee does not have to pay income tax on that portion. This practice is illegal and unethical.

Surveys of fraud

We can learn about the vulnerability of companies to fraudulent practices by examining the results of fraud surveys. We can discover the type of employees more likely to commit fraud and the best precautions to take to prevent it. Significant financial losses running to billions can now be attributed to fraud.

Certified fraud examiners

Scott (2002) reports that a study conducted by the Association of Certified Fraud Examiners (ACFE) found that in 2002 US organisations

- lost 6 per cent of their revenues to occupational fraud and abuse. Nationally this amounts to about $600 billion.
- more than 80 per cent of work frauds involve asset misappropriation, with cash being involved 90 per cent of the time.
- corruption schemes account for 13 per cent of all work frauds and cause, on average, more than $500,000 in losses annually.
- fraudulent statements are the most costly types of work fraud, with average losses of $4.25 million per scheme.

> "Sharpness does not earn one money, and honesty will not lose money."
> Chinese proverb

Businesses are the most vulnerable to work fraud. The report found that in small businesses the average loss is $127,500, whereas the average in large companies is $97,000. **According to the report frauds are usually detected through tips from employees, customers, suppliers and anonymous sources.** The second most common method of detection is by accident (18.8 per cent), followed closely by internal audit (18.6 per cent), internal controls (15.4 per cent), and external audit (11.5 per cent).

The report also found that frauds committed by managers averaged $250,000 and were much more costly than frauds committed by employees that averaged $60,000. This reflects the greater authority and power of the manager and thus more scope to commit fraud. However, where managers and employees colluded the average fraud was $500,000. Other findings of the report include:

- The typical perpetrator is a first time offender.
- Losses caused by perpetrators over 60 years of age are 27 times greater than losses caused by employees 25 years and younger.
- The average scheme lasts 18 months before it is discovered.

Verschoor (2004) reports on a more recent survey by the ACFE. This survey found that 508 fraud cases caused losses of more than $761 million. This represents 6 per cent of the total revenue of a US firm. As in the previous survey, the ACFE found that the most effective fraud detection mechanism is a tip from an employee, customer or supplier. Forty per cent of frauds were identified this way, with internal auditing only discovering about 24 per cent. Internal controls and external audit accounted for the rest.

A company with a hotline system in place had less than half the fraud of other companies. The average size of fraud in a company with an internal audit department was only 60 per cent of that of other companies. **These findings demonstrate that a whistleblowing policy in conjunction with an internal audit department is the most effective way of preventing fraud.**

Other surveys

Brune (2001) reports that most managers are aware of fraud in their workplace, but 40 per cent of them say they wouldn't report it according to a *Management Today* survey of more than 800 British executives. In fact, most managers believe that workplace fraud is inevitable, and many ignore unethical behaviour. For example, 75 per cent of those surveyed believe that making personal phone calls from work is acceptable. In addition, 48 per cent tolerate taking pens and pencils from work. Surfing the net for pleasure during work hours is condoned by only 22 per cent.

Conversely, taking a sick day after an office party and charging personal entertainment to company expenses were ranked as the least acceptable behaviour. The findings indicate that women typically have a more tolerant attitude than men towards questionable behaviour. Workers over 40 are less forgiving than their younger counterparts. Private sector employees are more tolerant of unethical practices than those who work in the public sector.

Honesty and probity should be actively encouraged as part of a company's culture. Ethical behaviour should be valued and rewarded by the company. Reinforcement theory says that rewarded ethical behaviour is more likely to be repeated. However, a 2003 survey, by the Society of Human Resource Management and the Ethics Resource Centre, found that nearly half of human resource professionals surveyed believe ethical conduct is not rewarded. The fate of whistleblowers would seem to support this view.

> "Honesty is the cornerstone of character. The honest man or women seeks not merely to avoid criminal or illegal acts, but to be scrupulously fair, upright, fearless in both action and expression. Honesty pays dividends both in dollars and in peace of mind."
>
> B.C.Forbes

The *Irish Times* (16/5/1998) reported that light-fingered employees are costing companies, around the world millions of pounds, every year, according to a survey of over 1,200 senior executives in 32 countries by

Ernst & Young. The survey, revealed that 84 per cent of the worst corporate theft is committed by a company's own employees. Employees with five years service committed half of the fraud. **It is often long serving, trusted employees who have been given too much freedom that commit white-collar fraud.**

O'Halloran (2005) reports that corporate crime by employees is costing Irish businesses an estimated €2.5 billion a year according to a Dublin Chamber of Commerce and consultants RSM Robson Rhodes survey (16/6/2005). Fraud, embezzlement, and cheque and credit card fraud cause the losses. The annual losses per company came to €450,000, while prevention cost each one a further €114,000. Prevention costs are incurred through increased security and higher insurance premiums. 34 per cent of the businesses survey said that they had taken disciplinary action against employees who had committed offences, while 44 per cent believed that the problem would get worse over the next three years.

Facilitating fraud

Fraud should never be condoned or tolerated in any circumstances. The culture of a company can provide a climate conducive to fraud. Lax management, bad example from the top, poor administration and inadequate accounting controls all aid the process. All frauds contain four basic elements: opportunity, economic or psychological need, moral justification and a perceived low chance of detection or inadequate penalties.

> "There are very many characteristics which go into making a model administrator. Prominent among them are probity, industry, good sense, good habits, good temper, patience, order, courtesy, tact, self-reliance, many deference to superior officers, and many considerations for inferiors."
>
> Chester A. Arthur

Preventative measures against fraud include good internal controls, reference checks on new employees and installing surveillance equipment. A drug habit, drinking, gambling or a high living life-style often provides the motivation. Moral justification is often rationalised on some basis such as everybody is doing it or that the insurance will cover the loss. In the long-term the chances of detection are probably high but the penalties for white-collar crime are still not severe. A petty shoplifter has a greater chance of being prosecuted and serving a prison sentence than someone caught for a white-collar crime.

Cybercrime

Government and corporate computer networks are now the potential targets of cyber-terrorists. Armstrong (2003) reports that money-laundering, drug-dealing, terrorism, hacking, fraud, child pornography and the distribution of objectionable material are crimes perpetrated on the Internet. The Internet remains largely unregulated and unpoliced. The FBI declared in 2003 that cyber-crime represented the most fundamental challenge for law enforcement in the 21st century. By its very nature, the cyber environment is borderless, affords easy anonymity and methods of concealment, and provides new tools to engage in criminal activity with less chance of detection.

Fear of cyber-crime is preventing some people from going online and engaging in e-commerce. This is one of the areas where the law and corporate systems have failed to keep up with the technology. Criminals may threaten and close down complete corporate networks. They are then in a position to use this power for blackmail or extortion purposes demanding cash for the return of the stolen data. For example, the *Irish Times* (8/12/2000) reported that the case against the perpetrator of the "Love Bug", a virus that jammed electronic networks, was dropped in the Philippines because of inadequate laws. Damages from that incident were estimated in billions of dollars. The communications systems of Ford Motor Co. and Lucent Technologies were severely disrupted. The problem has not gone away and since then many more viruses have emerged causing disruption to computer systems throughout the world.

The threat from hackers

Modern methods of fraud include hackers stealing confidential credit card details and bank account information from the Internet. Breaches of online banking security systems are not as isolated as the banks claim. Credit and debit card cloning in shops and restaurants and by organised criminals is a growing problem. The criminals then use the "skimmed" credit cards to withdraw large sums of cash. This problem has also surfaced at ATM machines where criminals use technology to skim details from unwary customers during withdrawals. Banks have warned customers to be very vigilant when withdrawing cash from ATM machines. They have also advised customers against letting credit cards out of their sight in shops and restaurants in case they are copied.

When making payments over the Internet people are afraid that their credit card details may be intercepted by hackers and used to defraud them. Apart from the damage and cost that hackers inflict, the anticipatory

fear that they engender is enormous. Banks assure us that their systems are completely secure but many people are not convinced. Hackers are viewed as criminals in most jurisdictions. They seem to be able to develop new ways all the time of breaking into computer systems, intercepting data and using it for fraud. Hackers also use their skills to spread viruses and bring down whole computer networks. They even sell their skills to organised crime rings. The threat exists not only from outsiders but from insiders as well, such as trusted employees and others who have access to the company's computer systems.

Malware

Malware is a type of cyber-crime and is the term for software that does bad things like clogging e-mail systems, stealing valuable information, and violating privacy. This costs organisations untold millions in lost productivity and down time. Fraudsters have been helped by the growth in broadband. The longer people are online the greater the risk exposure to fraud.

Spam is unsolicited e-mail sent to people to promote goods or services. It may be just a nuisance but it may have a more sinister purpose. Spam mail may be sent to overload corporate networks, causing systems to slow, freeze, crash, or fail. In response a whole industry of firewall and anti-virus software has been developed to deal with the threat of spam mail, viruses and worms. There has also been a huge increase for the services of IT security specialists. It seems that every cloud has a silver lining.

Computer scams have also appeared on our e-mail systems. Nigerians seem to be the main culprits. These people send you an e-mail with a promise of huge sums of money in return for bank account details. Their plausible story is designed to engage your sympathy and exploit your emotion of greed. Their real intention is to rob your hard-earned money by stealing from your bank account. Some people have fallen for this scam. Since this crime is not "up close and personal" the perpetrators probably feel less guilty about it than conventional stealing.

Computer fraud

Computerised accounting is now the growth area for existing and potential fraud. It is a double-edged sword in that in some cases it has made fraud more difficult and easier to detect while in others it has facilitated the process. Dhillon (1999) reports that in Malaysia, a senior bank official responsible for verifying and releasing interbank deposits gained access to passwords of his staff. He then transferred funds belonging to the bank to

his own account in another bank. The fraudulent transactions came to light only when he appeared on the local television as a proud owner of several sports cars.

> **"Opportunity makes the thief."**
>
> English proverb

There are many reasons why employees commit computer fraud. Some common reasons are seeking revenge for a perceived wrongdoing, personal debt, excessive gambling, funding a drug problem or a lavish life-style, and opportunity presented by a lack of internal controls. Business today is very competitive and employees are often stressed. As a result, some employees feel they are overworked, underpaid, and unappreciated.

Kelleher (2000) reports that when Timothy Allen was demoted, after nine years service by his employers in New Jersey in the USA he anticipated that it was only a matter of time before he was fired. So he designed, tested and loaded a small computer program on his employer's system. Two weeks after he was fired, his program went into operation and deleted all his employer's most important programs and cost the company more than $10 million. He was discovered, prosecuted, and in May 2000 convicted by the US Federal Courts. Revenge is a natural human reaction to a perceived wrong and employees with computer expertise have the means to sabotage their employer's computer systems if they so desire.

Dotcom bust

Many web companies when set up thought it was going to be a "get rich quick" situation and that the normal conventions of business would not apply. Like all businesses some were successful but many have gone to the wall. The dream and the reality did not match up. People were supposed to take to the Internet like ducks to water, but the process was slow and in the meantime many dotcoms were unable to survive.

Many investors lost their money in the dotcom boom. Many of the people who set up these companies were only interested in making money and didn't worry about the possible losses to shareholders. The *Guardian (18/5/2004)* reported that the United States securities watchdog had filed fraud charges against Lucent Technologies and nine former workers, for inflating its revenues by $1.1 billion in the dying days of the dotcom boom. Lucent shares once valued at $60 were now worth only $3.05. It has emerged that when the business suddenly fell away in 2000 the industry became a hotbed of fraudulent behaviour.

The *Irish Times* (2/7/2001) reported that global players like Intel, Yahoo and Cisco Systems axed thousands of jobs. Dotcoms around the world went out of business as the money ran out and the industry plunged into a recession. When initially set up many dotcoms were overvalued because the demand for their shares were high. It is a basic law of economics that when demand exceeds supply the price goes up. Consequently in the short-term fortunes were made on the stock exchange trading on their shares. When the bubble burst the result was just as dramatic.

The *Irish Times* (20/4/2001) revealed that a survey by Pricewaterhouse-Coopers found that a quarter of 400 dotcoms surveyed did not have cash flow forecasts or did not hold board meetings at least once a month – half of those surveyed did not hold proper board meetings. This is tantamount to reckless trading. When a dot.com goes bust it may have very little tangible assets. The main asset may be intellectual property, which may be difficult to sell. The result is that shareholders take a huge hit losing most of or all of their money.

The sector's biggest bankruptcy

Global Crossing was founded in 1997 to build an undersea broadband network that would link continents together. However, Global Crossing's anticipated revenues never materialised because of insufficient demand for broadband services. It was unable to meet its interest payments and was forced into bankruptcy in January 2002. It became the telecom sector's biggest ever bankruptcy. Like Enron, Global Crossing used the auditing firm, Arthur Andersen.

It transpired that Global Crossing was overstating its revenues through swapping capacity with other carriers. It misled investors by overstating the extent and capability of its networks. It has been accused of insider trading, making excessive political donations, and paying too much to its CEO and Directors. During its short life, it went through five CEOs, who were collectively compensated to the tune of $105 million. This case certainly demonstrates once again that it is the employees and shareholders that suffer most rather than the senior executives who usually finish up with their wealth intact.

Summary

Ethical issues inside the company concerning employees include white-collar crime such as the misappropriation of company assets and falsifying expense accounts. Surveys of white-collar crime demonstrate the substantial cost of this type of fraud to business. Companies can learn a lot of useful information by studying the results of these surveys.

E-commerce and the Internet have given rise to cyber crime. This is now the greatest potential source of fraud to a business. Computer fraud is also a problem in many companies.

Check Your Ethics Quotient

(circle the appropriate response)

1.	Poor internal controls can provide opportunities for employees to steal.	True	False
2.	Taking sick leave when you are well is illegal.	True	False
3.	More than 80 per cent of work frauds involve asset misappropriation.	True	False
4.	Auditors usually detect fraud.	True	False
5.	A whistleblowing policy in conjunction with an internal audit department is the best way of preventing fraud.	True	False
6.	Making personal phone calls at work is acceptable.	True	False
7.	The Internet is largely unregulated and unpoliced.	True	False
8.	Reinforcement theory says that rewarded ethical behaviour is less likely to be repeated.	True	False
9.	A significant number of managers turn a blind eye to unethical behaviour in the work place.	True	False
10.	Modern methods of fraud include stealing credit card details from the Internet.	True	False

Total the number of true and false responses and check Appendix 2 at the back of the book for the solution.

Case study: How the mighty fall

WorldCom started life as a small firm named Long Distance Discount Services in 1985. The company grew rapidly through acquisitions and in 1995 was renamed WorldCom. By this stage it was mainly involved in providing telephone and Internet services. In 1998, WorldCom merged with MCI, a company three times its size. The new company was named MCI WorldCom. This cost $37 billion paid for by overpriced stock and cost-cutting strategies. WorldCom Inc. became the largest bankruptcy in the history of the USA after admitting to overstating profits by $9 billion from 1999 to 2000.

It transpired that WorldCom was involved in massive fraudulent accounting. It was capitalising revenue expenses in order to overstate its profits and exaggerate its asset base. This led shareholders and financial analysts to believe that earnings were substantially greater than they actually were and that the company was reinvesting in upgrading and expanding its services. The share price reflected this false assumption. The infamous accounting firm, Arthur Andersen, auditors to Enron, were also auditors to Worldcom.

In July 2005 Bernard Ebbers, the former WorldCom chairman and chief executive, was sentenced to 25 years in prison for overseeing the demise of his company. A New York jury found Mr Ebbers guilty of conspiracy and securities fraud and seven counts of making false filings to the US Securities and Exchange Commission.

Mr Ebbers, who developed the Mississippi based group from an obscure long distance carrier to the second largest telecoms group in the US, was a hero in his hometown. He is unlikely to have the same standing with investors who lost billions when WorldCom collapsed.

Questions

- Why have so many Internet companies gone bust?
- Discuss Mr Ebbers personal standard of ethics?
- Is it ever right to mislead the investment community about the financial standing of the company? Discuss.

7. Ethical Issues: Customers

> ♦ What are the ethical issues relating to price-fixing?
> ♦ How does bait and switch operate?
> ♦ What are loss-leaders?
> ♦ What is churning?

"Tut, tut, child" said the Duchess. **"Everything's got a moral if only you can find it."**

Lewis Carroll, *Alice in Wonderland*

Ethical issues outside the company concerning customers include price-fixing, price discrimination, deceptive pricing, loss-leaders, bait-and-switch, over-pricing, unfair competition, dumping, hard sell, dangerous and defective products, misleading advertising, non-competitive practices, product-labelling, fraud, product-counterfeiting, excessive gifts and entertainment, shoplifting, safety and money-laundering.

Other issues concern the financial services industry, suppliers, dealing with other organisations, industrial espionage, bribery, outsourcing and human rights issues.

Price-fixing

Price-fixing occurs when competitors get together to co-ordinate pricing policies and agree retail prices. Cartels are often formed to monopolise and control the market and charge excessive prices to customers. In the past Microsoft has been accused of anti-competitive practices because of the near monopoly position its software enjoys in the market. Customers have the right to expect the lowest prices the market can offer. Price-fixing is rarely in the interests of customers and is illegal and unethical because it interferes with the customer's freedom of choice and market forces. Price-fixing is a particular problem in the retail, manufacturing, agriculture, banking and the pharmaceutical sectors.

Retail

Price-fixing charges have been taken against many companies. Price-fixing amounts to theft from consumers. The *Guardian* (20/2/2003) reported that the Office of Fair Trading fined Argos £17.28 million and Littlewoods £5.37 million for entering into anti-competitive agreements forcing consumers to pay artificially high prices over two years for toys such as the Monopoly board game and Action Man dolls.

The *Guardian* (31/10/2002) reported that the EU fined Nintendo, the Japanese video games manufacturer, £94 million for overcharging customers in Europe for most of the 1990s. The commission found that the UK market was one of the cheapest in Europe. However, Nintendo colluded with the UK distributor to ensure that cheap UK products were not re-exported to continental Europe where prices could be up to 66 per cent higher.

> "People of the same trade seldom meet together, even for merriment and diversion, but the conversation ends in a conspiracy against the public, or in some contrivance to raise prices. "
>
> Adam Smith

Corporate Watch (Dec 02/jan 03) reported that in June 2002 the Office of Fair Trading reached a provisional finding that Bacardi had breached competition law. In April 2002 it secured a £625,000 "sole supply" deal with the UK National Union of Students (NUS) under which the NUS would not stock any other white rum in its bars for three years.

Manufacturing

The *Guardian* (28/11/2002) reported that plasterboard manufacturer BPB and three of its European rivals were fined £300 million by the EU for operating an illegal price-fixing cartel for most of the 1990s. The price of plasterboard had fallen sharply in previous years because of intense competition and the companies concerned wanted to reverse the trend. The scam included passing sales information to each other and advance warning of price increases.

Agriculture

The EU's Common Agricultural Policy (CAP) has been criticised for bribing farmers to grow uneconomic products that keep domestic prices high. It penalises the taxpayer and hinders developing economies from growing. The CAP operates on three underlying principles:

1. A single market for farm products applies throughout the EU. Free movement applies across national frontiers and a system of common prices operates.
2. There is a common tariff barrier on agricultural imports from outside the EU.
3. The costs of the system are paid from a fund supported by all member countries.

The EU is currently overhauling the CAP system so that the link between subsidies and production will be broken. The US also subsidises its cotton growers and Canada subsidises its wheat growers.

Keegan (2004) maintains that abolition of subsidies would bring prices down, give money back to the taxpayer while giving developing countries a huge economic boost. The losers would be EU farmers growing uneconomic crops financed by taxpayers and consumers. The CAP still devours about $55 billion almost half of the entire EU budget.

The sugar industry

The *Guardian* (23/8/2002) reported that Europe's sugar industry is receiving a £1 billion handout from taxpayers and consumers. This allows it to dump millions of tonnes of subsidised sugar on international markets at the expense of the world's poorest farmers in developing countries like Mozambique and Senegal. The price-fixing deal set by Brussels pays farmers and firms up to three times the market price for sugar. The deal has enabled sugar beet farmers in Germany, Britain and France to become the world's largest exporters of white sugar despite being the most expensive producers. Guaranteed prices encourage farmers to be inefficient and to overproduce. The resulting sugar mountain is dumped on world markets depressing international prices.

However the EU is committed to opening up its sugar market to the world's least developed countries after 2009. It has already begun the process of phasing out its support for the sugar industry. In Ireland the Carlow sugar factory closed in January 2005. In the long-term when EU subsidies are phased out sugar production will no longer be a viable economic activity. It cannot compete with sugar produced from sugar cane

in tropical countries. Eventually Ireland and other EU countries will no longer be competitive producers of sugar. The subsidy system is unethical because it deprives farmers in developing countries a decent living and prevents consumers elsewhere of taking advantage of market prices.

Banking

The *Guardian* (12/12/2001) reported that five of Germany's banks were fined £63 million for operating a price-fixing cartel on foreign exchange transactions. The banks colluded in 1997 to fix a minimum charge of 3 per cent for a three year period to compensate them for the introduction of the euro. Banks are free to set the charges for exchanging currencies but it is illegal for them to get together to fix these charges.

> **"A reputation for good judgement, for fair dealing, for truth, and for rectitude, is itself a fortune."**
>
> Henry Ward Beecher

In Ireland there is so little difference between the two big national banks AIB and Bank of Ireland that for all practical purposes an oligopoly is operating. Interest charges on loans and current account charges are practically identical. Efforts by the government to free up the market have so far not been very effective although the entry of Bank of Scotland has made some banking services such as mortgages more competitive. The Irish government in January 2005 made it easier to switch current or cheque accounts from bank to bank thereby making it easier for customers to shop around for the best rates. The extent of dubious ethical practices prevalent in the banking sector in Ireland is probably facilitated by the lack of real competition.

Pharmaceutical

Pharmaceutical companies have a particular responsibility to price life-saving and life-enhancing prescription drugs reasonably and responsibly. In practice, this does not seem to be happening. Most people feel that medicines cost too much and that this is reflected in the huge profits that drug companies make. Medicine is a necessity for those who are ill. Most right-thinking people are disgusted when they see ill and dying people deprived of drugs that could save their lives. Drug companies are able to charge excessive prices for their products by taking advantage of vulnerable sick people who have little choice and are willing to pay any price to stay alive.

The high price of drugs is not hindered by the fact that many people are covered by medical insurance. This makes doctors and patients alike less cost conscious when it comes to paying for drugs, as the costs are refundable. Maitland (2002) reports that Dr Stephen Long, an economist at the RAND Corporation in Washington maintains that doctors assume that their patients want the best. Consequently and fearful of malpractice suits if they recommend anything else, they may disregard prices when prescribing drugs. Doctors sometimes prescribe an expensive drug when a cheaper generic one is just as good. Cardiologists continue to prescribe TPA, a drug that dissolves blood clots, for $2,000 a dose, even though studies have shown that streptokinase, at $200 a dose, is just as good for heart attack patients.

Critics of drug companies complain that they put profits before people and greed before need. They also criticise the fact that they get patents for their products giving them a virtual monopoly position and excessive profits for many years. During the patent period rival companies cannot copy the drug unless they get a licence to do so. As monopoly producers the drug companies are able to charge far higher prices than they would be able to do in a competitive market. The exorbitant price for anti-AIDS drugs is a case in point. The public outcry against this has forced drug companies to bring down their prices for the anti-AIDS drug somewhat. The plight of developing countries with AIDS problems that can't afford the drugs has also been highlighted and the ethics of leaving thousands of people die questioned.

> "What is a man if he is not a thief who openly charges as much as he can for the goods he sells?"
>
> Mohandas K. Gandhi

Some people think that healthcare is a basic human right and those medicines should be available on the basis of need rather than ability to pay. Hence the argument for public health services. On the other hand, drug companies claim that drugs are expensive to make and that profits are needed to fund the development of new drugs. They need to charge high prices in order to recover their research and development costs. However, critics claim that pharmaceutical companies spend more on promotion and marketing than on research and development. Unlike Jonas Salk, the inventor of the polio vaccine, who refused to take any royalties for his discovery, pharmaceutical companies are in business to make profits.

Pricing

Pricing issues include discrimination, recommended retail prices, price exploitation, dumping, bait and switch, loss-leaders, the hard sell approach and misleading customers.

Price discrimination

Price discrimination usually happens in a business-to-business situation. A seller offers generous discounts to a favoured buyer thereby giving the buyer an unfair competitive advantage. Sellers justify price discrimination because of the costs of production, delivery and selling. Keen prices may also be offered to compete successfully in competitive markets. Price discrimination is considered unethical by some because it puts small companies at a disadvantage in comparison to others who get big discounts. Multinationals justify different prices in different countries in relation to different distribution costs and economies of scale. In some countries such as the USA price discrimination is illegal. Different supermarkets in the same chain may also practice price discrimination. A supermarket in an affluent location may charge more for the same products than a supermarket in a less affluent area.

RRPs

Manufacturers' recommended retail prices (RRP) could be considered a type of deceptive pricing. When retailers mark down such prices customers think they are getting a great bargain. The RRP creates a fictitious basis of comparison. Such procedures though legal are unethical. A real reduction would be a lower price than the normal shop price. This is not deceptive because the basis of comparison is real and not fictitious. During sales some retailers operate deceptive pricing policies by pretending to lower prices when in fact they do not.

Price exploitation

Some companies may take advantage of unique situations to increase prices. Retailers may artificially create scarce situations to inflate the price of a particular product. After storms some builders may take advantage of the situation by charging more than normal to repair roofs. Demand for their service increase after storms and they know people are stressed and

under pressure to get their roofs repaired as quickly as possible. Because demand exceeds supply they are in a position to exploit the market.

Ferrell et al (2002) reports that Sydney hotels were accused of increasing their rates for the 2000 Olympics. Some Olympic officials were quoted a room rate for a three-star hotel during the games of $550 per night plus $45 for breakfast and $75 for lunch and dinner. In Ireland during international football matches and festivals and other busy periods it is common practice for hotels and bars to increase prices during the period involved. To say the least such practices are dishonest and unethical. Consumer bodies and the media are now taking a name and shame approach to these practices.

> **"More men come to doom through dirty profits than are kept by them. "**
>
> Sophocles

Supermarket shoppers are frequently overcharged by computer scanners that have not been programmed with the correct price. One assumes that these are genuine mistakes and that there are no hidden agendas or unethical practices going on. To be fair some supermarkets give the item free if the customer correctly points out to them that the item is incorrectly priced on the computer. However the vast majority of customers would not notice the incorrect price.

Dumping

This is the practice of selling products abroad at lower prices than at home. This might be done to capture a large market share or drive the competition out of the market. Alternatively, the level of demand at home might be insufficient to support production capacity and so to create economies of scale dumping abroad is resorted to. In other cases technologically obsolete products for which there is no demand at home may be dumped abroad.

Schlegelmilch (2001) reports that in the United States, a product found unsafe by the Consumer Product Safety Commission is not allowed to be sold in the country. This rule often provides a different motivation for US companies to dump the product abroad. For example, in 1989 the Commission outlawed three-wheel cycles as dangerous to the consumer. Many companies recalled their products and dealt with the large inventories by dumping them at low prices abroad. The firms involved were not prepared to incur large losses. Thus they put profit before the safety of their customers. They also decided that the safety of lives abroad hadn't the same value as the safety of lives at home. Dumping is unethical where

it damages competition, forces firms abroad to close, or puts the health and safety of customers at risk.

Bait and switch

This is the practice of enticing a customer into a shop with the offer of a bargain. The shopkeeper then attempts to persuade the customer to purchase a higher-priced item by pointing out the disadvantages of the lower-priced item. The hidden agenda all the time is to sell the higher priced items. If the customer insists on buying the bargain he may discover that the item is not really a bargain or is told that the item has already been sold out. It probably was never in stock in the first instance. Such tactics do nothing for the reputation of retailers. This is false and deceptive advertising and as such is a dishonest and unethical practice.

> **"Promise, large promise, is the soul of an advertisement."**
>
> Samuel Johnson

Loss-leaders

Loss-leaders are products sold below cost in order to attract customers into the shop. One such practice is known as BOGOF, or "buy one, get one free". The hope is that customers will buy sufficient other products to yield a good profit. Loss-leaders are not deceptive, though they can be considered suspect when other products are marked up to compensate for the below-cost selling. It is a type of robbing Peter to pay Paul. The use of loss-leaders has come under the scrutiny of the EU, particularly in relation to the sale of under-priced bread or milk. This practice is particularly unfair to farmers who are forced to supply their produce at ever lower prices cutting their margins until eventually it becomes unprofitable. Many complain that they can't make a reasonable living from farming and are being forced to leave. Small shops complain that the loss-leader policies of the large supermarket chains put them out of business. The smaller shops can't cross subsidise loss-making products from high margin products like the big supermarket retailers do.

The threat to the small shop is compounded by the fact that the larger retailers can squeeze better terms from their suppliers. France, Germany, Ireland and Spain have legislation to prohibit below cost selling. *Corporate Watch* (15/3/2002) reported that in 2000, Wal-Mart was found guilty of breaking German law by selling a range of grocery items at below their cost price. The world's largest retailer was ordered to halt the practice or face a substantial fine. In 2001, Wal-Mart decided to pull out of the German retail

market. Consumers complain that laws prohibiting below cost selling adds to the cost of their weekly groceries.

Hard sell

This is where excessive psychological pressure is put on customers to buy unneeded or unaffordable products or services. During periods of great emotional upset in their lives, people are particularly susceptible to this type of selling. Funeral directors can often exploit bereaved people at a time when they are emotionally vulnerable and incapable of making rational decisions for themselves. They want to give their loved one the best send-off possible, and so price is often not a consideration. As a consequence unnecessary debt and reckless expenditure is sometimes incurred. Similar situations arise when couples get engaged, parents arrange a wedding, or people borrow money to pay for life-saving medical care.

Salespeople may also try to sell expensive models with extra features that customers do not really want. The hidden agenda is to get the extra commission involved and reach sales targets quicker. The sales manager doesn't seem to care how the sales targets are achieved and at what cost to the customer. Managers should be concerned about ethical conduct and how goals are achieved.

Misleading customers

The senior citizens market is now seen as particularly lucrative. They have paid off their mortgages and own their own homes. Many have substantial disposable incomes. Their children have left the nest and they are often lonely, vulnerable and responsive to human conversation and contact. They can thus be taken advantage of by a friendly, talkative, diplomatic and unscrupulous salesperson.

> "The commerce of the world is conducted by the strong, and usually it operates against the weak."
>
> Henry Ward Beecher

Rogue traders, professional conmen, and dishonest tradesmen are just some of the people who try to cheat old people. Tradesmen take advantage of older people by charging them too much. Door-to-door salespeople convince them to buy products that they do not actually need or that are too sophisticated for them to use. They are easy to scam

because they get confused and fall victim to unscrupulous tradesmen or salespeople who blind them with technical jargon.

> **"He who wishes to be rich in a day will be hanged in a year."**
> Leonardo da Vinci

People with specialised knowledge can often convince the unwary customer to sanction unnecessary work, or overcharge for work done. Most people have only a vague idea of how things work. This means there is great room for exploitation of others by those with specialised knowledge. Electricians, plumbers, car mechanics, builders and computer technicians can exploit our ignorance. We assume that people are trustworthy and have our interests at hear. However, this is sometimes not the case.

Dangerous or defective products

A seller may be liable for damages when a customer is injured using their product. Before sale a seller is obliged to reveal possible dangers or substantial product defects to a buyer. Poor quality is unethical and quality is an ethical imperative. Thus a customer has a right to expect safety, protection and the necessary information to make informed decisions and to avoid serious harm.

> **"How many pretenses men that sell goods weave! What poor articles, with what a good face, do they palm off on their customers!"**
> Henry Ward Beecher (1813-1887)

Pace (2004) maintains that poor quality is not only unethical, but also an unwise business practice. Surveys have indicated that customers are demanding higher quality. Price is no longer the deciding factor in purchasing decisions. In the USA, for example, research has shown that 80 per cent of potential customers consider quality equal to or more important than price in their purchases. In practice sometimes the quality imperative is not met.

Customer safety

It is unethical to sell products injurious to health and safety. A person suffering from high blood pressure has a right to know the amount of salt in prepared foods. Without this information he will be unable to follow an appropriate diet to protect his health. Similar obligations exist with regard

to ingredients such as nuts that can cause allergic reactions in some people. Many of us do not realise the risks posed to our health by everyday products. It is often a question of *caveat emptor*, or "let the buyer beware". It may a wise safeguard to read the label and list of ingredients before you purchase.

The pressure to market products quickly and sometimes without adequate testing may pose dangers to the public. In rare cases unscrupulous people may surreptitiously tamper with the product such as in the Tylenol affair. A drug called Thalidomide was withdrawn during the early 1960s when it was realised that it caused major deformities in babies. About 12,000 babies were affected in Europe, Canada, Australia and Japan. The Food and Drug Administration had not approved it for use in the USA. It had been prescribed for women as an anti-sickness remedy during pregnancy. This tragedy gave rise to more rigorous testing of drugs before they were released for public consumption.

> "The large corporations, though still primarily a private economic entity, has such vast social impact (where it locates, whom it hires, what technology it pursues) that it has become a public trust with a communal constituency."
>
> Stephen B. Sheppard

Each year, particularly at Christmas time, unsafe toys are sold to children. Many of these are imported from developing countries where safety regulations are lax or non-existent. Teddy bears are sold with detachable eyes, which may be swallowed if they become loose and choke small children. Toys are sold with sharp edges that may cut children's hands. Others are painted with toxic substances, which may poison children if sucked. Some countries have regulatory bodies, which monitor the safety of toys and withdraw those deemed to be unsafe.

Pallister (2007) reports that half a million Chinese-made children's toys were recalled across the UK and Ireland after concerns that they contained a chemical which changes to the date rape drug GHB when swallowed. Reports had been received that at least six children in the US and Australia had become seriously ill and hospitalised after swallowing the beads. The symptoms of the drug are unconsciousness, seizures, drowsiness, coma and occasionally death. The incident highlights ongoing concerns about health and safety standards in China.

Producing quality products and service consistently is both ethical and good for business. Also, by not doing so you may break the law. It creates customer satisfaction, improves competitiveness, lowers costs, and promotes organisational and economic growth.

Pharmaceutical products and safety

Some drugs seem to induce suicidal and murderous tendencies. Raftery (2005) reports that on September 14, 1989, Joseph Wesbecker walked into his workplace in Louisville, Kentucky, produced an AK 47, shot 8 people dead, wounded 12 others and finally killed himself. It transpired that Wesbecker had a long history of depression and had been put on Prozac just one month before the killings. Relatives of his victims took a civil case against the pharmaceutical company Eli Lilly makers of Prozac. It argued that the drug was responsible for Wesbecker's murderous rampage. They lost their case. However, it has now transpired that documents have since come to light questioning the safety of Prozac. They indicate that Eli Lilly was aware of the possible side effects of Prozac and suicidal behaviour as far back as the 1980s and suppressed the information. It seems some pharmaceutical companies have been less than forthright and transparent about the side effects of their drugs.

> "Corporations, especially the large and complex ones with which we have to live, now appear to possess some of the qualities of nation states including, perhaps, an alarming capacity to insulate their members from the moral consequences of their actions."
>
> Paul Eddy, Elaine Potter and Bruce Page

Boseley (2003) reports that a coroner advised that Seroxat, the world's biggest antidepressant, should be withdrawn while its safety is fully investigated. The coroner has recorded an open verdict on a retired headteacher who killed himself within a fortnight of starting a course of the drug. Seroxat, is a class of drugs, with Prozac, termed SSRI or selective serotonin reuptake inhibitors. It has overtaken Prozac in sales. In 2001, the former SmithKline Beecham (now GlaxoSmithKline) was ordered by a Wyoming jury to pay £4.7 million to the family of Donald Schell, who killed his wife, daughter, baby grand daughter and then himself after two days on Seroxat. GlaxoSmithKline insists that the drug is safe.

Side effects of drugs

The *CBG Newsletter* (6/7/2004) published a press release from the Coalition against Bayer highlighting the dangers of drugs. It recommended independent studies on new drugs, the compulsory training of medical doctors without the involvement of the pharmaceutical industry, and government supervision on drugs after their release on the market. European governments need increased administrative and legal power to

systematically document the side effects of drugs and remove them from the market when necessary. They suggest advertising of drugs should be banned. They highlight the fact that companies spend twice as much on marketing as they do on research. They also claim that research shows that 250,000 people have to receive in-patient treatment because of the side effects of drugs. Out of this 12,000 patients die annually because of pharmaceutical side effects.

Corporate Watch (Spring 2000) reported that between 1946 and 1988 Glaxo made and sold a spinal x-ray contrast medium called Myodil. The drug is injected into the spinal canal to show up problems on x-ray. It was sold in approximately 50 countries including the UK. However, it has been found that Myodil, an oil-based yellow dye, is far from harmless. It causes a disease called Adhesive Arachnoiditis resulting in chronic pain. It has no known cure or treatment. It is estimated that tens of thousands of people have developed this disease. The sale of the product has been discontinued in the UK but is still manufactured and sold overseas.

"The commerce of the world is conducted by the strong, and usually it operates against the weak."

Henry Ward Beecher

Glaxo (now GlaxoSmithKline) always denied the links between Myodil and Adhesive Arachnoiditis. However, in an out of court settlement in 1995, whilst denying liability Glaxo Laboratories Ltd paid out an average £16,000 to each of 425 claimants suffering from the disease. A basic principle of business ethics is to at least do no harm. GlaxoSmithKline does not seem to be behaving very responsibly considering that its product is still being used in many countries throughout the world with the possibility of causing suffering and pain to many.

Recalling products

Recalling a product is a costly operation. However, the safety of the public should be protected irrespective of cost. Schlegelmilch (2001) reports that in 1999 the French manufacturer of Perrier bottled water had to remove its product from US retail stores. The product was found to contain benzene above the legal limit. Perrier maintained that the contamination resulted from an isolated incident. Other countries were influenced by the publicity and conducted tests of their own. Eventually Perrier had to withdraw its products in other countries resulting in a worldwide brand recall. The company was attacked by the media and accused of having

little concern for the safety of their customers. They procrastinated and put their own interests above those of their customers.

Schlegelmilch (2001) considers the example of good corporate social behaviour of a US company named H.B. Fuller. This company ran into trouble in 1995 when media reports claimed that thousands of Central American children were sniffing its shoe making glue and damaging their brains. Fuller responded to the misuse of its product by reformulating its glue and restricting its use in factories. It took the glue out of retail circulation and gave hundreds of thousands of dollars to social programmes. Fuller had taken a clear ethical stand balancing the need for profits with its social responsibility. It is another example of a principled morality stance.

The *Ethical Consumer* (Dec 03/Jan 04) reported that Greenpeace found toxic chemicals in children's Disney pyjamas and attached warning stickers to them. In tests on four pairs of Disney-branded pyjamas on sale at a Disney Store and other major retailers, a toxic chemical was found called nonylphenol, which can interfere with human DNA and affect sperm production in mammals. Also present in the pyjamas were phthalates, which can cause liver, kidney and testicular damage. These are already banned from teething toys under emergency EU legislation. As a result of the Greenpeace campaign, Disney Stores, along with Debenhams and Mothercare, have now withdrawn the offending garments

Principled morality

In 1982 seven people died after being poisoned by Tylenol. Some capsules had been interfered with and laced with cyanide. The CEO of Johnson & Johnson ordered that every single bottle of Tylenol should be removed from the shelves. The company openly admitted the problem and promised a replacement bottle for every one returned. He was not prepared to put the public's health and safety at risk despite the potential effects on profits. The cost of the recall was $100 million and the company's share price fell by 17 per cent. By his behaviour the CEO instilled the right values and behaviours in his employees by leading through example. This is an example of principled morality discussed in Chapter one.

"Business must be profitable if it is to continue to succeed, but the glory of business is to make it so successful that it may do things that are great chiefly because they ought to be done."

Charles M. Schwab

After the incident, faith in Tylenol was restored and it quickly regained its market share. The ethical response of Johnson & Johnson is considered the benchmark against which companies should compare their response in a crisis to. One good outcome of the incident was the new tamper proof bottle that is now universally available.

The high ethical image of Johnson and Johnson has since been tarnished somewhat by a case reported in the *Guardian* (29/7/2002). This report said that Johnson and Johnson was under criminal investigation over allegations that it made errors in drug manufacture and then tried to cover them up. A former employee claimed that in a wrongful dismissal case that he was pressured into changing key data to hide mistakes in making anaemia drug called Exprex at a factory in Puerto Rico. The news resulted in a dramatic fall in the company's share price. On the other hand, Proctor and Gamble displayed great environmental awareness when they redesigned their disposable diapers, which were not biodegradable, so that they decomposed more rapidly.

Genetically modified (GM) products

Many consumers are concerned about the safety of GM products. Some want to ban them until long-term independent research proves conclusively that such products are not harmful to humans, animals and the environment. The multinationals involved in the research on GM products assure us that they are safe. Naturally, the public does not trust or believe companies who employ public relations consultants for spin and are driven by the profit motive rather than the interests of consumers.

Many countries now require labelling of gm food products giving consumers the option of deciding for themselves whether or not they want these products. However they are being introduced into the food chain indirectly through feedstuffs. Sample (2004), reports that the British government plans to push ahead with the commercial cultivation of GM crops. The government's decision comes as the World Trade Organisation is considering a legal case brought by the US, Canada and Argentina, which maintain that the EU's effective ban on gm crops until they are proven safe is illegal and merely a smokescreen for a trade barrier.

Deception

Deception includes misleading advertising and customers, inadequate labelling, substituting lower quality materials, celebrity endorsement, and product counterfeiting. All of these are unethical.

> "Deceivers are the most dangerous members of our society. They trifle with the best affections of our nature, and violate the most sacred obligations."
>
> George Crabbe

Misleading advertising

Aggressive advertising supports consumerism and materialism. Some people maintain that all advertising is misleading since it exploits the basic human instinct of greed and causes many to buy goods that they want but that they do not really need. False and misleading advertising is illegal. Making exaggerated claims may not be illegal but it is unethical. However, the definition of misleading is vague. Dishonest advertising exaggerates the product's performance and raises expectations to unrealistic levels which cannot be fulfilled, creating dissatisfaction and the inevitable badwill which follows. Thus in pursuing today's profits unethically, a company might be sacrificing tomorrow's business success.

> "Never write an advertisement which you wouldn't want your family to read. You wouldn't tell lies to your own wife. Don't tell them to mine. Do as you would be done by. If you tell lies about a product, you will be found out – either by the Government, which will prosecute you, or by the consumer, who will punish you by not buying your product a second time. Good products can be sold by honest advertising. If you don't think the product is good, you have no business to be advertising it. "
>
> David M. Oglivy

A bank that promoted a cheque card as having no annual fee in fact charged a monthly fee. Customers only became aware of this on checking their bank statement. Misleading advertising can be subtle where advertisers link an unhealthy product like alcoholic drink or cigarettes with sports activities and attractiveness to the opposite sex. When selling breakfast orange juice using the term fresh when the product is processed or pasteurised would be misleading. In the recent past one company was prosecuted for selling filtered tap water as spring water.

> "The whole idea of image is soon confused. On the one hand, Madison Avenue is worried about the image of the players in a tennis tour. On the other hand, sports events are often sponsored by the makers of junk food, beer, and cigarettes. What's the message when an athlete who works at keeping her body fit is sponsored by a sugar-filled snack that does more harm than good?"
>
> Martina Navratilov

Product labelling

This also provides opportunities for unethical actions for business organisations. False labelling is relatively rare, but misleading labelling is commonplace. The *Observer* (2/2/2003) reported that in 1983 the California supreme court gave the green light to an action brought by a health organisation against General Foods concerning their breakfast cereals called Sugar Crisp and Cocoa Pebbles aimed at children. The plaintiffs argued that the product promoted and labelled as cereals could in fact be more accurately described as sugar products or candies. The court suggested advertisements that even implicitly claimed such products were nutritious or healthy made plausible lawsuit targets. The case was settled.

Manufacturers may substitute lower quality materials for higher quality materials to reduce costs. Ferrell et al (2002) reports that the Beech-Nut Nutrition Corporation took this concept to an extreme when it used a lower-cost concentrate in making its apple-juice product. The concentrate was merely a chemical concoction that had the taste, smell and look of apple juice. They labelled the product as 100 per cent apple juice. The issue here is that consumers are denied the facts to enable them to make a good buying decision based on the truth.

Creating false expectations

When a product is bought it doesn't always live up to the expectations created in a child's impressionable mind. Thus some countries have laws controlling the type of advertising aimed at children and the times during the day when it can be advertised on TV. The more ethically minded supermarket chains have removed sweets from near the checkouts. The ethical position here is that supermarkets and advertisers should not exploit the vulnerability of children.

As a customer, one notices packages being only partially full with the product. There are two ethical concerns here. One is the actual waste of

packaging and the environmental consequences of added waste disposal. The second is misleading the customer regarding the contents of the package. However, we must give the benefit of the doubt as in some cases the slack fill may not be as a result of an intention to deceive but may be a natural settling down of the product during transit.

> "Whoever buys
> Should have two eyes,
> But one's enough
> To sell the stuff."
>
> Anon

Pharmaceutical companies have a particular duty not to engage in misleading advertising as the health and welfare of their customers is at stake. They should not overstate the effectiveness of a drug or minimise the risks attached to using it. Customers are now able to purchase all kinds of prescription drugs online often without the need for a prior prescription. The ethical propriety of selling prescription drugs over the Internet is doubtful and this is an area that needs to be regulated to safeguard the health of the public. It is another example where the law has not yet caught up with the technology.

Counterfeiting

Counterfeiting is a huge problem particularly in designer clothes, pharmaceuticals, CDs, DVDs and computer software. Companies try to protect their intellectual property rights through patent or copyright. However, in many underdeveloped and developing countries where patent law and copyright is lax or non-existent this strategy offers little protection. The Internet has facilitated the downloading and counterfeiting of CDs.

Firms that engage in product counterfeiting justify their position on the basis that they provide goods at a price that the market can afford. Computer software and pharmaceutical companies justify their high prices on the basis that they are obliged to recover the high research and development costs incurred in developing the product in the first instance.

O'Rourke (2004) reports that counterfeit products cost up to $350 billion according to the International Chamber of Commerce. These include not only obvious street-vendor forgeries but also complex black market operations involving major retailers as part of a worldwide counterfeiting market. Companies fear counterfeiting not only for the loss of revenue, but because a shoddy fake may have a detrimental effect on a company's reputation. Consequently, the International Counterfeiting Coalition spends

an average of $2 to $4 million annually to fight it. Product counterfeiting is a type of stealing and is unethical and illegal in many jurisdictions. However, in some jurisdictions it is still legal.

Shoplifting

Shoplifting is now prevalent and mirrors the low ethical standards operating generally in society. Very few offenders seem to consider the ethics involved – that shoplifting is wrong. Shoplifting is not a victimless crime. It results in large security and insurance costs that are passed on to the customer in the form of higher prices. Firms can be put out of business, employees can lose their jobs and some can even be wrongly accused of such crimes.

To counteract the prevalence of shoplifting even small stores now have at least one security person. There has been a huge growth in the security industry in both manpower and equipment. Closed circuit television cameras are omnipresent on our streets, in our workplaces and in our shops. The *Guardian* (5/3/2002) reported that in 2001 British retailers lost £746 million to customer theft, 22 per cent was committed by under 18's. According to Home Office figures, shoplifting makes up an eighth of recorded offences and, for the first time, more women than men are being cautioned for the crime. It is particularly prevalent among young women.

Some young women rationalised shoplifting on the basis that the retailers were charging too much and making excessive profits. Some steal as an antidote to depression particularly older women. Compulsive shoppers who shoplift are often middle-aged, middle-class women who feel enormous guilt and shame when caught. Some people shoplift for the thrill involved or to support a drug or gambling habit.

Financial services

There are many issues giving rise to ethical concerns in the financial services sector. These include price-fixing, loans, selling to the elderly, deceit, churning, money-laundering, and lack of transparency

Financial services fraud

Nick Leeson is infamous as the man who brought down Barings Investment Bank in 1995 with losses of £850 million on futures and options trading. His managers didn't understand what Nick was up to and thus he was able to bluff them until the losses became so obvious that

they could no longer be concealed. Leeson was also given too much authority and freedom. He controlled the front and back office in Singapore. Good control would demand that one office should be used to check the activities of the other.

> "There are two times in a man's life when he should not speculate: when he can't afford it, and when he can."
>
> Mark Twain

Leeson was sentenced to six and a half years in jail in Singapore and Barings was subsequently sold to Dutch Bank ING. Mismanagement, lack of controls and failure to ask the right questions facilitated the fraud. Managers failed to probe the scam because they did not want to appear ignorant about derivatives, futures and options trading. They were confused by the jargon of options trading and failed to probe by asking the right questions. In addition many managers and directors did not really understand the risks associated with derivative trading. Leeson now lives in Ireland where he writes on financial issues and occasionally makes radio and TV appearances. In recent times he has reinvented himself in a management role with Galway United FC.

> Conscience tells you what to do
> And puts you in a tizzy;
> But when it tries to get to you,
> The line is sometimes busy.
>
> Anon

John Rusnak worked for a subsidiary of AIB in the USA called Allfirst and made $691 million in losses in a similar situation to Nick Leeson. History repeated itself. AIB Bank had not taken on board the lessons of the Nick Leeson affair who also lost millions with complex derivative-backed bets against the Japanese yen. John was sentenced to seven and a half years in prison in 2003 after pleading guilty to a single count of bank fraud. He did not embezzle any of the money but fraudulently claimed bonuses and salary for revenues that he did not earn. He was ordered to pay restitution of $1,000 a month for five years after his release. John was active in his local church and was a pillar of the local community. Poor management supervision and inadequate bank controls facilitated the fraud.

Seymour (2008) reports that a rogue trader at MF Global Ltd made $141.5 million losses on the broker's account. The loss has cost the company almost a fifth of its market value. Evan Dooley, the trader, was operating beyond his authorised limits while trading in wheat contracts.

MF Global fired Dooley. This comes just weeks after Jerome Kerviel, a trader at Société Générale, lost more than $7 billion in losses on his company's account by placing unauthorised bets on European stock indexes. These scandals raise questions about the banks' lax control procedures. In the case of Société Générale, management failed to act on an internal report warning about questionable trades. Kerviel maintains that his superiors must have known what he was doing but turned a blind eye as long as he was making money.

The *Observer* (7/2/1999) reported that a survey by accountants Ernest & Young found that **three in five frauds are uncovered purely by chance, while less than 10 per cent are detected by auditors.** Despite the huge foreign exchange fraud and the lack of management controls the chief executive of AIB did not resign. The days of the concept that "the buck stops here" seem to be gone. Managers can help to reduce the incidence of fraud by making sure that employees take their annual leave as planned and that staff are rotated frequently.

> The problem of money dogs our steps throughout the whole of our lives, exerting a pressure that, in its way, is as powerful and insistent as any problem of human existence. And it haunts the spiritual search as well.
>
> Jacob Needleman

Subprime mortgage lending

A subprime mortgage lender is one who lends to borrowers who do not qualify for loans from mainstream banks. Some lenders are independent, but most are subsidiaries of mainstream banks operating under different names. To cover the higher risk involved they charge higher interest rates and commission fees. The borrowers usually have poor credit histories and potentially adverse financial circumstances.

Johnson & Neave (2008) found that a combination of greed, perverse incentives to borrow, inadequate risk controls and lax regulation has resulted in a crisis in the subprime market. The whole basis of the market for subprime lending is suspect. It doesn't make sense and is certainly unethical to give loans to financially vulnerable people who can ill afford them and charge them exorbitant interest rates and fees for the privilege. It seems nothing less than the exploitation of the less well-off. When interest rates increased and property prices fell, increased repayments were faced by those least able to afford them without the cushion of home equity. This meant that more borrowers were unable to pay the repayments on their loans.

In September 2007, Northern Rock, the UK's fifth largest mortgage provider had to be baled out by the Bank of England. This was a direct result of problems caused by the subprime lending crisis in the US. Northern Rock offered mortgages of up to 125 per cent of the value of a home and loans of up to six times salary. Prudence would suggest mortgages of up to 90 per cent of the value of a home and loans of up to three times salary. Northern Rock's financial base depended on the wholesale money market rather than customer deposits. When the crisis started banks refused to lend to each other and thus the source of Northern Rock's finance dried up. Hence its problems.

Mortgage fraud

Mortgage fraud occurs where an applicant for a mortgage materially misrepresents information on a loan application form. This may take many forms:

◆ Borrowers may overstate their income to qualify for a larger loan. This highlights the need for a careful verification process by the lender.
◆ Borrowers may fail to disclose the extent of their liabilities. The debt to income ratio is a key criterion for loans. The omission of liabilities will allow the borrower to qualify for a larger loan.
◆ The borrower may collude with the estate agent to overstate the value of the house to get a larger loan.
◆ "Shotgunning" is the process when a person takes out multiple loans on the same property. In 2007 Michael Lynn, a Dublin based solicitor and property speculator, took out multiple loans on a number of his properties with different banks. He has absconded leaving estimated liabilities of €80 million behind. In December 2007 his Dublin practice was shut down by the Law Society and the police in Ireland have issued a warrant for his arrest. His whereabouts are unknown.

Loans to executives

Most people are not financially literate and thus easily deceived in matters relating to money. The financial services sector often takes advantage of this fact. Thus the real cost of a loan is hard to determine for the layperson when service charges, methods of repayment and different ways of calculating the rate of interest are taken into account. Service charges are often hidden in the small print escaping the notice of the customer. Banks

must now, under law, disclose the real cost of borrowing. This law was brought in to stop banks from exploiting the ignorance of borrowers.

> Commerce is, in its very essence, satanic. Commerce is return of the loan, a loan in which there is the understanding; give me more than I give you.
>
> Charles Baudelaire

Banks in the past have been accused of making the availability of loans too easy. In particular they have targeted students knowing that once caught they have a customer for life. Students are offered loans that are repayable when they graduate and get a job. As a result loans are often acquired for spurious purposes. The wide use of credit cards has facilitated the creation of even greater debt. Excessive interest rates charged on these cards magnify the problem. Consequently students are in debt for many years after starting work putting them under considerable financial pressure. This is at a stage in their lives when other costs may come into play such as housing, childcare and health.

Selling to the elderly

People selling financial products have been accused of taking advantage of the old by selling them products completely unsuitable to their needs. Many of these have been high-risk bonds linked to stock market indexes and the people who invested in them may have been left penniless. People were promised high returns but weren't made aware about the possible downside – that they could lose all their money. These products pay extremely high commission to the broker and usually occur because the old person investing in the product doesn't really understand what they are buying.

> The voice of conscience has a difficult time making connections with the ears.
>
> Edgar Watson Howe

AIB in Ireland has been criticised for selling unsuitable investment products to old people. One case that came to light in 2005 concerned the sale of an equity-based savings product to two very elderly sisters – both were in their nineties. The product lost €31,000 because it was linked to the stock market, which did very badly. Their advanced years would suggest that long-term investments were completely unsuited to their needs. The bank consistently advised its elderly customers to think long term, as the return on equities in the long term is better than any other

form of investment. The sisters maintained that AIB described the investment as low risk. Many vulnerable people have lost some or all of their life savings in such schemes.

Financial institutions that sell flexible mortgage plans downplay the risk that they may not earn sufficient cash to pay off their mortgages when they mature. They have been accused of systematically mis-selling mortgage endowment policies. Many customers are not sophisticated enough to understand the risks involved and often it is not clearly explained. Most are led to believe that they will have sufficient to pay off the mortgage and have a small surplus to booth. The only people who gain from the above transactions are the financial institutions who pocket generous commission and administration fees regardless of the outcome of the investment.

In the long-term the unethical hard sell approach does not pay. If such practices get into the media the prestige of the company will be tarnished. In addition, there is always the danger that a legal action will be taken against the company resulting in more bad publicity and the possible loss of future sales. The solution is to train sales representatives in ethical selling methods and not to take advantage of vulnerable investors.

Deceit

The independence of the advice from investment analysts employed by brokers has come under scrutiny. Most of them are only interested in earning commission rather than in giving their clients good investment advice. Some recommend their clients to buy when correct impartial advice would be to sell. In fact it is well known in the world of finance that the so-called "Chinese Wall" that is supposed to protect investment analysts from being pressurised by bankers does not exist. Some of the firms of brokers are subsidiaries of the financial institutions or tied to them commercially. Investment analysts have been pressured to upgrade ratings from "neutral" to "buy" in order to win lucrative business.

The *Irish Times* (12/4/2002) reports that a ten-month investigation of Merrill Lynch by the New York chief prosecutor turned up deceitful e-mails. These showed that high profile analysts were promoting poor investments to clients. The firm's Internet research group, led by star performer Mr Henry Blodget was recommending "buys" on failing start-ups. Mr Blodget first gained prominence when he predicted, accurately, in 1998 that Amazon would rise to $400 from $232. As the stock collapsed when the dotcom bubble burst, he continued to recommend clients to buy. The stock was eventually trading for less than $10. The investigation showed that the "Chinese Wall" between Merrill Lynch's analysts and its bankers was

fictitious. The brokerage firm used the prospect of a favourable assessment as an inducement to obtain their business. Merill Lynch was fined $100 million because their Internet analysts recommended investors to buy stocks they knew were poor investments.

Churning

Suiter (1999) said that a report into the insurance industry revealed widespread churning in Irish Life. **Churning is the process of cancelling one policy in favour of another solely to earn the salespeople commission.** In a review in 1998, 75 policyholders were found to be victims of mis-selling and received compensation. There was no evidence that senior executives were aware or encouraged the practice. However, churning was a problem in Irish Life since 1994. Irish Life has paid €139,557 to policyholders who were disadvantaged by churning between 1993 and 1998. Disciplinary action was taken against 5 salespeople. Brokerage firms have also been found to be engaging in churning – needlessly trading accounts in shares in order to charge commission on the deals.

> It is difficult but not impossible to conduct strictly honest business. What is true is that honesty is incompatible with the amassing of a large fortune.
> Mohandas K. Gandhi

Money-laundering

Money-laundering happens when people go to extreme measures to hide or camouflage the source of their money. Legislation has been enacted in many countries to counteract money-laundering activities engaged in by criminals, drug dealers and terrorists to hide their ill-gotten cash. Banks and financial institutions must notify the police of suspicious transactions.

Embezzlement, insider dealing, bribery and computer fraud schemes can also produce large amounts of cash which people may wish to conceal through money-laundering. Those who do not wish to pay tax may launder their money through an offshore tax haven. In addition various financial instruments, property, luxury assets, or business ventures may be used.

Dealing with other organisations

It is important that ethical standards are maintained when companies deal with other organisations including suppliers and competitors. Taking an excessive amount of time to pay suppliers, industrial espionage,

outsourcing, take-overs and mergers, bribery, and human rights abuses are just some of the conduct giving rise to unethical behaviour.

Suppliers

Large supermarket groups are often accused of exploiting their powerful position by taking excessive periods in which to pay their suppliers. In the meantime suppliers have to organise bank overdraft facilities in order to keep afloat. Supermarket chains may also abuse their power by demanding rock bottom prices from their suppliers. In the past they have been known to charge suppliers fees for shelf space or for using the more visible places on the shelves. This practice is unethical as it exploits the supplier's need to access the marketplace on a fair basis.

On the other hand, suppliers may perpetrate fraud against a company by over-billing, double billing, short shipment of goods, or misrepresenting the quality and value of goods supplied.

> When a man sells eleven ounces for twelve, he makes a compact with the devil, and sells himself for the value of an ounce.
>
> Henry Ward Beecher

Farmers complain that there is a huge difference between what they get for their meat and vegetables and what the customer finally pays in the shop. Lower costs are not being passed on to the customer but instead are being kept by the retailers to increase their profit margins.

Subcontracting

A company may be criticised for obtaining products from offshore manufacturers who pay their employees sub-living wages. A company may have to police their contractors from the outset to ensure that they aren't exploiting their workforce. Arnold et al (2003) reports that in Haiti apparel manufacturers such as L.V. Myles Corporation, producing clothing under license with the Walt Disney Company in several contract factories, paid workers substantially less than the Haitian minimum wage. These clothes were sold in the US at Wal-Mart, Sears, J.C. Penney and other retailers. This practice continued until the National Labour Committee documented and publicised this violation of Haitian law.

Arnold et al (2003) also reports that a Guatemalan Ministry of the Economy study found that less than 30 per cent of factories in export processing zones, supplying multinationals make the legally required payments for workers into the national social security system giving

workers access to healthcare. The Ministry of the Economy did not make the report public due to its "startling" nature.

Outsourcing

Some companies have no hesitation in outsourcing work to third world countries where labour costs are low, working conditions are poor, and environmental laws lax. This is quite legal but may be unethical. There is an ethical dilemma here. On the one hand outsourcing results in loss of jobs for the home base. This can be devastating for some employees while others are given the opportunity to start up their own businesses or get alternative employment. Many companies have a value statement stating that they value their employees. Outsourcing may be seen as a contradiction of such statements resulting in a loss of jobs for employees and a loss of credibility for the company.

On the other hand it creates jobs abroad even if they are low paid. Outsourcing also gives consumers a greater variety of goods at lower prices. This is balanced by the fact that the lower prices are achieved by exploiting labour. If the outsourcing is needed to remain competitive and keep the company in business then it probably is ethical. However, if the outsourcing is motivated by the greed and selfishness of the top executives to make even more money when the company is already profitable then it probably is unethical.

Industrial espionage

Because of intense competition companies may resort to corporate espionage. Espionage is considered unethical because it gives one company an unfair advantage over competition. Ferrell et al (2002) reveals that General Electric (GE) was the victim of a conspiracy to steal drawings and diagrams of its turbine parts. Investigators discovered that, over a period of years, several small manufacturing firms bribed GE employees for confidential drawings of turbine parts. This enabled them to manufacture identical spare parts to those made by GE. By acquiring these drawings unethically the companies avoided spending millions of dollars in research and development. The fraud was discovered.

Take-overs and mergers

Managers have a responsibility to run the business in the interest of the owners or shareholders. Take-overs and mergers are often done to increase the power and remuneration of senior executives rather than in

the interests of employees or shareholders. Senior executives have a responsibility to undertake a due diligence exercise before proposed mergers and take-overs to ensure that the arrangement is good value for money. A poor deal can spell future financial disaster for a company.

The effects of hostile take-overs on the workforce are often particularly serious. The acquiring company may seek to recoup some of its cost of purchase by selling portions of the company or by restructuring. This often involves plant closures and layoffs.

Bribery and corruption

A bribe is a payment made to a person to do something contrary to their responsibilities. Bribery is common in some countries. It is almost impossible to get work done in such countries without resorting to grease payments. For example bribery is endemic in Eastern European countries, Russia, Arab and African countries. There are some fine distinctions to be drawn, for example, some managers regard political contributions as bribery. If the payer initiates the payment it is a bribe. If the receiver demands the payment it is extortion. Foreign officials have been known to threaten companies with the complete closure of their local operations unless suitable payments were made. Some people also make a distinction between bribery and grease payments.

> "The accomplice to the crime of corruption is frequently our own indifference".
>
> Bess Myerson

Grease payments

Grease payments are small amounts given to bureaucrats or administrators to do their jobs. Multinationals are sometimes unable to obtain services to which they are legally entitled because of deliberate delays by local officials. Cash payments to the right people may be enough to oil the machinery of bureaucracy. In the USA bribery is illegal. However, in many developing countries it is an acceptable way of doing business and of supplementing a meagre income. In fact bribery seems to be widespread throughout the world, even in the developed nations. Weber et al (2004) reports that a 1997 World Bank survey found that 40 per cent of 3,500 firms in 69 countries admitted to paying bribes. The bribe averaged about 20 per cent of the transaction amount.

CEOs in India admit that their companies engage constantly in bribery. They claim it is very hard to get business done without resorting to grease

payments. It is very difficult to get goods through customs smoothly and quickly if one does not bribe. All Southeast Asian countries have laws against corruption and bribery. Nevertheless they tend to view corruption as a normal and necessary way of life.

"The first sign of corruption in a society that is still alive is that the end justifies the means".

George Bernanos

Bribery for public contracts

Bribery has been the downfall of many managers, legislators and government officials. Some Presidents, Prime Ministers, Ministers and politicians have been involved in bribery. Obviously the person giving the bribe hopes to gain some favour such as a chance to influence legislation or be awarded large and profitable public contracts. Moorhead et al (1998) reports that in 1995 Lockheed-Martin paid $24 million in fines. They clinched the sale of three aircraft to the Egyptian government because they made a $1.5 million payment to a government official who helped them get the contract.

Weber et al (2004) reports that in South Korea, Kim Hong-up, son of former President Kim Dae-jung, was sentenced to three and a half years in prison for accepting bribes. He was also ordered to return the bribe money and pay a fine of over $1 million. Another presidential son, Kim Hong-gul, received a suspended sentence and a fine for the same offence. Both sons had accepted bribes in return for accepting a company win a lottery license. Their close ties to the president did not save them when their corrupt behaviour was discovered.

Bribery is an added cost and may reduce foreign investment. Bribery is anti-democratic as it may influence public officials to act contrary to the public interest. Bribery is like a virus, which may affect the whole political process from minor officials to top politicians pervading all aspect of political life.

Many organisations are now trying to tackle and eliminate bribery. In December 1997, OECD ministers signed the Convention on Combating Bribery of Foreign Public Officials in International Business Transactions. The Convention makes it a crime to offer, promise or give a bribe to a foreign public official to obtain or retain international business deals. It also effectively ends the practice of allowing bribes as tax deductible expenses.

Human rights

In the past, Levi Strauss has demonstrated its commitment to good ethical principles. The *Irish Times* (21/6/1999) reported that in 1993 its chief executive countermanded an executive committee decision to expand trade and investment in China. He defined the company as one that set such a high priority on human rights that trade with a regime allegedly carrying out gross human rights abuses was unacceptable, despite economic and even ethical arguments to the contrary. In 1998 he reversed the decision when China's human rights record had improved and when it was shown that trade with the country under certain conditions would help to improve it further.

> "The superior man seeks what is right; the inferior one, what is profitable."
> Confucius

Corporate Watch (Feb/Mar 2003) reports that ExxonMobil is being sued by the International Labour Rights Fund for complicity in human rights abuses committed by the Indonesian army in the province of Aceh, including supplying excavators allegedly used to dig mass graves. The lawsuit, filed on behalf of eleven Aceh residents, claimed that the Indonesian troops, hired by ExxonMobil to provide security for its Arun gas facility, had committed torture, rape, kidnapping and murder. A multinational has to be careful that it does not become guilty of abusing labour rights by association.

Summary

Ethical issues outside the company concern customers, suppliers and competitors. Those relating to customers include price-fixing, price exploitation, dumping, bait and switch and loss-leaders. Other ethical issues relating to customers include the sale of defective and dangerous products, misleading advertising and bribery.

The special safety issues relating to the pharmaceutical industry were explored. The ethical problems encountered in the financial services industry including loans, deception, churning, and money-laundering, were discussed.

Those relating to suppliers include paying on time, and subcontracting. Those relating to relations with other organisations include exploitation of labour, outsourcing, industrial espionage, bribery and take-overs and mergers.

Check Your Ethics Quotient

(circle the appropriate response)

1.	Price-fixing is legal and ethical.	True	False
2.	Banks must disclose the real cost of borrowing.	True	False
3.	Price discrimination is illegal.	True	False
4.	Bait and switch operations are unethical.	True	False
5.	A seller is obliged to reveal possible dangers or substantial product defects to a buyer.	True	False
6.	False and misleading advertising is illegal.	True	False
7.	The use of celebrity endorsement is legal.	True	False
8.	Bribery may be acceptable in some cases.	True	False
9.	Money laundering is illegal.	True	False
10.	Churning is ethical.	True	False

Total the number of true and false responses and check Appendix 2 at the back of the book for the solution.

Case study: Fraud in the financial services sector

The *Irish Times* (9/5/1997) reports that shipping tycoon Abbas Gogal was convicted of masterminding a corrupt web of loans of $1.2 billion that toppled the Bank of Credit and Commerce International in 1991. He had forged huge numbers of letters, guarantees, and minutes of meetings to make possible the loans. The illicit cash was laundered through two New York banks. Simultaneously the bank was able to book vast fictitious profits from the interest on the loans. The fraud was facilitated by the fact that BCCI had two auditors for its two main arms ensuring that no one firm would have an overview of its tangled affairs. In response to rumours of losses the regulators tightened their grip on BCCI in 1987. Price Waterhouse was appointed auditors and the whole scam came to light.

Gogal was sentenced to 14 years in prison for what is believed to be one of the world's greatest banking frauds. He was the largest single borrower from BCCI and used the money to fund a lavish lifestyle, jetting around the globe in private aircraft and enjoying occasional spins in his two Rolls Royce cars – one in Geneva and one in London. The judge said that Gogal had sought to conceal the instability of BCCI so that investors continued to deposit money with the bank.

Numerous British councils and local authorities lost millions of pounds when BCCI collapsed, together with thousands of small businesses and individual savers. Private investors lost their life savings. They would not have parted with their money if they knew the truth about what was going on. During the investigation police discovered that the London HQ of BCCI falsified documents to cover the fraud. The bank had also been involved in laundering money for drug barons.

Treanor (2003) reports that the creditors of BCCI are to receive another $1 billion. The cost of the 11-year liquidation is now more than $1.2 billion. This means that 75 per cent of all claims have now been met. This is considerably more than the 5 to 10 per cent that the liquidators Deloitte & Touche predicted after they were appointed in 1991. Former employees of BCCI have agreed to the

settlement of their claims that they were tarnished by the stigma of having worked for the bank and found it hard to get employment. The liquidation is predicted to last another five years. About 100 accountants and lawyers are still working full-time on the liquidation. It seems that the accountants and lawyers always gain from these situations. Deloitte & Touche revealed it had received almost $300 million for its work in the English jurisdiction alone.

Questions

♦ How can the excesses of senior management be curbed?
♦ Why do senior executives often treat company property as their own?
♦ Should loans to senior executives be made illegal?
♦ Discuss the laundering of money and how the authorities have tackled the problem?

8. Departmental Ethics

- Why do different departments need their own codes?
- What are the particular ethical issues relating to HRM?
- What are the particular ethical issues relating to other functions?
- What actions should managers take to support business ethics?
- Who is responsible for ethics in a business?

"The quality of moral behaviour varies in inverse ratio to the number of human beings involved".

Aldous Leonard Huxley

The HRM function has a special role to play in setting, encouraging and maintaining ethical standards throughout the company. Ethics are also necessary in departments such as purchasing, finance, manufacturing, marketing, public relations, and research and development. There are ethical issues peculiar to each of these functions that should be addressed.

Industries have their own unique ethical issues and dilemmas. Departments need their own specific code of ethics to deal with the unique ethical challenges facing them. Disciplinary action should be taken against those who break the ethical code.

HRM ethics

Ethics within the HRM agenda are concerned with issues like training, privacy, appraisals, discipline, equality, nepotism, sexual harassment, sex discrimination in promotion, reverse discrimination, rewards, promotion, dismissal, discipline, personality tests, electronic eavesdropping, industrial relations, health and safety, wages and conditions, trade union recognition, redundancy, and whistleblowing. These are ethical issues

because they concern fairness and respect for the individual. Many of them are legal issues as well and mishandling them can bring litigation cases against the company. The HRM manager must ensure that the law is adhered to at all times. If things go wrong the cost incurred by the company can be enormous not only in terms of finance but in a damaged reputation and demoralised staff as well.

> "Reputations are longer in the making than the losing."
>
> Paul Von Ringelheim

The HRM manager has a particular responsibility for the company's code of ethics. Ethics training and communication programmes should be organised and the code promulgated throughout the company. HRM policies have an important role in determining employee trust and loyalty. Good credible communication about the financial situation of a company, its ethics, corporate mission and personnel policies are crucial. The HRM manager should be a role model regarding fairness, equality, and confidentiality.

Discrimination

Employees must not be discriminated against on the basis of age, sex, religion, race, sexual orientation, family connections, social background or personal habits. Ethical issues may arise for a HRM manager when asked to discriminate against a minority or to give preferential treatment when hiring a relative of a senior executive. Discrimination occurs when people with the same qualifications are treated differently. Discrimination on the basis of gender, colour, race, religion or age is illegal as well as being unethical. In Ireland economic success known as the "Celtic Tiger" has brought with it the problem of workplace diversity and accusations of racism and unfair treatment of immigrant workers particularly in relation to pay and conditions.

> "Feelings of worth can flourish only in an atmosphere in which individual differences are appreciated, love is shown openly, mistakes are used for learning, communication is open, rules are flexible, responsibility is modelled and honesty is practised – the kind of atmosphere found in a nurturing family."
>
> Virginia Satir

Amnesty International has published human rights principles for business including one for freedom from discrimination (www.web.amnesty.org).

This states that companies should ensure their policies and practices prevent discrimination based on ethnic origin, sex, colour, language, national or social origin, economic status, religion, political or other conscientiously held beliefs, birth, or other status.

A case taken against a company for discrimination can be very costly in terms of money and reputation. The morale of other employees can also be adversely affected. Sexual harassment, bullying and ageism are common examples of discrimination. Employees are often afraid to speak out in case they are victimised. Some employees suffer from post traumatic stress disorder as a result of the sexual harassment or bullying.

Discrimination is often rife in developing countries even when it is illegal under local law. Arnold et al (2003) reports that Human Rights Watch has revealed that in the Mexican export processing zones US companies such as Johnson Controls and Carlisle Plastics require female job applicants to submit to pregnancy screening. Women are refused employment if they test positive. Employment discrimination based on pregnancy is a violation of Mexican law.

Companies should have policies in place to deal discretely with such situations. However, multinationals are faced with an ethical dilemma in some countries. It is difficult to formulate hiring practices for gender equality in the workplace where the local culture disapproves. This is the situation in Arab countries like Saudi Arabia, and in other countries like Japan. To adopt such policies may offend the values of the host country.

The glass ceiling

It is well known that one of the reasons why there are so few women in senior management positions is because of the so-called "glass ceiling". **The glass ceiling is the organisational and attitudinal barrier that prevents women from progressing as quickly as men up the management hierarchy.** It is the ethical duty of the HRM manager to make sure that a glass ceiling does not operate in the company. The Chartered Institute of Personnel and Development (CIPD) has drawn up a Code of Professional Conduct for its members.

Women are often discriminated against in the workplace when they become pregnant. Sometimes they are made redundant or forced out of their jobs. When they return from maternity leave they may find that their job has gone or that they have missed out on a promotion. Others may find that they have forfeited a bonus or missed out on training opportunities. Some employers ask women inappropriate and biased questions during a job interview. In addition they may be reluctant to hire young women because if they get pregnant they may leave after the company has

incurred considerable costs in training them. Under equality legislation this treatment and attitude towards women is both unethical and illegal and the company may find itself paying out large sums of money in damages. Therefore, HRM managers should ensure that this sort of thing does not happen.

Nepotism

Nepotism is showing favouritism towards relatives, spouses or children of employees when hiring new employees. It is not illegal but may be unethical. It might also include giving preference to relatives or friends when making promotions. Obviously the fairest approach is to hire and promote people on merit irrespective of family connections. Nepotism is not something new. During the Renaissance popes made their nephews bishops regardless of their qualifications. The havoc this practice caused to the church in terms of efficiency, morale and morals is similar to the type of problems experienced by modern business who practice nepotism.

> "I weep for the liberty of my country when I see at this early day of its "successful experiment" that corruption has been imputed to many members of the House of Representatives, and the rights of the people have been bartered for promises of office."
>
> Andrew Jackson

Some companies have anti-nepotism policies in place to ensure an even playing field in selection, recruitment and promotion. Such policies will help to eliminate nepotism from the workplace. People employed may develop feelings of lack of confidence due to the fact that they're unsure if they've been hired on merit or purely by family connection. Family-dominated firms may fail to attract suitably qualified and ambitious managers to join the company.

Waterfield (2008) reports that Den Dover, the chief whip of the Tories in the European Parliament, lost his position following questions about payments to his wife and daughter. The Conservative leader, David Cameron, has told Hugh Thomas the party's new "head of compliance", a former ethics supervisor at Deutsche Bank, to go to Brussels to scrutinise how Tory Euro-MPs claim annual expenditure of more than £280,000 per head. Mr. Cameron maintains that MEPs, like MPs should meet the highest possible ethical standards with accountability and transparency. The sacking of Den Dover came the day after the resignation of Giles Chichester, the leader of Conservative Euro-MPs, following a controversy over expenses. Den Dover's daughter, Amanda, earned between £20,000

and £30,000 as a part-time parliamentary secretary even though she also worked a four day week as a travel agent in Radlett, Herts, close to her home. It is unethical but permitted within European Parliament's rules that family members can be paid up to £60,000 a year without proper scrutiny on the quality or level of work provided. The door is thus left open for the creation of fictitious jobs and nepotism. At the same time it is known that some MEPs employ real assistants on exploitation wages without any social security provision.

At home, Kirkup (2008) reports that the Committee on Standards in Public Life plans to investigate MPs' perks amid concerns that lavish expenses have undermined voters' faith in parliamentary democracy. MPs are able to claim thousands of pounds of taxpayers' money to furnish their homes. Prime Minister Gordon Brown claimed expenses for a second home even though he is provided with a home in Downing Street.

Kirkup (2008) reports that under Government proposals to clean up parliamentary allowances MPs will be banned from employing their children. Mr. Derek Conway, who has lost the Tory whip, was found to have overpaid one of his sons for his work as parliamentary researcher, and ordered to pay back more than £13,000. At least 22 other MPs currently employ their children according to parliamentary sources. It will still be allowed to employ spouses. MPs have an annual allowance of £100,000 to hire staff.

Conflicts of interest may arise and fraud may be facilitated when relatives work closely together. Thus the employment of relatives in the same site or same department may not be allowed. Conflicts of interest also arise when incompetent members of the family are promoted into senior managerial positions. In addition, there may be sibling rivalry over management succession. Non-relative employees may be suspicious that relatives will act as spies for management.

Some people also claim that nepotism has some advantages, especially for the small firm. It provides an identifiable source of dedicated and loyal employees and creates a family oriented business boosting morale and job satisfaction. However, employing relatives of executives is no guarantee that they will do their jobs well or be committed to the company. The practice of nepotism is rampant in Arab countries where tribal and kinship relations are still viewed as very important. It is also rampant in developing countries but less prevalent in the western economies.

Selection

Recruitment candidates they have a right to be treated fairly and with respect and consideration. Ethical practice would include that they should be informed about the selection without undue delay. It is important that tests used in selection should be used ethically. Only suitably qualified personnel should administer psychometric tests. The results of tests are confidential and should be securely filed. The test results of those candidates who failed to secure employment should be destroyed. Applicants who request should have the right to get the test results. The tests should be administered in a suitable environment. An ethical company will be interested in attracting ethical candidates of good character. By recruiting the right people the company can avoid ethical and litigation problems in the future and build up a reputation as an organisation that places a high value on honesty, integrity and trust.

> "A man may not always be what he appears to be, but what he appears to be is always a significant part of what he is."
>
> Dr Willard Gaylin

Reward system

The reward system in the company should be fair and in line with general market conditions. The reward system is a key component and reinforcement of the ethical culture of the company. So it is important that ethical conduct is rewarded in the long-term and unethical behaviour discouraged and disciplined. In the public sector reward systems tend to be open and transparent. This is often not the case in the private sector where secrecy may be the norm.

> "Discipline isn't just punishing, forcing compliance or stamping out bad behaviour. Rather, discipline has to do with teaching proper deportment, caring about others, controlling oneself and putting someone else's wishes before one's own when the occasion call for it."
>
> Lawrence Balter

Sexual harassment

The HRM manager has a special responsibility to create a work environment in which sexual harassment will not be tolerated. **Sexual harassment has been defined as any unwelcome sexual advances, requests for sexual favours, or other verbal or physical conduct of a sexual**

nature. As well as being unethical sexual harassment in the workplace is also illegal. It is not just a female issue as males can also be sexually harassed.

Trevino et al (2004) reports that in June 1998, Mitsubishi Motors' North American division agreed to pay $34 million in settlement of a sexual harassment case. The settlement was based on charges brought by 350 female factory workers at the Illinois plant. The women alleged that co-workers and supervisors kissed and fondled them. They called them "whores" and "bitches," posted sexual graffiti and pornography, demanded sex, and retaliated if they refused. They complained that managers did nothing to stop the harassment. In addition to paying the fine the company fired 20 workers and disciplined others. They also agreed to provide mandatory sexual harassment training, to revise sexual harassment policy, and to investigate future sexual harassment allegations within three weeks of a complaint.

Confidentiality

The HRM manager is likely to come across very sensitive, personal and private information about employees. Such information must remain confidential. Revealing information given in confidence is a violation of trust and a most serious matter.

> "No virtue is more universally accepted as a test of good character than trustworthiness."
>
> Harry Emerson Fosdick, D.D.

Training

The HRM manager has the responsibility to develop employees to reach their potential and meet the organisational needs of the company. Employees should be given an equal opportunity to take advantage of the training and development opportunities in the company. In practice it is often those who need training the most that get the least.

Security of employment

Although the concept of a job for life may not be feasible in most organisations, it is still ethically incumbent on a company to try and achieve security of employment. If it ever becomes necessary to make some employees redundant, the scheme should be handled in a fair and sensitive manner. Every effort should be made to find the employees

alternative employment. In the normal course of events employees should only be dismissed for a just reason and due process must be observed. A just reason might include automation, disciplinary reasons, and prolonged absenteeism. Every effort should be taken to mitigate the harmful effects of the dismissal. Due process means that the agreed and recognised procedures are followed. This ensures that decisions to dismiss employees cannot be taken arbitrarily and are done in a fair manner.

Employees expect to be consulted about issues concerning their jobs and thus companies should pursue high involvement policies. Employees expect to be treated fairly and consistently and have the right of union representation if desired.

Performance appraisal

Performance appraisal should be honest and based on sufficient and relevant information. Winstanley et al (1996) recommends that performance management should operate in line with the following ethical principles:

- ◆ Respect for the individual – people should be treated as "ends in themselves" and not merely as "means to other ends".
- ◆ Mutual respect – the parties involved in performance management should respect each other's needs and preoccupations.
- ◆ Procedural fairness – the procedures incorporated in performance management should be operated fairly to limit the adverse effect on individuals.
- ◆ Transparency – people affected by decisions emerging from the performance management process should have the opportunity to examine the basis upon which decisions were made.

Walton (1986) points out that Deming, the quality guru, condemns evaluation systems that leave people "bitter, despondent, dejected, some even depressed, all unfit for work for weeks after receipt of rating". People should be made to feel that they are winners rather than losers.

Moonlighting

Moonlighting is where an employee has a second job. A conflict of interest may arise when the second job is with a company that is in direct competition with the primary employer. Even when this is not the situation a second job divides loyalties, interests and time and drains energy. It may also be interpreted as a lack of commitment to the primary employer.

Moonlighting is not illegal and not necessarily unethical. Two factors may make moonlighting acceptable. If the work you do with your second employer does not compromise your position with the first and if both employers know about your activities and have indicated that they don't mind. In addition, the employee may have no choice but may have to work at a second job to provide a reasonable standard of living for his family.

Discipline

It is important that due process is adhered to in the disciplinary procedure. Employees should be treated the same for similar breaches of discipline with the discipline appropriate to the offence. The discipline should be constructive and fair and done in a professional sensitive and respectful manner. The discipline should be done in private and not in front of other employees. Employees should be given the opportunity to discuss the issue so that their point of view is considered. The same principles apply to a grievance procedure.

Terminations

There must be just cause for the termination. This may differ from company to company but usually includes theft, fraud, forgery, assault and gross insubordination. Other reasons may include poor performance, downsizing or layoffs. Whatever the reason due process must be followed so that everything is handled in a just manner. It is important that the person being terminated is treated with dignity and respect. The law must be adhered to, and best ethical practice followed.

Organisation behaviour

Organisational behaviour (OB) techniques may be used to modify the behaviour of employees. Critics have raised ethical issues about the use of OB to modify employee behaviour. The use of such techniques infringes the individual's freedom of choice and may be considered a type of manipulation or brainwashing. Managers may employ reinforcement techniques to mould people's behaviour for the advantage of the organisation rather than in the best interests of the employee.

Thus employees may be rewarded for working hard and putting in long hours. This may be stressful for the individual, detrimental to their long-term health and disruptive to family life. At the same time behaviours promoting personal growth and development may be ignored. Thus an employee's behaviour is being manipulated or shaped in a certain way in

the interests of the company but ultimately to the detriment of the employee. Many critics consider this to be an abuse of power on the manager's part and should be considered unethical.

Ethics of research

There are ethical considerations to be observed by those who conduct research within organisations such as HR managers, internal business analysts and management consultants. A person's right to privacy should be respected. The surreptitious observation of employees is unethical. Employees should be free to decide whether or not they want to take part in a research study.

If they do decide to partake employees should be given information about the purpose and scope of the study before it starts. They should be informed of their right to withdraw from the study at any stage if they wish. Confidentiality should be maintained and thus the anonymity of the respondent is crucial. Employees should not be subjected to pressures or any experimental conditions that could harm them in any way physically or psychologically.

The other issue concerns the way the researcher reports the results. The research procedure and methodology should be reported in a transparent way so that studies can be replicated. This is standard practice within the academic scientific community. Ideally the results should be made freely available to interested parties. Sometimes unfavourable research findings are not released. The researcher has a particular obligation to tell the truth and not to tamper with data.

Accounting ethics

Accountants may come under pressure from senior executives to report information in a certain way so as to ignore discrepancies and present a favourable financial picture. They may also be asked to avoid commenting on creative accounting practices that are legal but quite misleading. Auditors have a particular obligation to tell the truth about a company's financial difficulties. In recent times auditors have failed to fulfil this duty and faced criminal charges following inaccurate statements regarding the financial state of companies that they have audited. Already there is a substantial literature concerning ethics in accounting – including corporate social reporting, environmental accounting, and auditing. For example, the annual report is recognised as a key document that must accurately reflect an organisation's ethics and ethos.

The UK's Consultative Committee of Accounting Bodies (CCAB) offers guidance on ethical matters for accountants in business, based around five fundamental principles:

1. Integrity (not merely honest, but fair and truthful).
2. Objectivity (having regard to all considerations relevant to the task in hand).
3. Competence (undertaking professional work only with the required competence).
4. Performance (carrying out work with due skill, care, diligence and expedition).
5. Courtesy (showing courtesy and consideration towards all).

Just like accountants in public practice, accountants working in industry have the same responsibility to abide strictly by their professional code of ethics. In recent business scandals both internal and external accountants connived in fraudulent accounting practices.

Marketing ethics

Marketing situations rank as those causing the most ethical conflict among executives. Issues which have already been touched upon in previous chapters include biodegradable packaging, unfair pricing, price-fixing, the giving and receiving of gifts, gratuities and bribes, misleading advertising, loss-leaders, bait and switch, and cheating customers.

Furthermore, in advertising we have sexism, persuasion, deception, and the unethical use of psychology such as subliminal advertising and brainwashing. Using scantily dressed young women to advertise products is hardly ethical. A person dressed in white in a TV advertisement may give the impression of medical endorsement. The false impression created is dishonest and unethical. Market research findings may be manipulated to provide the desired result.

> "Advertising may be described as the science of arresting the human intelligence long enough to get money from it."
>
> Stephen Leacock

Manufacturing ethics

Managers of manufacturing and operational units have a special interest in the health and safety of their employees. Transport, construction and

agriculture are particularly dangerous industries to work in with very high rates of death and injury due to industrial accidents. Managers have a duty of care towards their employees and may be prosecuted for breaches of health and safety legislation. They have a responsibility to create a safe working environment and workers should not be exposed to unnecessary risk.

The *Irish Times* (30/10/04) reported that Smurfit News Press Ltd has been fined €1 million for health and safety breaches linked to accidents in the workplace. One worker lost a leg and another had skin ripped off his hand. The accident took place in 2002 in almost identical circumstances at its printing plant in Kells, Co Meath. The judge said that the company had shown a "cavalier" attitude towards safety and had placed the pursuit of profit ahead of worker's safety. He also maintained that the second accident would not have taken place if the lessons from the first incident had been learned and put into practice.

Arnold et al (2003) reports that critics of multinationals argue that many workers are vulnerable to workplace hazards. These include repetitive motion injuries, exposure to toxic chemicals, exposure to airborne pollutants such as fabric particles, and malfunctioning machinery. Fire safety is one of the most common workplace hazards.

In factories throughout the world workers are locked in to keep them from leaving the factory. When fire breaks out workers are trapped. This is what happened in 1993, when a fire broke out at the Kader Industrial Toy Company in Thailand. More than 200 workers were killed and 469 injured. The factory produced toys for US companies such as J.C. Penny, and Fisher Price. In Bangladesh alone, there have been seventeen fires resulting in fatalities since 1995.

Lax health and safety standards violate the moral requirement that employers be concerned with the physical safety and welfare of their employees. Some of these practices may be legal in developing countries or tolerated by corrupt or repressive regimes. However, this does not exempt multinationals from acting responsibly when operating abroad. Some of them take their responsibilities very seriously. For example, companies like Levi Strauss and Motorola make sure that their employees abroad have comparable health and safety standards to those at home. Levi Strauss stipulates that "We will only utilise business partners who provide workers with a safe and healthy environment." Motorola operates to a strict business code at home and abroad.

In the "Valuejet" air disaster of 1996 hundreds of people lost their lives in the Everglades of California. The low cost fare airline allegedly

compromised safety standards by cutting corners in terms of safety checks and staff safety training.

Purchasing ethics

A purchasing manager who pays a higher price than normal to a supplier from whom he accepts a bribe is acting unethically. Similarly if he accepts lavish gifts and entertainment he is acting unethically because it is difficult to maintain independence of judgement and act in the interests of the company in such circumstances.

Public relations ethics

Some people maintain that the PR stands for perception restructuring. The phrase probably exemplifies the low public esteem of public relations. *Corporate Watch* (3/8/2004) reported that widespread cynicism about spin and advertising are now leading PR companies to look for ways to improve their own image with the Institute of Public Relations (IPR) working hard to remedy the situation.

The IPR is applying for a Royal Charter. If granted it should give PR practitioners an image of professionalism and integrity, and help distance them from the more shady elements involved in the industry. Unfortunately spin-doctors hired by politicians and prominent business people to befuddle issues and tell half-truths haven't exactly enhanced the reputation of the PR industry.

> "Integrity is not something that you should have to think about ... consider doing but something in the heart that is already done."
>
> Doug Firebaugh

Industry ethics

Industries will have unique ethical issues and dilemmas particular to their type of business. Some industries are more regulated than others are.

◆ Chemical companies will need to pay particular attention to environmental and safety issues.
◆ Banks and financial services companies will need to pay particular attention to fiduciary, confidentiality, money-laundering, conflict of interest and customer service issues.

- ♦ A manufacturing company will need to look at worker safety, product quality, product liability, and labour relations.
- ♦ A retail company will have particular concerns like pricing, selling and customer service.
- ♦ Multinationals will have ethical issues relating to relocation, bribery and corruption.

Managerial action for business ethics

Brenner and Melander (1977), based on a Harvard Business Review Survey of 1,200 US readers, suggested five aspects of managerial action for business ethics:

1. Fair dealing with customers and employees is the most direct way to restore confidence in business morality.
2. Corporate steps taken to improve ethical behaviour clearly must come from the top and be part of the reward and punishment system.
3. If an ethical code is developed and implemented, have an accompanying information system to detect violations. Then treat violators equitably.
4. Test decisions against what you think is right rather than against what is expedient.
5. Don't force others into unethical conduct.

> "The generality of men are naturally apt to be swayed by fear rather than reverence, and to refrain from evil rather because of the punishment that it brings than because of its foulness."
>
> Aristotle

Who is responsible for ethics?

In a business all are responsible for the practice and maintenance of good ethics including chief executives, directors, senior managers, middle managers, supervisors and employees. Outside, the government, industry, commerce, the professions and the church have their own unique ethical challenges.

The values, beliefs and ethical conduct of the chief executive will set the standard for the rest of the company. The chief executive is responsible for the major strategic decisions of the company and the ethical response taken provides the example for the rest of the company.

> "Today we are afraid of simple words like goodness and mercy and kindness. We don't believe in the good old words because we don't believe in the good old values anymore."
>
> Lin Yutang

At the tactical and logistical level, ethics are the concern of middle managers and supervisors making ordinary everyday business decisions. These individuals often have to reconcile the company's values with local business rules and customs. Often there are no clear guidelines for making these decisions. However, managers as leaders must demonstrate good judgement, integrity and exemplary behaviour in everything they do. At the operational level the character and values of the individual employee will determine the ethical stance taken.

Many professions including the Legal, Medical, Accountancy, Engineering, HRM and the Marketing profession have drawn up their own codes of ethics. Members who break these may be penalised or have their practising certificates withdrawn.

Summary

The HRM manager has a special role to play in ensuring that ethical standards are maintained throughout a company. Within the personnel area he must ensure that ethical practices operate in the selection, recruitment and training of staff. Psychometric testing must be carried out in a fair and equitable way. Information acquired by the HRM manager during the course of his work must be kept confidential.

Industries such as banking and financial services have their own unique ethical issues. Within a company each department has its own specific ethical challenges and each therefore needs its own unique code of ethics. Thus finance, marketing, purchasing, operations, information technology, and public relations will have their own specific code of ethics. The staff employed in these functions are especially exposed to temptations requiring ethical consideration.

Fair dealing with customers and employees is the best way to restore confidence in business morality. Those guilty of unethical behaviour should be subject to disciplinary measures. Nobody should feel compelled to carry out unethical acts to achieve business results. The feeling that everything is fair in love or war is inappropriate in business. In a business all are responsible for the practice and maintenance of good ethics including chief executive, directors, senior managers, middle managers, first line managers, supervisors and employees. Senior management team will set the tone for the ethical climate in a company.

Check Your Ethics Quotient

(circle the appropriate response)

1. In HRM many ethical issues are now legal issues as well.   True   False

2. Discrimination is unethical but legal.   True   False

3. The glass ceiling is the organisational and attitudinal barrier that prevents women from progressing as quickly as men up the management hierarchy.   True   False

4. Sexual harassment is illegal and unethical.   True   False

5. Moonlighting is illegal.   True   False

6. Using OB to modify employee behaviour is illegal.   True   False

7. Professional accountants have their own code of ethics.   True   False

8. Managers have a duty of care toward their employees.   True   False

9. Only senior executives and managers are responsible for ethics in a company.   True   False

10. In many practical situations there are no clear guidelines for making ethical decision.   True   False

Total the number of true and false responses and check Appendix 2 at the back of the book for the solution.

Case study: A purchasing manager's fall from grace

The *Sunday Business Post* (9/11/2003) reported on the activities of a purchasing manager named Howard Napier employed by Irish Rail. Napier had managed the purchase of forklift tyres for ten years at the state-company. During his tenure with Irish Rail, Napier received gifts and junkets from the company's supplier of forklift tyres called Advance Pitstop. It was alleged that the tyres had been invoiced at an inflated price. The business was worth €561,700 over three years. In 2000, it had a profit margin of almost 40 per cent on the account. The norm for a similar sized account with a state company would have been closer to 10 per cent. It is estimated that Irish Rail lost up to €165,000 on the fork lift tyres by not getting the standard 10 per cent mark up over the three years to the end of 2000.

The scam by Napier came to light when other companies complained about his behaviour. For example, one company said that it was propositioned by Napier in 1992 for €500 supposedly for a golf sponsorship. When the company requested that he put it in writing they never heard from him again.

The junkets included trips to some of the country's top golf courses with hotel accommodation. The gifts received by Napier included a tie press, an electric jigsaw, an electric knife sharpener, a home sound system, an electric belt sander and a clothes drier. At Christmas 1998 he received a dishwasher, a television, a mini-disc player and a blender. Napier resigned from Irish Rail in 2003. In November 2003 Irish Rail invited a number of companies to tender for the new tyre contract at the company.

Questions

- Discuss the ethical issues raised in this case?
- Design a policy in relation to the receiving of gifts by employees that would have prevented the above from happening.

- Before his resignation, Napier consistently denied any inappropriate dealings. Discuss the need for personal values and ethics in business.

9. Environmental Issues

- How do companies abuse the environment?
- Why is the public concerned about radiation?
- What are the environmental hazards of asbestos?
- How does global warming arise?
- What is the Kyoto protocol?

"When the world is destroyed, it will be destroyed not by its madmen but by the sanity of its experts and the superior ignorance of its bureaucrats".

John Le Carré

The earth's resources are finite and should be protected. Companies driven solely by the profit motive have depleted natural resources, destroyed landscapes and polluted rivers and air. People are now more conscious than ever before about the negative consequences of environmental pollution particularly in relation to their health. Being ethical should be seen as good for business, good for the customer and good for the environment.

Global warming is caused by the greenhouse effect. Rising temperatures and vulnerability to storms and flooding has been attributed to this phenomenon. The World Bank has been criticised for its lending policies, which in some cases has caused the resettlement of indigenous peoples.

Environmental abuse

In the 1960s space exploration presented mankind with the first pictures of the earth as seen from outer space. Some people who saw these at the time underwent a paradigm shift. They now saw the planet earth for the first time as a tiny blue globe with finite resources that should be

conserved and protected. This change in perspective motivated many non-governmental organisations to become advocates for conservation. Despite this most companies still prioritise profitability ahead of conservation.

> "The practice of conservation must spring from a conviction of what is ethically and aesthetically right, as well as what is economically expedient. A thing is right only when it tends to preserve the integrity, stability, and beauty of the community, and the community includes the soil, waters, fauna, and flora, as well as people."
>
> Aldo Leopold

In the past some companies have exploited and abused the environment. They have depleted natural resources, marred scenic views, destroyed landscapes, polluted rivers and streams, emitted toxic fumes into the atmosphere, and created unpleasant smells. They have carelessly disposed of waste by dumping, generated traffic congestion, destroyed forests, and generally pursued policies inimical to human and animal life. Mining, chemical, electricity generation, transportation and other industries have all contributed to what has now become known as the "environmental crises".

Other environmental issues include the destruction of the ozone layer, the accelerating loss of tropical forests, the threat to wildlife, and the waste from excessive packaging and consumption. Plastic containers are a particular problem. Because plastic does not rot it is taking up more and more of the limited landfill space. All of these issues demand urgent attention. The disposal of waste and pesticides are just some of the current environmental issues being discussed in the media.

Disposal of waste

Manufacturing companies should reclaim their used products for reuse and recycling. EU legislation is already in force to ensure that this is done in relation to appliances like fridges, washing machines and computers. In August 2005 Ireland implemented this directive. Waste disposal is now a huge environmental issue and companies who create much of it with their products and packaging have an ethical duty to put policies in place to help deal with it. Companies have a responsibility to respect and conserve the environment in which they operate.

> "These men of the technostructure are the new and universal priesthood. Their religion is business success; their test of virtue is growth and profit. Their bible is the computer printout; their communion bench is the committee room. The sales force carries their message to the world, and a message is what it is often called."
>
> John Kenneth Galbraith

The illegal disposal of waste has become so profitable that criminals have become involved in it. Some have taken advantage of poor regulations abroad and cheap labour in countries like China and India to export their waste. It is of course unethical to be dumping your waste disposal problems in somebody else's backyard irrespective of the low cost of doing so.

Pesticides

The spraying of pesticides and the use of artificial fertilisers on crops cause major damage to the environment, to the workers who spray and also to the health of those in the food chain who consume the produce. The concern of consumers for their health has given rise to the demand for organic fruit and vegetables.

The *Guardian* (30/6/2004) reports that environmental campaigners have won a legal battle against Bayer, a German multinational company, on the right to publicise the potential hazards of pesticides. Bayer markets many pesticides world wide posing a threat to the environment and health. For example, the Bayer weed killer IPU is frequently detected in public water supplies. It has to be filtered out by the water companies at a high cost to the taxpayer to comply with EU standards. Bayer has been forced to drop a court action against Friends of the Earth (FoE). FoE believes it is an important victory in its campaign for greater transparency about pesticides. Bayer tried to use their massive financial resources to prevent access to important health and environmental data about substances that are sprayed on crops everyday inimical to public health.

Hoffman et al (1986) highlight the case of the Velsicol Chemical Company of Chicago, manufacturers of a pesticide called Phosvel. The World Health Organisation classified this product as extremely dangerous due to its delayed neurotoxic effects – it could cause paralysis for some time after exposure. The Environmental Protection Agency did not approve Phosvel for sale in the USA. However, Velsicol sold it to developing countries where there were no import restrictions. Irrespective of the law the basic universal ethical principle of "do unto others as you would have

them do unto you" should apply. In this case this principle was ignored. Different standards for different cultures are unethical.

Topical environmental issues

Topical issues include pollution and traffic congestion. The nuclear industry and the radiation emitted by electromagnetic fields and mobile phone masts is currently an issue. Because of misinformation in the past the public remains sceptical of the pronouncements from these industries.

> "The great fault of all ethics hitherto has been that they believed themselves to have to deal only with the relations of man to man. In reality, however, the question is what is his attitude to the world and all life that comes within his reach. A man is ethical only when life, as such, is sacred to him, and that of plants and animals as that of his fellow men, and when he devotes himself helpfully to all life that is in need of help. Only the universal ethic of the feeling of responsibility in an ever-widening sphere for all that lives – only that ethic can be founded in thought... The ethic of Reverence for Life, therefore, comprehends within itself everything that can be described as love, devotion, and sympathy whether in suffering, joy, or effort."
>
> Albert Schweitzer

Pollution

Pollution is one of the dreadful side effects of modern industrialisation. Noise, air, land and water pollution and traffic congestion are the most common problems caused by business. Ecologists now warn that there is a finite amount of fresh good quality water available on the planet and so it is important to respect and conserve it like any other natural resource.

People have the basic human rights of expecting to drink clean water and breathe clean air and this must be respected. Weber (2002) reports that in 2001 the United Nations Commission on Human Rights declared that everyone has a right to live in a world free from toxic pollution and environmental degradation. Those who pollute or destroy the natural environment are not only committing a crime against nature, but violate human rights as well.

> "Human beings have rights, because they are moral beings: the rights of all men grow out of their moral nature; and as all men have the same moral nature, they have essentially the same rights."
>
> Angelina Grimke

Air pollution

Ahmed (2003) reports that in a report on the next 30 years of air travel, the British Department of Transport in Britain finds that increases in the number of flights taken each year creates unsustainable levels of noise and air pollution. Passenger flights emit more than 8 million tonnes of damaging carbon dioxide gas every year according to the report. As airports expand and the number of flights increase, the figure will rise to 19 million tonnes in 2030. Green organisations maintain that the growth of cheap flights – many cities in Europe are now reached for under £50 return – has meant that passengers are not paying the true cost of flying.

The general public also causes major air pollution through the use of cars. Car manufacturers have reduced CO_2 emissions from new cars. Some such as the Toyota Motor Company have even developed environmentally friendly electric cars. Unfortunately the demand for such cars is still very small. On the other hand car companies have been criticised for marketing Sports Utility Vehicles (SUVs) which are not efficient energy users. There is a growing demand for these types of vehicles. For example, Ford has been criticised by the environmental group Bluewater Network for failing to meet its pledge to increase the fuel efficiency of its SUVs by 25 per cent. In an advertisement it depicted Chairman William Ford Jr. as a long-nosed Pinocchio. The ad stated "Don't buy his environmental rhetoric. Don't buy his cars."

In the UK, the Chancellor's Budget in March 2008 announced plans to raise vehicle excise duty for the more polluting cars next year. A congestion charge came into operation in parts of Central London on 17 February 2003 and was extended into parts of West London on 19 February 2007. It is claimed that it has cut traffic by 15 per cent and reduced air pollution.

In Ireland, from 1 July 2008 Vehicle Registration Tax (VRT) will be based on CO_2 emissions rather than engine size. Motor tax rates will increase by 11 per cent for cars with an engine size above 2.5 litres. The rate for other vehicles will increase by 9.5 per cent. Incentives were also introduced for the purchase of hybrid models. These changes are designed to encourage people to buy low-emission cars.

People have become very conscious of the damage that pollution causes to our health. They are now demanding that business take a more responsible attitude to environmental issues and that they are held accountable for any damage that they cause. Some industries are taking heed. Paper manufacturers now plant more trees than they cut down and mining companies reinstate and landscape the land that they disfigured. Business has the minimum moral obligation not to harm society.

> "We already have the statistics for the future: the growth percentages of pollution, overpopulation, desertification. The future is already in place."
>
> Gunter Grass

Oil pollution

Ethical Consumer (Feb 2003) reports that exploration for oil can involve deforestation, forcibly removing people from their land and polluting waterways and fragile ecosystems. A lot of oil exploration takes place in oppressive regimes with a higher regard for oil companies' money than the wellbeing of their people or their environment.

Pipeline and tanker spills, with their devastating consequences for wildlife and the environment, are commonplace. The refining of crude oil is energy intensive and causes pollution through the emission of toxic substances into the air. In addition many of the end products of the oil industry are themselves highly toxic such as petrol, chemicals and pesticides. Oil spills at seas are not uncommon.

Valdez

Consider the grounding of the Exxon oil tanker Valdez in Prince William Sound, Alaska. The accident was caused by among other things an inadequately trained crewman piloting the tanker. In the meantime the captain, who had been drinking, was below deck. Some time previous to the incident the captain had been disqualified for drunken driving, nevertheless he was deemed competent to pilot a ship!

Exxon only spent about 6 months attending to the effects of the spill. It seems that fighting lawsuits and making settlements is cheaper than cleaning up the mess. *Corporate Watch* (Feb/Mar 2003) reports that ExxonMobil had to pay $1.1 billion in fines and damages over the spill in 1991. Some maintain that this is only a fraction of the real cost of the environmental damage caused. The company now describe the Sound as "healthy, robust and thriving", although ten years after the spill only Pacific

herring and sea otters had recovered and an estimated 20,000 gallons of crude remained buried in the area.

Sea Empress

Corporate Watch (Spring 1997) reported that on the 15 February 1996 the Sea Empress tanker ran aground on rocks at the entrance to Milford Haven in South Wales. Over 175 miles of fragile coastline – including 35 sites of special scientific interest, 20 National Trust properties and a marine reserve – were affected by the massive oil slick. Tourism and fisheries were badly affected. The spill was one of the largest in the UK to date. Of the 75,450 tonnes officially spilled, only about 3,000 tonnes have been recovered during the clean up operation. A series of human errors, poor organisation and slow decision-making meant that the scale of the disaster was compounded.

A comprehensive report by Friends of the Earth on the Sea Empress disaster found that **"the massive kill of marine animals will cause long term ecological changes, including a change in species diversity and population numbers."** Some sensitive ell-grass beds may not recover for two centuries, if at all. There were major fish kills and 25 different species of birds were affected. A conservative estimate is that up to 20,000 birds died either from drowning, hypothermia or swallowing toxic oil while preening.

Suspicion of big business

People are suspicious of big business. Their response through their public relations people is made to protect the interests of the company and to undermine the credibility of critics. It is often better to come clean than to risk the public distrust that results from denials, half-truths and cover ups. In the past we were assured by big business that nuclear power was safe, that smoking did not damage our health, that all additives were harmless, that lead in petrol was fine and that asbestos was safe to use as insulation material.

> "Today every inhabitant of this planet must contemplate the day when this planet may no longer be habitable. Every man, woman and child lives under a nuclear sword of Damocles, hanging by the slenderest of threads, capable of being cut at any moment by accident or miscalculation or madness."
>
> John Fitzgerald Kennedy

We now know that nuclear power is potentially very dangerous, that smoking kills, that some additives are carcinogenic and that asbestos causes cancer. We also know that unrestricted economic growth is unsustainable because of the finite nature of the planet on which we live.

The nuclear industry

The infamous Chernobyl accident was caused by human error, not by a faulty plant. It is only in recent years that the scale of this tragedy has become known. More than 100 emergency workers on the site of the accident on 26 April 1986 suffered radiation sickness and 41 of them died. Hundreds from the surrounding area have also died and more than half a million are sick from only a 3 per cent radiation release. The biggest direct consequence of the radiation is increases in childhood thyroid cancer with an estimated 1800 cases in all. For years the Russian government tried to cover up the extent of the catastrophe rather than confront its ethical responsibilities.

> "I durst not laugh, for fear of opening my lips and receiving the bad air."
>
> Shakespeare

Sellafield

Sellafield is a major potential health hazard of Chernobyl magnitude to the Irish nation. British Nuclear Fuels (BNF) own the plant. The potential for radioactive discharges into the Irish Sea has created outrage in Ireland. An accident in one of Sellafield's high activity waste tanks could release up to ten times more radioactivity than Chernobyl. Like Chernobyl, all we are waiting for is another human error. Can we trust managers to put the health and safety of the general public before profit? Managers at Sellafield say the plant is quite safe. However, *Corporate Watch* (Winter 1996) reported that in Sellafield's 44-year history it has seen nearly 1,000 nuclear accidents. According to Greenpeace its discharges have made the Irish Sea the most radioactively polluted sea in the world. Unusual clusters of cancers have been found around Drogheda and Dundalk on the East coast of Ireland.

Sellafield has a history of accidents. In 1983, 25 miles of the Cumbrian beach were closed for six months due to a radioactive leak at Sellafield discovered by Greenpeace and members of the public. Even though members of the public were contaminated BNF was fined a miserly £10,000 with £60,000 costs. In 1986 a plutonium mist escaped into the atmosphere contaminating 11 workers, and forcing an Amber Alert. In

1992, 6 gallons of plutonium nitrate was leaked, halting reprocessing for several months. The Irish Government has made representations to the British Government and the EU to close the Sellafield plant but to no avail.

Radiation

Some community groups have objected to the erection of high-tension electricity masts. Pylons mar the scenic landscape while others are concerned about possible health dangers from radiation. There is much current debate and concern about the potential of electomagnetic radiation associated with electric power to cause ill-health, particularly cancer, and most notably leukaemia. There is conflicting scientific evidence about the dangers involved and it is very difficult for ordinary members of the public to make an informed choice one way or another. Those strongly opposed to new transmission lines can quote research, which appears to show that electromagnetic radiation can be linked to cancer. On the other side, electricity companies counter by presenting a vast body of scientific work rebutting such claims. So the jury is still out and in the meantime many potential consumers would prefer power lines to be located as far as possible away from their homes.

Some people are worried about the health risks of using mobile phones while others have campaigned against the erection of mobile phone masts near homes or schools. The *Irish Times* (7/3/1998) reported that the scientific jury is still out on the issue of the safety of mobile phones. Expert opinion is currently heavily weighted in favour of the view that there is no evidence of health damage to users. Dr Alistair McKinlay, who chaired the European Commission's expert group on mobile phones and is vice-chairman of the International Commission on Non-ionising Radiation Protection, found no convincing evidence of long-term hazards from mobile phones. But further research is necessary to allay concerns including long-term cancer studies and evaluation of possible effects on sleeping patterns, immune systems and people who may be EMF-sensitive.

> "It is impossible, except for theologians, to conceive of a world-wide scandal or a universe-wide scandal; the proof is the way people have settled down to living with nuclear fission, radiation poisoning, hydrogen bombs, satellites, and space rockets."
>
> Mary McCarthy

Global warming

In the mid 1980s scientists first observed a "hole" in the ozone layer over the Antarctic. They believe this has been caused by the widespread use of ozone-depleting substances such as chlorine and bromine. These include chlorofluorocarbons (CFCs) mostly used in refrigeration and air-conditioning and in halons, used to extinguish fires.

In September 2001, the UN Intergovernmental Panel on Climate Change (IPCCC) concluded through its studies that the Earth's climate is changing. An extract from its report states **"The Earth's climate system has demonstrably changed on both global and regional scales since the pre-industrial era, with some of these changes attributable to human activities."** This is primarily caused by the burning of fossil fuels and that the world is likely to become much warmer than previously thought. The IPCCC concludes that unless action is taken to reduce our emissions of carbon dioxide and other climate changing pollutants:

♦ We will experience more heat waves and floods.
♦ Glaciers and polar ice will continue to melt.
♦ Sea levels could rise by up to six metres.
♦ Many plant and animal species will become extinct.
♦ Outbreaks of diseases will become more common.
♦ Millions of people will be forced to move.

There is strong scientific evidence for global warming. Many scientists believe that global warming is caused by the emission of gases when we burn oil, coal and other fossil fuels including car emissions. These gases contribute to the greenhouse effect as they accumulate in the atmosphere and trap the outgoing heat radiated from the surface of the earth. Pumping greenhouse gases into the atmosphere is like having an extra blanket over the Earth making it warmer. One of the consequences of this is the increased risk to flooding, which has actually happened in various parts of the world over the past few years. The great ice caps of Antartica and Greenland are also melting adding to our ecological problems and may cause flooding of low-lying coastal areas.

The Environment Agency (2/9/2004) reported that scientists predict that the average number of people whose homes are flooded along coastlines will increase from a few million each year today to between 75 and 200 million by 2080. Billions of dollars worth of damage will be caused annually in countries like Egypt, Vietnam and Poland. Many islands in the South Pacific could disappear beneath the waves by 2100. In Britain, sea level rise is likely to have a greater impact in the south and

east, where the land is already sinking slowly. Many countries feel that something should be done about global warming before disastrous consequences happen.

Kyoto Protocol

The 1997 Kyoto Protocol is an attempt by the developed world to control the damage caused by development on the environment by cutting down on greenhouse gas emissions. The protocol came into force on 16th February 2007 and has so far been ratified by 182 parties, with the notable exception of the US who signed the original agreement but have yet to ratify it. The cuts agreed by the developed countries averaged 5 per cent off 1990 levels to be achieved by 2008-2012.

> "In the past we have perhaps depended too much on the hope that creating new wealth would automatically provide us a better life. Now we are finding that growth itself causes problems."
>
> Charles B. Reeder

As referred to above, the USA has so far refused to ratify the protocol. However, it is known that USA contributes 25 per cent of the pollution causing global warming despite having only 4 per cent of the world's population. The protocol has been vigorously opposed in the US by the powerful oil lobby. The major political contributions that the oil companies make to the Bush administration means that the president is on their side.

Ethical Consumer (Feb 2003) reports that one of the largest and most aggressive lobby groups the US Global Climate Coalition (GCC), has been instrumental in blocking US ratification of the Kyoto agreement. GCC members include Exxon, Mobile and Texaco. Exxon gave a political contribution of over $1 million to the Republicans in the 2000 election. Coincidentally when George Bush became president he pulled the US out of the Kyoto Protocol. Exxon also funds scientific research to undermine the case for global warming. Despite the obvious conflict of interest involved Exxon maintains that its scientific research is independent.

However some oil companies are not prepared to go along with the scam. BP, Shell and Amoco have left the GCC and are investing in renewable energy. BP and Shell have both set targets for reducing their carbon dioxide emissions by 10 per cent from 1990 levels. BP wants to regain the moral high ground by positioning itself as an environmentally friendly company interested in exploiting alternative energy sources. Nevertheless Greenpeace criticises it for its meagre investment in

renewable energy sources in comparison to its investment in oil exploration.

In the meantime, Romm (2008) reports that the Recent G8 meeting of July 2008 seals President Bush's legacy as the president who opposed all serious efforts to reduce greenhouse gas emissions. For more than seven years he has opposed states like California from reducing their emissions and stopped Congress from adopting greenhouse gas controls and the international community from developing a serious follow on to the Kyoto protocol.

Conservation

We know that the energy resources in the world are finite, so it is obviously important to conserve what we have to make it last as long as possible. Some governments have introduced taxation policies to discourage the use of energy such as oil and petrol. People generally are more aware of the need to conserve energy. Houses and buildings are better insulated. Over the years machinery and cars have become more energy efficient. There are energy efficient electric appliances aimed at the conservation and ethically aware customer. Consumers worried about global warming are prepared to pay more for green electricity produced from renewable resources such as sun, wind and wave power.

Britain and Ireland have enough wind to power their countries several times over. One 1.8MW wind turbine produces enough electricity for 1,000 households every year. An EU renewable directive has set targets to generate 20 per cent from renewable sources by the year 2020. The EU directive obliges member states to give priority grid access to renewables. America is the biggest producer of wind power and yet it only provides about 1 per cent of US electricity. Although the capital costs of wind power are greater than conventional plants, the operating costs are comparable to fossil fuels like coal and oil. When constructed wind plants have no fuel costs compared with coal and natural gas.

> "Over the long haul of life on this planet, it is the ecologists, and not the bookkeepers of business, who are the ultimate accountants."
>
> Stewart L. Udall

Being efficient aids conservation, reduces costs and improves profitability. *Ethical Consumer* (Dec 02/Jan 03) reports that making new paper from recycled paper uses 30-50 per cent less energy than making paper from

trees and it reduces contributions to air pollution by 96 per cent. Many manufacturers are investigating ways of producing the same or more from less inputs of energy.

Some companies willingly pursue environmentally friendly policies. Some even carry out environmental audits to ensure that they are complying with the law and best environmental practice. Others have the necessity thrust upon them by events. Stainer et al (1999) reports that British Telecom as part of their mission want to exploit technologies that are environmentally friendly. They are committed to minimising the impact of their operations through a programme of continuous environmental improvement. After the Brent Spar disposal saga, Shell UK learnt its lesson and now stresses corporate commitment to the improvement of environmental performance and reporting. They also have set out strategies to win back public trust.

Peat bogs

Peat is extracted from bogs for fuel and for horticulture. In Ireland peat is used for the generation of electricity and moss peat is exported for horticultural purposes. Ornaments for the tourist industry are also made from peat. Peat is a substantial business in Ireland and the main player in the market is Bord na Mona. It is now realised that peatbogs are of great cultural and archaeological interest because of their preservation qualities. They therefore are a living museum of past climate, unique wildlife, vegetation and human activity going back thousands of years.

Perfectly preserved artefacts and human mummies dating back centuries and even thousands of years have been found in peatbogs. In addition, peatbogs play an important role in the regulation of the world's climate. There is therefore a strong argument that the remaining peatbogs should be preserved as a unique natural heritage rather than be exploited further. Therefore conservation and preservation is becoming an issue in countries with this natural resource.

Corporate Watch (4/4/2002) reports that the peat extraction works on Hatfield Moor in the UK was the focus of demonstrations by activists campaigning against the continued destruction of lowland bogs. In March 2002 the UK government paid Scotts, the US multinational owner of the plant, £17 million in compensation to stop mining peat at two other sites and to phase out production at the Hatfield site. However, Scotts still intends to mine peat there for a further two years. Campaigners argue that this will destroy the remaining wildlife on the site and that the mining should stop now.

World Bank projects

The World Bank has been criticised for the adverse environmental and social impact of its lending policies. As a result of their lending policies people have been forced to leave their native lands and resettle elsewhere. Clark (2002) reports that the Bank's history of involvement with involuntary resettlement has been a well-documented failure. It has resulted in forcible impoverishment of displaced communities with particularly severe impacts on indigenous peoples and ethnic minorities. The Bank is frequently criticised for providing financial backing and an aura of legitimacy to repressive and corrupt regimes. On its part the Bank's ignores the political dimensions of human rights in its lending policy.

The World Bank has been involved in hundreds of projects, such as the construction of dams and power plants throughout the developing world. Consequently, tens of millions of people have been forcibly displaced. They have been rendered landless, jobless, and without the skills or capacity for future income. It has failed to restore livelihoods of those who have lost their homes.

Displacement of people

In the Singrauli region of India, hundreds of thousands of people have been displaced. They have suffered repeated waves of evictions over the past forty years. This was necessary to make way for eleven open-pit coalmines, six coal-fired power plants, hundreds of associated industries, and a dam project. Since 1977, the World Bank has provided core financing for the industrialisation of Singrauli, and has loaned more than $4 billion to India's National Thermal Power Corporation (NTPC).

> "When we depend less on industrially produced consumer goods, we can live in quiet places. Our bodies will become vigorous; we discover the serenity of living with the rhythms of the earth. We cease oppressing one another."
>
> Alice Bay Laurel

The World Commission on Dams has documented the heavy toll that the displacement of indigenous peoples has caused. It maintains that for the vast majority the experience has been extremely negative in cultural, economic, and health terms. The outcomes have included loss of assets, unemployment, debt, hunger, and cultural disintegration. For both indigenous and non-indigenous communities, studies show that displacement has disproportionately impacted on women and children.

The impoverishment and disempowerment of displaced persons violates the Bank's mandate of poverty alleviation and its policy that the standard of living of displaced people should be improved or at least restored. The unfortunate reality is that peoples whose rights have been harmed have only limited access to recourse and remedy. It also directly contradicts the provisions of international human rights law regarding the right to an improved standard of living, the right to adequate housing, the right to property, and the right to work. The World Bank should be an exemplar of business ethics to other organisations and must be seen to be above reproach.

Clark (2002) concludes that if the World Bank is to play a constructive role in promoting human rights and the rule of law, it must take responsibility for ensuring that its activities do not undermine the rights of affected communities. Failure to respect the rights of local people and the health of ecosystems leads to impoverishment, ineffective development, and social and environmental injustice.

> "Russian forests crash down under the axe, billions of trees are dying, the habitations of animals and birds are laid waste, rivers grow shallow and dry up, marvellous landscapes are disappearing forever. Man is endowed with creativity in order to multiply that which has been given him; he has not created, but destroyed. There are fewer and fewer forests, rivers are drying up, wildlife has become extinct, the climate is ruined, and the earth is become ever poorer and uglier."
>
> Anton Pavolovich Chekhow

Summary

We now realise that the resources of the earth are finite and should be protected. In the past many companies have exploited and abused the environment. They have depleted natural resources, marred scenic views, destroyed landscapes and polluted countryside, rivers and air.

People have become very conscious of the ethical issues involved and the negative aspects of environmental pollution on health. Particular concerns are the possible negative health effects of transmission lines and mobile phone masts. Asbestos, which was used extensively as an insulator, is now known to be carcinogenic and is therefore banned.

Global warming is caused by the greenhouse effect as gases accumulate in the atmosphere trapping the outgoing heat radiated from the surface of the earth. Some of the consequences of this are increased temperatures and risk of flooding. The Kyoto Protocol is an international agreement aimed at cutting down on greenhouse gas emissions. One way of doing this is by conserving energy and implementing environmentally friendly policies.

The World Bank has been criticised for the adverse environmental and social impact of its lending policies. Their policies mean that native people have been forced to resettle. Failure to respect the rights of local people and the health of ecosystems leads to impoverishment, ineffective development, and social and environmental injustice.

Check Your Ethics Quotient

(circle the appropriate response)

1. Most companies prioritise profitability ahead of conservation.   True   False

2. People are now demanding that companies take a more responsible attitude to environmental issues and are held accountable for any damage caused.   True   False

3. The exploration for oil does not involve a heavy environmental cost.   True   False

4. The resources of the world are infinite.   True   False

5. The health risk of using mobile phones is uncertain.   True   False

6. There is no scientific evidence for global warming.   True   False

7. The USA has refused to take part in the Kyoto protocol.   True   False

8. Being efficient aids conservation, reduces costs and improves profitability.   True   False

9. Some companies do an environmental audit.   True   False

10. The World Bank has been criticised for the adverse environmental and social impact of its lending policies. True   False

Total the number of true and false responses and check Appendix 2 at the back of the book for the solution.

Case study: The World's worst industrial accident

In the Bhopal tragedy in 1984 poor regulatory, safety, maintenance, design and training standards, together with cost-cutting measures, were at the root of the problem. More than 3,800 people died and more than 200,000 were injured when toxic gas seeped from the Union Carbide insecticide plant. It is estimated that 11,000 more died in later years due to ailments resulting from inhaling the gas. It was the world's worst industrial accident. The people who suffered most were slum dwellers, the poorest of India's poor, who lived near the Union Carbide plant. Survivors still complain of ailments ranging from breathlessness, chronic fatigue and stomach pain to cardiac problems and tuberculosis.

The Bhopal episode cost Union Carbide at least $470 million paid to the Indian Government as compensation. The lax standards in Bhopal would not have been tolerated in the parent company in the USA. Different standards were acceptable and tolerated outside the USA. Siting of a potentially dangerous chemical plant in a densely populated area also could not be morally justified. In addition, the regulatory framework in third-world countries is often inadequate or non-existent. Where laws do exist they are often not consistently enforced.

Union Carbide's chairman, at the time of the disaster, Mr Warren Anderson, has refused to appear in an Indian court on manslaughter charges and the authorities have been unable to extradite him from the United States. The company has accepted moral responsibility for the disaster, but claimed at the time that a disgruntled employee sabotaged the plant.

Experts maintain that several factors made the accident inevitable. For example, the plant used carbon steel valves, which corroded when they came in contact with acid, allowing the toxic gas to escape. The cooling system that kept the gases at a low temperature also had not been working for a month when the leak occurred. The company did not quickly make information about the chemical properties of methyl isocyanate available. Consequently, the Indian health officials did not immediately know how to treat

the victims of the poisoning. The company also failed to notify the government and health officials that such large amounts of the toxic methyl isocyanate, used to make pesticides, was being stored underground at the Bhopal site.

Questions

♦ Discuss the ethical issues raised in the Bhopal case.
♦ How in your opinion could the world's worst industrial accident been prevented?
♦ Should the chairman be charged with corporate manslaughter or murder in the USA as well as India?

10. Organisational Ethics

> ◆ What are the well-known political scandals?
> ◆ What are the ethical issues in the health industry?
> ◆ What ethical problems have arisen in the church?
> ◆ What is the model for resolving ethical problems?
> ◆ How does the law impact on business ethics?
> ◆ How have trade unions highlighted ethical abuses?

"Those who cannot remember the past are condemned to repeat it."

George Santayana

Ethical scandals have also come to light in our most revered institutions and professions including healthcare, church, politics, the law and medicine. Although most are registered as charities and therefore pay no corporation tax, these are organisations in their own right with huge budgets and hundreds of thousands of employees. They have revenues and expenditures, finance departments, HRM departments, Public Relations and even some have taken on the philosophy of marketing with their customer orientation approach. To all intents and purposes they are substantial businesses though operating in the non-commercial sector. They play a pivotal role in the economy.

In healthcare these organisations are represented in both private and public sectors. Unethical practices have left the health boards and church open to claims by victims of abuse for compensation. Institutional and professional reputations have been destroyed and political careers have been ruined with some politicians made bankrupt. Trade unions and non-

governmental bodies have been active over the years in bringing ethical abuses to the attention of the public.

Organisations in the non-commercial sector are subject to the same ethical challenges as the commercial sector. Where people gather in organisations they are subject to the same temptations. We should learn from these ethical scandals and draw lessons from them. **Personal character and values, codes of business ethics, the law and professional standards will help us to be more ethical in our business dealings.**

Political scandals

Unethical behaviour in politics is not confined to just one country. It is a worldwide problem. The following which are only the tip of the iceberg cover prominent political scandals in the US, Britain and Ireland.

"Since a politician never believes what he says, he is surprised when others believe him."

General Charles de Gaulle

US political scandals

In the US, political scandals have happened at the highest levels. President Nixon resigned after being impeached because of the Watergate affair and President Clinton barely survived the sexual scandals surrounding him. Even Presidents have lied under oath. The general public no longer trusts politicians. It seems to be standard practice now that election promises are made to be broken and lies and half-truths are the norm rather than the exception.

"Politicians are the same all over. They promise to build a bridge even where there is no river."

Nikita Khrushchev

In the Watergate affair burglaries were authorised and sanctioned by President Nixon. Months of congressional hearings, testimony, and denials by the president and his staff concluded with Nixon's resignation to avoid impeachment and various jail terms for many of his closest associates. Nixon is reputed to have said that he was not sorry for any of the lying and cheating, he was only sorry that he got caught. President Clinton was threatened with impeachment for his sexual adventures. He engaged in half-truths, lies and deceptions to conceal the affair. Character and

honesty seem to be a thing of the past. People at the top no longer provide the example to inspire the rest of us. They seldom practice what they preach.

Political contributions

There is little doubt that political contributions are made by companies to government in order to influence public policy in their favour. Pilhofer et al (2004) says that according to an new report by the Centre for Public Integrity the US energy industry has lavished more than $440 million over the past six years on politicians, political parties and lobbyists in order to protect its interests in Washington. The study found that oil and gas companies overwhelmingly favoured Republican over Democrats in their campaign. Just over 73 per cent of contributions have gone to Republicans candidates and organisations.

In the US Enron made huge contributions to the Republican and Democrat parties probably to influence the administration's energy policy. The *Guardian* (8/3/2002) reported that Global Crossing also made significant contributions to both parties. Over five years, it spent $3.6 million on political donations. During the 2000 elections alone, it contributed $2.8 million, split evenly between Republicans and Democrats. This was more than the Enron contribution that year. In Ireland the amount of contributions given by business to political parties has been limited to curb the influence business had on the political process.

British political scandals

The *Guardian* (20/7/2001) reported on the spectacular fall from grace of Jeffrey Archer as peer and former Conservative deputy chairman. He was sentenced to four years after one of the most serious cases of perjury in British criminal history. He was convicted on two counts of perjury and two counts of perverting the course of justice. During the seven-week trial the best-selling author was exposed as a calculating liar who corrupted his friends and employees to make sure he won the 1987-libel action against the *Daily Star*. The judge concluded that Archer had sworn an affidavit dishonestly and gave false evidence in court. Jeffrey Archer was one of Margaret Thatcher's bright-favourites to become Lord Mayor of London.

David Blunkett the British home secretary resigned in December 2004 after weeks of controversy over his relationship with a married woman and accusations of abuse of office. He gave free railway tickets to his lover at the taxpayers expense and fast tracked the visa for his lover's nanny. Such

transgressions in Ireland such as the Cullen affair do not incur the same repercussions.

Irish political scandals

Concurrently, in Ireland Martin Cullen the transport minister awarded a huge public relations contract to a lady friend after being appointed to the cabinet in 2002. He breached EU rules by failing to put the contract out to tender. The contract was worth €300,000 considerably more than similar contracts awarded to other public relations companies. Calls by the opposition for resignation have been ignored and an official enquiry into the affair has been carried out. This showed that what was done was not illegal but it did raise ethical concerns. The ethical standards for integrity in office are taken much more seriously in Britain than in Ireland.

> "It has now become the doctrine of a large clan of politicians that political honesty is unnecessary, slow, subversive of a man's interests, and incompatible with quick on ward movement."
>
> Anthony Trollope

In Ireland, scandal surrounded an ex Prime Minister Charles Haughey during his period in office. He has been accused of corruption and tax evasion. He presided during an era of cash in brown bags, wholesale bribery of councillors, some politicians and local government officials, and when hundred of millions of Irish pounds flowed into offshore bank accounts. Like Alice in Wonderland, nothing is what it seems. Politicians classified blatant bribes as political donations, management consultancy fees, or unsolicited gifts. Tribunal after tribunal has been set up in Ireland revealing the murky underside of politics.

Tribunals

In response to intense public pressure tribunals were set up in the late 1990s to investigate, expose and report on the various scams going on. Their findings to date has astonished and dismayed the Irish public. Bribery and corruption seemed to have been rampant throughout certain parts of the political system. Planning permissions were influenced by businesspeople bribing local government officials, local and central politicians alike. Fortunes were made on land redesignated for development. Land often quadrupled in value making corrupt politicians and land speculators rich overnight. Tribunals have found that it was a

systematic and organised affair with votes being bought at county council meetings to get the land redesignated.

> "There is an increased demand for codes of ethics in politics, although most office holders are sworn in with their hand resting on one."
>
> Bill Vaughan

According to a survey by Transparency International published on 9th December 2004 Irish people view political parties as the most corrupt sector in Irish society. This is not surprising considering what has come to light. On a scale of 1 to 5, where 1 represents zero corruption and 5 represents extreme corruption, political parties ranked worst with a score of 3.9. The survey, done between June and September 2004, found that the next most corrupt institution was the legal system and judiciary, closely followed by Dail Eireann, the Irish Parliament. Irish people's view of political parties reflected worldwide opinion with 36 out of 62 countries polled rating political parties as the most corrupt.

Medical scandals

One rightly expects the medical profession to have the highest ethical standards. However, this is not always so as the following German, UK and Irish cases illustrate. Like most professions the vast majority of medical practitioners are people of great integrity but there are always exceptions to mar the reputation of the profession generally. Cases have come to public attention of doctors involved in mass murder and professional misconduct. A new area with ethical concerns is cosmetic surgery. There have been allegations that some practitioners operate from just a financial perspective often performing unnecessary procedures and promising unrealistic outcomes.

> "Ethics, too, are nothing but reverence for life. That is what gives me the fundamental principle of morality, namely that good consists in maintaining, promoting and enhancing life, and that destroying, injuring, and limiting life are evil. "
>
> Albert Schweitzer

German medical scandals

Sherwin (2004) reported that Hitler in 1939 sanctioned a euthanasia programme to murder severely disabled children. The murders began in

July 1939 when a family petitioned the German government to authorise the "mercy killing" for their baby born with major deformities. Using this case as a pretext, Hitler ordered that any infant born with deformities were to be reported to the authorities. These deformities included idiocy, hydrocephaly, spina bifida, or paralysis of any significant kind.

The parents were deceived, by being told that high quality treatment centres would be provided for these children. In fact most of the children were murdered or left starve to death. In each case, the parents were notified that the children died of natural causes. Five thousand children lost their lives. Three Berlin paediatricians supervised the murders. This euthanasia programme could not have been done without the connivance and active participation of the medical profession. What happened to the Hippocratic oath? The excuse of following orders is not tenable. This was only the start.

In October, 1939, Hitler authorised euthanasia for adults in German asylums. Because of the large numbers involved carbon monoxide delivered through fake showerheads became the technique of choice for mass murder. Between January 1940 and August 1941 some 70,000 adults patients were gassed, their only crime being that they were unproductive members of the Nazi state. Specially selected physicians and nurses staffed these facilities. Medical staff were also involved in the concentration and death camps where medical experiments were practised and millions of Jews murdered. This became known as the Holocaust. In addition, there is no doubt that hundreds of bureaucrats were involved in the organisation and administration of the whole diabolical scheme.

"When Hitler attacked the Jews ... I was not a Jew, therefore, I was not concerned. And when Hitler attacked the Catholics, I was not a Catholic, and therefore, I was not concerned. And when Hitler attacked the unions and the industrialists, I was not a member of the unions and I was not concerned. Then, Hitler attacked me and the Protestant church – and there was nobody left to be concerned."

Martin Niemller

Irish medical scandals

Carolan (2003) reports that in Ireland a Dr Michael Neary was found guilty of professional misconduct and struck off the medical register. In total, at least 65 women had claimed that Dr Neary performed unnecessary Caesarean hysterectomy operations on them during the 1970's, 80's and

90's. Dr Neary was suspended from the hospital in 1998. Their wombs were removed following childbirth in a procedure usually used only in an emergency where the mother's life is at risk from haemorrhaging. The rate of Caesarean hysterectomies at Our Lady of Lourdes Hospital in Drogheda aroused suspicion, as they were higher in relation to comparable hospitals. Significant amounts of money have already been paid out in damages to compensate patients.

The *Irish Times* (3/9/2003) reported that a Mr Justice Finnegan confirmed the decision of the medical council to strike Dr Neary off the medical register. The Judge said that the committee had 15 cases referred to it and, in respect of these, seven allegations of professional misconduct against Dr Neary had been made:

1. That he failed to show and apply the standards of clinical judgement and competence required of a person in his position.
2. That he carried out operations when he knew or ought to have known there were insufficient grounds for them.
3. That he made findings in respect of patients when he knew or ought to have known there were insufficient grounds for them.
4. That he made inaccurate or misleading entries in patients' notes.
5. That he acted in a rude and insensitive manner towards some or all of his patients.
6. That he failed to act in their best interests.
7. That he acted in a manner derogatory of the medical profession.

In February 2006, a report on the case was issued by Judge Maureen Harding-Clarke. Her report confirmed many of the findings of the Medical Council but was more detailed. The Health Service Executive issued an apology to the women who suffered through the malpractice of Dr Neary. Dr Neary has paid a high price for his unethical behaviour. He has been labelled a "monster" and a "mutilator of women" by the press and will never practice again. He is also likely to be the subject of numerous personal injury claims.

"No man can be a pure specialist without being in a strict sense an idiot."
George Bernard Shaw

The MRSA scandal

Raftery (2004) reports that the Irish Minister for Health was amazed that she had to issue guidelines to medical staff about hand hygiene to contain MRSA (methicillin resistant staphylococcus aureus). MRSA is resistant to penicillin. Inappropriate use of antibiotics is blamed for the development of resistant bacteria. Ireland has the second highest rate of infection in Europe, with the figure rising each year. MRSA is an infection that lives primarily in hospitals and it targets the sickest of patients. The primary route of transmission is from dirty hands, clothing and equipment of medical personnel. Overcrowding in hospitals and old buildings which are more difficult to keep sterile and clean also contribute to the problem.

In the UK they have become so alarmed by MRSA figures that they have introduced league tables comparing each hospital's incidence of the infection. Crucially, they also include MRSA information on death certificates. It is now estimated that the death rate from hospital acquired infections in the UK may be as high as 5,000, or about one in ten of hospital deaths. In Ireland there are no figures available for MRSA deaths and each hospital's incidence of the infection remains secret. The MRSA problem leaves hospital authorities open to claims for substantial damages from patients.

British medical scandals

The *Irish Times* (19/7/2001) reported that a report found that a "club culture" of powerful but flawed surgeons at the Bristol Royal Infirmary (BRI) led to one-third of its patients receiving inadequate care. A "poisoned" atmosphere between management, surgeons and other staff meant that people who raised concerns about the scandal at the hospital were ignored and threatened.

The inquiry chairman, Professor Ian Kennedy said that up to 35 babies under a year old died unnecessarily at the BRI between 1991 and 1995 as a result of sub-standard care. Surgeons were able to cover up high death rates by claiming they were on a "learning curve". Their powerful positions both on the wards and at management level meant that nobody dared to question them. Parents were given "partial, confusing and unclear" information and were kept in the dark about major concerns about the heart unit at the hospital. The hospital's chief executive, Dr John Roylance and Mr James Wisheart, a surgeon, were struck off the medical register for serious professional misconduct.

Dr Harold Shipman, a general practitioner, was Britain's most prolific serial murderer and was jailed for life in 2000 on 15 murder counts. He

was found hanged in his cell in Wakefield prison in January 2004. The 57-year-old was serving 15 life sentences. Shipman is thought to have murdered at least 215 patients by administering doses of diamorphine (pharmaceutical heroin). In this case several doctors who signed cremation certificates failed to notice anything wrong even though all the deaths were sudden, unexpected or in unusual circumstances. Undertakers who were alarmed at the number of deaths involving Shipman's patients alerted the police but their investigations were less than thorough. His crimes eventually came to light when he forged the will of one of his patients.

> "If a man is good in his heart, then he is an ethical member of any group in society. If he is bad in his heart, he is an unethical member. To me the ethics of medical practice is as simple as that."
>
> Dr Elmer Hess

Sexual misconduct of doctors

Boseley (2004) reports that a 46 year old GP, Dr John Razzak was struck off the medical register by the General Medical Council (GMC) at his own request claiming he was unsuitable to be a GP because of his numerous affairs with patients. Five days before Staffordshire GP Keith Bevan was thrown out of the medical profession for a 14-month affair with a farmer's wife. He seduced her in his surgery while her husband was sitting in the waiting room. She was having marital problems and wanted the doctor to prescribe Viagra for her husband. Bevan told the GMC hearing that she was avid for sex. The GMC concluded that his behaviour undermined the confidence that the public is entitled to place in doctors and constituted a gross abuse of his position.

Boseley (2004) also reports that in July 2004, the GMC struck off a 66 year old GP Dr Iain MacLeod who drove around his local town in a Jaguar with the number plate TSM IT, which stood for "The Sexiest Man in Town". He had a 22-year affair with a woman he had been treating for depression. In February, Dr Anthony Leeper, 48, was given a two year supervision order after he admitted having a 11 month sexual relationship with a patient who was being treated for anxiety and emotional problems.

There are obvious ethical implications in these cases. First there is the power imbalance between a doctor and a patient. The doctor should not exploit this relationship for his own personal gratification especially when patients are at their most vulnerable. There is also the question of professional boundaries that the doctor should not step across. Having sex with a patient can affect a doctor's ability to make an objective medical

diagnosis. Not least there is the question of moral standards expected of a professional. Every doctor knows that having sex with a patient is a breach of trust and a career ending offence.

Ghostwriters

Barnett (2003) reports that hundreds of articles in medical journals are written by ghostwriters paid for by drug companies rather than by academics or doctors. In February 2003 the New England Journal of Medicine was forced to retract an article published last year by doctors from Imperial College in London and the National Heart Institute on treating a type of heart problem. It emerged that several of the listed authors had little or nothing to do with the research. The deception was revealed only when German cardiologist Dr Hubert Seggewiss, one of the 8 listed authors, called the editor of the journal to say he had never seen any version of the paper. It is alleged that drug companies pay medical writers to write review articles supporting particular drugs. They will then find a recognised medical doctor to put their name to the article without anybody realising that a ghostwriter or a drug company is behind it. This is dishonest and a highly unethical practice.

Blood transfusions

Just like any product, people getting blood transfusions are entitled to get a quality product and service not injurious to their health and safety. The *Guardian* (27/3/2001) reported that more than 100 people infected with the hepatitis C virus through blood transfusion won compensation worth millions of pounds. The total bill for the NHS could reach £10 million. Mr Justice Burton said that the public was entitled to expect clean blood. Blood contamination with hepatitis C was defective, and anyone who caught the virus as a result was entitled to compensation because the NHS knew about the risk. The NHS should have acted earlier to reduce the risk of transmission, and should have introduced routine screening of all blood transfusions by March 1, 1990.

The claimants included women who received transfusion immediately after childbirth, and patients given blood during surgery or as a treatment for a blood disorder. Several children became infected while being treated for leukaemia. Similar cases in Ireland revealed a culture of secrecy and buck-passing in the national blood transfusion service. Huge sums were paid out to compensate patients.

Medical sponsorship and gifts

It is well known that pharmaceutical companies sponsor many medical events including postgraduate medical education. Dr Houston (2004) reports that sponsorship includes clinical meetings, medical association AGMs and conferences at which research is presented. Doctors are often put up overnight in expensive hotels as part of the deal. It is also the practice to pay the travel expenses of consultants attending conferences and educational events abroad. Drug companies even sponsor patient advocacy groups. Rumours that pharmaceutical companies pay for lavish trips abroad to exotic locations if doctors prescribe their products abound.

> "Every clique is a refuge for incompetence. It fosters corruption and disloyalty, it begets cowardice, and consequently is a burden upon and a drawback to the progress of the country. Its instincts and actions are those of the pack."
>
> Madame Chiang Kai-Shek

There is no such thing as a free lunch and pharmaceutical companies are motivated by the favourable attitude from the medical profession towards their products that such largesses earn. There is no doubt that doctors need to be kept informed about new drugs, new medical procedures and developments. However, it would be better if the relationship were kept at arms-length so that the position of the medical profession is not seen as compromised. Ideally medical doctors should not accept money, gifts or hospitality that could create a conflict of interest in their dealings with pharmaceutical companies and patients.

Cosmetic surgery

Cosmetic surgery is now widely advertised in popular magazines. It is often marketed as a life-choice event. There is a wide range of services offered. These include penis and breast enlargements, Botox fillers and laser treatment to iron out wrinkles, tummy tucks, nose jobs, liposuction, and facelifts. There is a changed attitude to cosmetic surgery so that it is not only the rich and famous who take advantage of such treatments. Everybody is now a potential customer. Some people are even prepared to go deep in debt to finance such treatments.

It is also well known that customers are likely to be customers for life as the benefits of the treatment wear off with the passage of time. Eventually new treatments are needed in the perpetual search for the nirvana of youth and beauty. The risks involved are never mentioned but

may be fatal. There have been numerous scares about breast implants and some have even been removed. The media from time to time has highlighted operations that have gone wrong with dire consequences such as disfigurement and even death. Concerns of cancer from leaking or ruptured implants are also prevalent.

Cosmetic surgery is often traumatic and patients may need a great deal of post-operative care. People are going to feel sore and bruised afterwards and so it is important that they get the best of after care. The Observer (14/3/2004) reported that in January 2004 novelist Olivia Goldsmith, author of The First Wives Club, died during an operation for a chin tuck. In March 2004, Lorraine Batt's family were awarded compensation for her death in a north London hospital following a tummy tuck. Deaths from liposuction operations in the US are running at 20 per cent per 100,000, according to research carried out by the plastic surgeon Frederick Glazer

Ethical issues with cosmetic surgery

The ethical issues with cosmetic surgery are numerous. Critics say that cosmetic surgery exploits people's insecurities. Many of the people who go for this type of surgery are very vulnerable with low self-esteem. The media and magazines are presenting unattainable images as the way people should aspire to look. Like the models and film actresses they see on television they should have nice breasts, a nice bum, a nice nose, large beautiful eyes, a well-proportioned face and a thin waist. These ideals are unlikely to be ever realised. Even if cosmetic surgery addresses the physical issues the deeper psychological issues remain and will inevitably come to the fore again.

> "Industrial societies turn their citizens into image-junkies; it is the most irresistible form of mental pollution. Poignant longings for beauty, for an end to probing below the surface, for a redemption and celebration of the body of the world. Ultimately, having an experience become identical with taking a photograph of it."
>
> Susan Sontag

There are also concerns about the qualifications of the people performing such surgery and about the misleading type of advertising used to attract customers. Even if doctors perform the surgery there is no guarantee that they have any formal training in cosmetic surgery. The cosmetic surgery industry is largely profit driven. So far the industry remains largely unregulated.

Church scandals

A wave of scandals has hit the Church in the past few years. Sexual abuse cases have emerged in the USA, Canada, Australia, Britain and Ireland and other European countries. It would be wrong to assume that it is only the Catholic Church that has been affected as other churches and religions have been confronted with sexual abuse cases as well. At first most people just didn't believe the stories about priests and religious sexually abusing children until it was conclusively proved. The potential claims against the Church runs into millions of Euro, some of which have already been conceded.

The reputation of the Church has been damaged by the hierarchy's efforts to cover up the sexual abuse by moving the culprits around from parish to parish. Contrast this with lay people who if caught molesting young children are removed from society and handed over to the police to be tried by the criminal justice system. The power of the Church has diminished while Church attendance and collections have fallen.

Fall from grace

Priests were held in the highest esteem and seen as paragons of truth, integrity, spirituality, virtue and justice. However when confronted with their crimes priests proved to be no better than the worst of mankind and resorted to lies, deceit and half-truths. Their bishops aided and abetted in the cover up. They seemed to be more interested in protecting the reputation of the Church than in protecting the innocence and rights of the children abused. But they forgot that these young children would grow up to blow the whistle and confront them with their abuse. It was only after a long and vigorous campaign by the victims that justice eventually was won.

> "Whatsoever things are true, whatsoever things are honest, whatsoever things are just, whatsoever things are pure, whatsoever things are lovely, whatsoever things are of good report, if there be any virtue, and if there be any praise, think on these things."
>
> Philippians 4:8

The clergy are now viewed as potential deviants. The priest's pastoral role and perceived power gives them privileged access to people. It is a breach of trust and unethical if this role and power is used to sexually exploit people. One always thought that the religious would have the highest sense of ethics but unfortunately the evidence suggests otherwise.

Priests have been defrocked and some bishops who turned a blind eye have been forced to resign. Although it is generally acknowledge that there is only a small minority of priests who abuse, unfortunately their actions has tarnished the priesthood generally. Even Cardinals have been found guilty of sexual abuse.

US Church scandals

The US Catholic Church has been rocked to its foundations with scandal after scandal. Kaiser (2002) reports that Cardinal Bernard Law, the archbishop of Boston ignored a massive amount of evidence of child abuse against Father Paul Shanley. Shanley was allowed to come in contact with young boys for years after the church knew he had been abusing them. Church officials even knew that Shanley had attended a meeting of the North American Man-Boy Love Association.

Dreher (2002) reports the following high profile US cases:

♦ In Dallas, Rudy Kos, a former priest, was convicted in a criminal court of the serial molestation of altar boys and sent to prison. During the trial, it was revealed that Church officials were repeatedly warned that Kos was a danger to children. However they did nothing. Michael Sheehan, the seminary rector who was advised time and time again about Kos's attraction to children, but allowed him to remain, continued to rise in the hierarchy, and is now archbishop of Santa Fe.
♦ In 1999, the Diocese of Santa Rosa, California, already paying out $5.4 million in child sex abuse settlements from the early 1990s, was astounded when DNA and taped evidence proved that Bishop G. Patrick Ziemann had been having sex with one of his priests. The priest claimed that he was blackmailed into the relationship with Zieman. It emerged that Ziemann, who resigned, had lost millions of the diocese's funds in shady investment schemes. He was never prosecuted for the fraud because Church officials refused to co-operate with local law enforcement officials.
♦ John Bollard, a former Jesuit seminarian in San Francisco, filed a sexual harassment lawsuit against the Society of Jesus, claiming his superiors in the order pressed him constantly for gay sex. When their claim to be immune for religious reasons from sexual harassment law failed, the Jesuits settled the lawsuit.
♦ Bishop J. Keith Symons, resigned in 1998 as head of the Palm Beach Florida, diocese after five men came forward accusing him of having molested them decades earlier when they were altar boys in his parish.

Symons admitted the charges and left his post. Two years later, to the dismay of victims' rights groups, he resurfaced in Michigan, living in a convent and conducting spiritual retreats for adult Catholics.

> **"I am not sure how many 'sins' I would recognise in the world. Some would surely be defused by changed circumstances. But I can imagine none that is more irredeemably sinful than the betrayal, the exploitation, of the young by those who should care for them. "**
>
> Elizabeth Janeway

Dreher (2002) also claims that there is a network of discreet but powerful homosexual networks within seminaries. A. W. Richard Sipe, a psychiatrist and former Benedictine monk has treated scores of sexually abusive priests and has written extensively about the problem. He maintains that the reality of the gay network is well known to clerics and others closely familiar with the workings of the Catholic Church, though difficult to prove from public sources. In Ireland the president of St Patrick's seminary at Maynooth had to leave his job prematurely amid allegations of sex abuse.

O'Clery (2002) reports that the 157-year-old order of the Oblates of Mary Immaculate in Canada declared itself bankrupt in April 2004 after being hit with thousands of sexual abuse claims. In Los Angeles Cardinal Roger Mahoney retired up to a dozen priests connected to sexual abuse. However, when he declined to name them, the chief of police demanded compliance with laws requiring that all reports of sexual abuse be referred to the police. Agnew (2002) subsequently reports that Cardinal Roger Mahoney revealed that he had been accused of sexual misconduct with a teenage girl more than 30 years ago.

Irish & other Church scandals

In Ireland a succession of scandals has come to light, each one worse than the last. In 1992 the public were scandalised when it discovered that the Bishop of Galway, Eamonn Casey, had fathered a son after an affair with Ms Annie Murphy. He quickly went into exile to South America after revelations that he had an 18-year-old son and that he had misappropriated church funds to support him.

In Scotland a similar case came to light in 1996. It concerned a Bishop Wright who was linked to a divorced mother of three, Kathleen MacPhee. He also had a son Kevin born in 1981 with his former lover, Joanna Whibley. It appears that the Bishop was not afraid of publicity as he sold his story to the News of the World.

A Father Michael Cleary fathered a son with his housekeeper, Phylis Hamilton. Father Cleary had a radio programme on which he preached about high moral standards and that sex outside marriage was wrong. He kept secret his own sexual encounters that broke his vow of chastity. Father Cleary and Bishop Eamonn Casey were very much involved in the ceremonies to welcome the Pope to Ireland in 1979. With hindsight the hypocrisy of both is remarkable.

> "Among the best traitors Ireland has ever had, Mother Church ranks at the very top, a massive obstacle in the path to equality and freedom. She has been a force for conservatism, not on the basis of preserving Catholic doctrine or preventing the corruption of her children, but simply to ward off threats to her own security and influence."
>
> Bernadette Devlin

Paedophile priests

A Father Brendan Smith in 1997 was found to have been abusing children since the 1950s. His own order, the Norbertines, turned a blind eye to his activities over many years. Even Cardinal Daly knew about his activities but failed to intervene because he insisted that he had no authority to interfere in the affairs of the Norbertine Order. Smith died before charges could be levied against him and was buried in the middle of the night for fear of retribution.

The *Irish Times* (3/12/1997) reports that a former priest, Tony Walsh, was jailed for a total of 10 years at Dublin Circuit Court for indecently assaulting six boys in the 1980s. He committed five of the offences in the presbytery of the Church of the Assumption in Ballyfermot, Dublin, where he was a popular curate during the 1980s. The court was told that Walsh befriended the victims' families while a curate in Ballyfermot. He rationalised that he was not harming the boys, who were aged between 8 to 14, because he believed they did not understand what he had done to them.

The fallout

Bishop Brendan Comiskey of the Diocese of Ferns in Co. Wexford, resigned in 2002 after acknowledging that his handling of the serial sex abuser, Father Sean Fortune, was inadequate. Initially, allegations of clerical sex abuse were met with denial, deception and delay. Despite numerous complaints made to the Bishop about Father Fortune's sex abuse, the priest was allowed to remain in contact with young people. Father Fortune

committed suicide in 1999 rather than deal with 29 charges of child sex abuse, a likely jail sentence and being publicly branded as a paedophile. In the late 1980s Father Fortune had been treated for paedophilia in a clinic in England but on his return was given another parish with access to young children.

Austrian scandals

Traynor (2004) reports that the Austrian Catholic Church was plunged into its second big sex scandal in a decade when a seminary was alleged to be the site of orgies among young priests and their teachers. The Vienna newsmagazine *Profil* published pictures of priests and students engaged in sexual acts. The pictures were part of a cache of some 40,000 photographs and child pornography videos found by Church officials on computers at the seminary in 2003.

This latest scandal comes on top of the crises in 1995 when the head of the Austrian Catholic Church, Cardinal Hans-Hermann Groer, was accused of paedophilia. Senior Church figures eventually found that he had been molesting boys for years. He was forced to retire and died in 2003.

The Jersey childcare scandal

Stewart (2008) reports that police are looking into about 97 allegations of abuse at a former children's care home in Jersey and say there are more than 100 suspects. Investigations started in February 2008 after the discovery of what was initially believed to be part of a child's skull. Following the find, scores of people came forward claiming they were drugged, raped and beaten at the home. Six people have been arrested. Three have been charged with child abuse while the others have been released on bail pending further investigations. Charred remains from at least 5 children have been found at the site. They were found in a hidden dungeon described as "punishment rooms".

Judicial scandals

The legal profession are supposed to be the upholders of law and the implementers of justice. One doesn't expect them to be involved in illegal and unethical behaviour. Coulter (2004) highlights the need for legislation to regulate judicial conduct and ethics. She reports that a Circuit Court

judge, Judge Curtin was accused of the criminal conduct of possessing child pornography. He was acquitted on a technical irregularity. The judge resigned in November 2006 but retained entitlement to a lump sum of €57,000 and an annual pension of €19,000. Nevertheless he has suffered considerable stigma and has been shunned by the local community in Tralee where he resides.

> **"In civilised life, law floats in a sea of ethics."**
>
> Earl Warren

A Circuit Court judge deals with family law, criminal cases, personal injury and other litigation. Lack of credibility might arise if Judge Curtin were to sit on family law case or a criminal case involving any kind of sexual assault. The legal system would be brought into disrepute if such a case were brought before him because of the perceived lack of impartiality and integrity. The Irish government has called on Judge Curtin to resign.

The *Irish Times* (24/5/1996) reports that solicitor Elio Malocco, and a director of Irish Press Group was jailed for five years for fraud, forgery and deceit. He subsequently lost his appeal against conviction and sentence in the Court of Criminal Appeal. A jury at Dublin Circuit Court convicted Malocco in May 1996 on fraud charges involving £68,500. This money had been given to him by the Irish Press to deal with libel cases. The judge found that there had been no attempt at restitution. Malocco had been entrusted with funds and the jury had found him guilty of dishonesty. A former partner of Malocco, Conor Killeen, pleaded guilty to five charges of being an accessory after the fact to forgery.

> **"Dishonesty is a forsaking of permanent for temporary advantage."**
>
> Christian Bovee

The Sheedy affair

In October 1997 Philip Sheedy a Dublin based architect was sentenced to four years in prison after pleading guilty to drunk and dangerous driving. Sheedy was driving the car that killed a young Dublin mother. The subsequent premature release of Sheedy by Mr Justice Cyril Kelly led to a judicial enquiry that found that two judges were guilty of judicial misconduct. Kelly had suspended three years of Sheedy's four-year sentence. The two judges at the centre of the controversy, Mr Justice Hugh O'Flaherty and Mr Justice Cyril Kelly both resigned. The Dublin County Registrar, Mr Quinlan also resigned.

The judicial enquiry by Chief Justice Hamilton described Mr Justice O'Flaherty's conduct in the Sheedy affair as "inappropriate and unwise" and accused him of "damaging the administration of justice". It was claimed that O'Flaherty's intervention had been done on humanitarian grounds. Apparently O'Flaherty had summoned Quinlan to his chambers to discuss the case. Critics maintain that Sheedy was treated favourably because of his middle class background. In an addendum to the scandal the Irish government subsequently nominated Mr O'Flaherty to fill the post as vice-president of the European Investment Bank but because of public outrage it was withdrawn.

Trade unions

Trade unions want recognition and representation rights in order to negotiate with employers on behalf of their members. Membership of trade unions should be voluntary. Trade unions have campaigned actively against the wrongs of sweatshops and child labour. They have been in the forefront of highlighting ethical abuses by employers. On a worldwide basis non-governmental bodies such as the Fair Labour Association and Transparency International have taken up the cause.

> "With all their faults, trade unions have done more for humanity than any other organisation of men that ever existed. They have done more for decency, for honesty, for education, for the betterment of the race, for the developing of character in man, than other association of men".
>
> Clarence Darrow

Recognition

The unique nature of trade unions is recognised and protected by law. Their main role is to enhance the wages and working conditions of their members. They do this in collective bargaining with the employer. They act as a counterbalance to employers and so help to minimise labour abuses. In some economies they are a major political force and can influence government policy in relation to taxation and wage increases. In Ireland they are partners in national wage agreements. However, some multinationals, mainly in the US, still refuse to recognise trade unions and discourage their employees from joining them. Some even sack employees for joining one. Ryan Air as a matter of policy refuses to deal with trade unions.

Representation rights

Trade unions have the right to represent their members when negotiating with management. Amnesty International published human rights principles for business in 1998 (www.web.amnesty.org). It has one covering the freedom of association and right to collective bargaining. This states that companies should ensure that employees, without penalty, could exercise their rights to free expression, collective bargaining, and peaceful assembly and association.

Trade unions have a right to strike to achieve the objectives of their members. Unofficial strikes are illegal and may be unethical. Official strikes may be unethical if other alternative courses of action have not been exhausted. Secondary strikes are illegal in many countries. By law, the Union must operate in the interest of all workers whether they are members of the union or not. This is only fair in equity as otherwise you could have two workers getting different rates of pay for doing exactly the same job.

Voluntary membership

Nobody should be forced to join a trade union as a condition of employment. Such closed shops are anti-democratic, unethical and illegal. Union busting and the systematic denigration of trade unions by employers are also unethical. Such a stance creates bad industrial relations and negative publicity for the company.

Unions and sweatshops

Trade unions and human rights organisations often highlight companies throughout the world who run sweatshops or exploit child labour. Amnesty International have a basic human rights principle covering freedom from slavery (www.web.amnesty.org). It states that companies should ensure that their policies and practices prohibit the use of chattel slaves, forced labour, bonded child labourers, or coerced prison labour.

> "Men and women are not yet free... The slavery of greed endures. Little child workers, the hope of the future, are sacrificed to industry. Young men are sent out by the billion to die for profits... We must destroy industrial slavery and build industrial democracy... The people everywhere must come into possession of the earth."
>
> Sara Bard Field

In sweatshops workers are paid insufficient basic wages to live on, forced to work overtime, prevented from taking advantage of medical assistance while on the job, and discouraged from joining a trade union. In some instances union activists are threatened, blacklisted and even fired. Arnold et al (2003) reports that workers in a Bangladesh factory said that they are expected to work virtually every day of the year. Overtime pay, a legal requirement, is often not paid. Employees who refuse to comply are fired.

McDougall (2008) reports that the huge fashion store Primark (trading under the name "Penneys" in Ireland) sacked three of its suppliers in June 2008 after an investigation for the BBC's Panorama and the Observer uncovered children labouring long hours in dire conditions in Indian refugee camps to produce some of its cheapest garments. Campaigners are now demanding that the UK government acts to force companies to be responsible for the welfare of workers in their supply chains. Primark claims it is an ethical organisation, as evidenced by their swift response to the BBC's Panorama investigation. Critics are not convinced. Primark give value for money, but at what cost? Customers should be aware of the ethical issues involved in buying clothes from retailers like Primark.

Unions network with other trade unions throughout the world to monitor labour abuses and so are aware of unethical working practices in different countries. A company with good ethics will have a code of conduct and will also ensure that its contractors abide by it.

Unions and public awareness

The actions of trade unions have brought labour abuses to the attention of the general public from time to time. During the period of apartheid in South Africa unions were very much instrumental in highlighting the injustice of segregation to the rest of the world and organising boycotts of produce. This eventually made the apartheid system unsustainable. The International Labour Organisations also tries to improve labour practices throughout the world.

Unions put subtle pressure on retail clothes shops and government departments to desist from doing business with sweatshops overseas. If this doesn't work they often boycott retail outlets who stock the products of such companies or who deal with oppressive regimes. Responding to union pressure, companies such as Nike and Gap have endeavoured to get rid of the worst labour practices from their contract factories.

Unions and some consumers are concerned about the appalling working conditions and low pay that workers in third level countries have to endure to meet the needs of the rich developed world. TV documentaries have been produced highlighting the problems. The toy and garment

industry, in third world countries, employ labour practices that are little better than slavery. Employees work twelve to sixteen hour shifts for little or no pay. By outsourcing work to such sweatshops suppliers are able to supply toys and clothes to retailers at very competitive prices.

> **"A man's true wealth is the good he does in this world."**
>
> Mohammed

Most retailers are unaware or not interested in knowing the conditions under which the clothes they sell in their shops are produced. They should confront the ethical issues involved in supporting suppliers who underpay and exploit their work force and force them to work in inhuman conditions. Besides the ethics involved, being linked to a supplier who violates human rights can be very damaging to a company's image and reputation.

Unions and multinationals

Multinationals have no hesitation moving elsewhere to take advantage of cheap labour, gain tax advantages and take advantage of less strict or non-existent environmental regulations. Alcoa, the world's largest producer of aluminium exploits local labour in Mexico. *Ethical Consumer* (Sept/Oct 2002) reported that in August, 2001, when Mexican workers made it known that they wanted to organise, the company threatened to take its operations to other countries such as China. At the time it was building a 5,000-employee factory in Nicaragua where it hopes to pay workers as little as 38 cents per hour.

Ethical Consumer (July/August 2004) reported that American workers' rights group, the National Labour Committee (NLC), released a new report in March about the Niagra factory in Bangladesh, which produced clothes for Disney and ASDA. Twenty-two union members at the factory who demanded their legal overtime pay were allegedly beaten, fired, and imprisoned on false charges. The factory apparently requires 19 hour shifts, pays no overtime and denies maternity leave and benefits. The NLC wants the basic legal rights of workers to be respected. It seems that otherwise ethical companies are prepared to turn a blind eye to the activities of their suppliers in third world countries.

Arnold et al (2003) reports that an El Salvadoran Ministry of Labour study, funded by the United States Agency for International Development, found widespread violation of labour laws, including flagrant violation of the freedom to organise and unionise, in factories that supply multinationals. The Ministry of Labour suppressed the report after factory owners complained. It is not unusual that multinationals may seek to

exploit local labour conditions as after all the reasons they went to these areas was probably because of a cheap and a plentiful labour supply, lack of labour law enforcement and poor health and safety standards.

Unions and child labour

Ethical Consumer (June/July 2003) highlights a recent report by Human Rights Watch, based on interviews with local children. It showed that the average age at which children started on the Dole Food Company's supplier plantations in Ecuador was around eleven and a half, with some starting as early as eight or nine. Even more worrying were the serious violations of their rights: pre-teen girls were subjected to sexual harassment and exposed to a range of pesticides, generally without adequate protection, resulting in health problems.

> "You never expect justice from a company, did you? They have neither a soul to lose, nor a body to kick."
>
> Sydney Smith

Cocoa is a major ingredient of chocolate. *Ethical Consumer* (Oct/Nov 2002) reported that a survey published in July 2002 into child labour carried out by the International Institute of Tropical Agriculture in Ivory Coast, Cameroon, Ghana and Nigeria found the majority of children working on cocoa farms were under 14. About one third of school age children living in cocoa producing households had never been to school. Famous brand names, Mars and Nestlé buy large amounts of cocoa from the Ivory Coast. The ethical issues here are about the exploitation of children – a practice that would be unacceptable in the developed world.

Innovative solution to ethical dilemma

However, the situation is not all bad as the following case illustrates. Arnold (2003) reports that even companies with sound codes of conduct, and appropriate methods of verifying compliance, still confront labour practice challenges and ethical dilemmas. For example, if child labour is discovered in a supplier factory, the easy solution may be to end the employment of children. However, without school as an alternative the children may end up working under substantially worse circumstances such as prostitution and street begging. When confronted with such a situation Levi Strauss came up with an innovative solution. It made an unprecedented arrangement whereby children under the age of 14 at the factory would continue to receive their wages, but would attend school at

the factory site. Levis paid for tuition, books, and uniforms. The factories promised to offer the children a job at the plant when they turned fourteen.

Fair Labour Association (FLA)

Geller (2003) reports that the FLA found that workers in some overseas factories making products for Adidas, Levi's, Reebok and other international brands were forced to work overtime and fired after becoming pregnant or trying to form a union. The FLA was founded in 1999. It promotes a code of conduct based on international labour standards, conducts independent monitoring of labour practices and co-ordinates public reports by factory inspectors. Its board members include representatives of US colleges and universities, as well as human rights and consumer groups. It grew out of a government task force formed during the Clinton Administration that looked at working conditions of apparel makers after negative media publicity beginning in 1996.

The report, which charts findings from 185 visits to factories in 30 countries by FLA, inspectors lists numerous instances of poor working conditions, underpayment, overwork and other abuses. Some of the problems and violations listed in the report include:

♦ Employees at a Vietnam factory that makes bags and accessories for Adidas told inspectors they were often barred from leaving the plant and made to work overtime. Also, workers were disciplined for visiting the toilet outside permitted hours.
♦ Workers at factories in the Philippines, one making products for famous brands Levi Strauss & Co. and the other for Nike, reported being required to take pregnancy tests when applying for the job and while being employed. Those found to be pregnant were not hired. Similarly, workers at the Adidas plant in Vietnam said women who got pregnant were fired.
♦ At a plant in El Salvador that makes sportswear for Reebok International Ltd. and Adidas, inspectors were told that workers who tried to form a union were fired.
♦ At the Nike plant in the Philippines, workers who were late by a half-hour to an hour were docked 30 per cent of a day's pay.
♦ An Indonesian firm making goods for Reebok didn't think it necessary to put finger guards on its sewing machines.
♦ A Hong Kong sweatshop supplying socks to Adidas employed children, fired its workers if they didn't show up for five days, and withheld 60 per cent of their wages until the end of the year to stop them from leaving.

- Chinese factories routinely confiscate new workers' residency papers, making it hard for them to leave. Also, workers are not allowed to form unions.

All the news is not bad, however. Foster (2004) reports that FLA gave Reebok its stamp of approval after it verified that the shoe and apparel maker had implemented standards protecting workers in its footwear factories around the world. Standards included banning child labour, forced labour, abuse and discrimination, and guaranteeing health and safety of workers and freedom of association and collective bargaining. The FLA's workplace code of conduct covers such issues as forced labour, child labour, harassment or abuse, non-discrimination, health and safety, freedom of association and collective bargaining, wages and benefits, hours of work and overtime compensation.

Transparency International (TI)

TI is the best known and most highly regarded non-governmental organisation dedicated to the fight against bribery and corruption. TI works through more than ninety national chapters worldwide to prevent corruption and encourage systematic reform. Its mission is to curb corruption through international and national coalitions encouraging governments to establish and implement effective laws, policies and anti-corruption programmes.

It provides information and conducts research into bribery and corruption. Its best-known reports are the Corruption Perceptions Index and the Bribe Payers Index. These are used to chart the scale of worldwide corruption. Generally the index shows that rich countries have the least amount of corruption while poor countries have the most. International organisations such as the EU, World Bank, the United Nations and the OECD have adopted many of TI's ideas and principles on bribery and corruption.

TI's influence on business

TI's business principles for countering bribery have been adopted by many of the world's largest companies. It has formulated a set of anti-money-laundering principles for the banking industry. In politics it has promoted greater financial transparency in election campaigning. It has worked with businesses and governments to fight corruption in public contracting. It has campaigned alongside other non-governmental bodies for international oil companies to publish payments to governments and other

state oil companies. This will give a more transparent picture of the source of state revenues. In many instances oil payments have disappeared into the offshore bank accounts of politicians and other public officials.

> **"Secrecy is the badge of fraud."**
>
> Sir John Chadwick

Generally it has encouraged business to eschew all forms of bribery and corruption in domestic and international trade. TI concludes that corruption in large public contracts is a major obstacle to sustainable development. It causes a significant loss of public funds for education, healthcare and poverty alleviation, both in developed and developing countries.

Summary

Major scandals in politics, health, the medical profession and the church further highlight the inherent weaknesses of the human condition and the need for public awareness and vigilance. The most esteemed professions and institutions have fallen from their pedestals.

The scandals in the various professions and the breach of trust involved now means that people are left with serious reservations as to whom to trust. The former role models and pillars of society have all taken a tumble including politicians, doctors, lawyers, and priests.

Ethical issues affecting trade unions include recognition, and representation rights in order to be able to negotiate with employers on behalf of their members. It is only right that membership of a trade union should be on a voluntary basis. Trade unions have vigorously campaigned against the wrongs of sweatshops and child labour. The FLA was founded to improve working conditions in overseas plants. They have drawn up their own workplace code of conduct that members agree to abide by. Transparency International is a non-governmental body dedicated to the fight against corruption in business and government.

Check Your Ethics Quotient

(circle the appropriate response)

1. Unethical behaviour in politics is a worldwide problem. True   False

2. FLA was founded to improve working conditions in overseas plants. True   False

3. Bribery is a problem in political life. True   False

4. Medical doctors always abide by the Hippocratic oath. True   False

5. Professions tend to close ranks when confronted with ethical complaints from the public. True   False

6. Sexual abuse has proved to be endemic in the Church. True   False

7. In handling ethical complaints the Church proved to be open and transparent. True   False

8. Cosmetic surgery though legal may be considered unethical. True   False

9. Telling lies or being economical with the truth is endemic in politics. True   False

10. Because of its training the legal profession does not engage in unethical practices. True   False

Total the number of true and false responses and check Appendix 2 at the back of the book for the solution.

Case study: Father John Geoghan's abuse has cost millions of dollars.

Dreher (2002) reports that a Father John Geoghan spent 36 years molesting scores of children in at least three Boston area parishes. These included a four-year-old boy and seven boys in an extended family. Documents show that the top levels of the archdiocese had long been aware of Geoghan's abuse of children but failed to take any action. Cardinal Law's predecessors knew about Geoghan and Law was told about him when he took over in 1984. Law nevertheless approved Geoghan as pastor of St Julia's parish, where he would go on to molest more children.

Geoghan had been treated at institutions for sexually abusive priests but it didn't seem to do him much good. After more treatment the archdiocese returned him to the parish where he went on to abuse more children. After leaving parish work in 1993, Geoghan was assigned to the chaplaincy of a nursing home, but continued to seek out and abuse children. By the time Geoghan was convicted in the first of three criminal trials more than 130 people had come forward, claiming to have been sexually assaulted by Geoghan when they were children. The Church has paid millions of dollars to settle civil suits for Geoghan's abuse, and faces 90 more suits. Pope John Paul 11 defrocked Geoghan in 1998. Geoghan was imprisoned but was murdered in prison by a fellow prisoner.

Questions

- ◆ Why do you think that even though Geoghan's superiors knew about what was going on, they did nothing about it?
- ◆ Do you think sexual abuse is endemic in the Church or is it just as likely to happen in other professions such as teaching?
- ◆ What action should the Church take to stamp out the problem of sexual abuse within its ranks?

11. Corporate Governance

> ◆ What is corporate governance?
> ◆ What are the best practices of corporate governance?
> ◆ What are the six guiding principles of governance?
> ◆ Why are audit committees necessary?
> ◆ What is the function of a remuneration committee?

"The biggest corporations, like the humblest private citizen, must be held to strict compliance with the will of the people".

Theodore Roosevelt

Just like countries companies need to be governed in a democratic, accountable, equitable and transparent way. The implementation of good principles of corporate governance will go some way in ensuring that this is done. Audit committees and remuneration committees are needed to oversee the process and to make sure that good principles of business ethics are adhered to.

Definition of corporate governance

The structure of companies creates a gap between the shareholders who own the company and the senior executives who manage the company on their behalf. Corporate governance is the term used to describe the regulation and control of the way a business is managed, including in particular the way in which boards of directors oversee the running of a company by its managers. The objective of good corporate governance is to ensure that senior executives act not only in the interests of shareholders but also in the interests of stakeholders generally. Unless the shareholder owns a big block of shares he will have little power to influence executive decisions and hold the executives accountable.

Companies that are well governed generally outperform others and are better able to attract investors and qualified staff to meet the growth needs of the business.

Corporate greed

Corporate greed is alive and well and thriving in our boardrooms. Gordon Grekko, the financial wizard in the film *Wall Street* famously said that greed is good. It seems that some senior executives believe in this saying. Huge executive salaries, unjustified bonuses, generous stock option plans, golden handshakes, enormous pensions and fraudulent accounting are just some of the issues highlighted in the recent past.

> "The avaricious man is like the barren sandy ground of the desert which sucks in all the rain and dew with greediness, but yields no fruitful herbs or plants for the benefit of others."
>
> Zeno of Citium

Greed often motivates ambitious expansion plans funded by excessive debt, which eventually brings down the company. In the past executives have failed to exercise due diligence (i.e. making sure the proposed purchase is value for money) when taking over other companies. Such investments often drain the cash resources of the company and may eventually result in financial ruin.

Despite auditors and shareholders boards of directors seem to be able to invest in unduly risky projects and award themselves excessive remuneration packages. Think about the more prominent business scandals and the lavish executive life-styles, high-risk strategies and massive fraud within the senior management ranks often with the active complicity of auditors and other board members. Some executives were able to treat corporate assets like their own personal fiefdom.

> "From top to bottom of the ladder, greed is aroused without knowing where to find ultimate foothold. Nothing can calm it, since its goal is far beyond all it can attain. Reality seems valueless by comparison with the dream of fevered imaginations; reality is therefore abandoned."
>
> Emile Durkheim

The concept that the board of directors represents shareholders and the CEO reports to the board is sometimes a myth. In practice the board often reports to and represents the CEO. Thus the exorbitant reward packages

that have come to light in recent financial scandals often with the blatant approval of the board. It is obvious that some constraints on the power of the CEO are necessary.

If all CEOs and directors were ethical there would be no need for regulation. Since this is not the case we have a definite need for good corporate governance. Greed, dishonesty, corruption and selfishness are just as prevalent in the ranks of senior executives as they are in the general population. The frailty of the human condition with its tendency to be dishonest is a feature of life.

"Greed is all right, by the way ... I think greed is healthy. You can be greedy and still feel good about yourself. "

Ivan F. Boesky

Best practice

The best practices in corporate governance recommended by the Cadbury report, other reports and an amalgam of good practice adopted by the best companies, provides as follows:

Directors

♦ Only independent non-executive directors should sit on the board committees that oversee the three functions central to effective governance, audit, corporate governance, and compensation.

♦ A majority of board members should be independent non-executive directors. It is important that they were not previously executives with the company to prevent conflict of interests. Non-executive directors bring an independent outside view and special expertise.

♦ The performance of the CEO should be regularly and formally evaluated. The reward package should be based on performance and comply with good ethics. In practice we have seen senior executives being rewarded even when the company is doing badly.

♦ Remuneration committees should be appointed to set realistic but ethical salaries for senior executives. No one individual should be in a position to influence their remuneration level. Senior executives' salaries should be published in the annual report and accounts. Golden handshakes and executive retirement packages should come under scrutiny to ensure that they are reasonable and appropriate.

♦ Potential conflicts of interest should be made public. Every employee and director has a duty to avoid business interests which conflict with

those of their company's business and which may undermine and compromise their loyalty to the company.

♦ Loans to directors and corporate officers should be prohibited. Some of the big companies that collapsed had loans outstanding to directors.

♦ The positions of chairman and chief executive officer should always be separate. It not a good idea to combine the two roles in one person. The chairman should review the performance of the chief executive and the board. This ensures that no one person has unfettered powers of decision and control. If the two roles are merged there is a loss in checks and balances that may result in a decrease in vigilance in the company's management. Power may centre in one individual who may use the position for personal gain at the expense of the stakeholders of the company. A culture of greed and corruption may ensue.

♦ Directors should get appropriate training to equip them for their role. They particularly need training in financial literacy as some claimed during recent financial scandals that they did not understand the financial statements.

♦ Board members and the chief financial officer should accept ultimate responsibility for the contents of the financial reports rather than the auditors. Under US law they must certify the financial statements. These statements should be timely, relevant and easily understood by users.

♦ Senior executives should not compromise personal character and values for power and prospects of promotion. They are just as prone to temptation as the rest of us.

♦ High turnover of senior executives – often an early warning sign that serious ethical problems are arising in the company – should be investigated rather than ignored.

♦ Directors should make sure that the company operates within the law and that senior executives set the right example. The only way to prevent scandal is to have strong values of honesty and integrity emanating from the top.

> "Faultless honesty is a sine qua non of business life. Not alone the honesty according to the moral code and the Bible. When I speak of honesty I refer to the small, hidden, evasive meanness of our natures. I speak of the honesty of ourselves to ourselves."
>
> Alice Foote MacDougall

♦ Fraud of any kind by senior managers must be prevented, and immediately litigated if discovered.

- Recruitment criteria for executives should include character values such as honesty and integrity, and extensive reference checks should be part of the process.

> **"Honesty is the first chapter in the book of wisdom."**
>
> Thomas Jefferson

Shareholders

- Shareholders should approve of stock options and the restriction of stock option plans in which directors or executives can participate. Stock options should be accounted for in the financial statements.
- Shareholders should actively monitor ethical practice, and should raise concerns if they become aware that the company engages in unethical practices such as creative accounting. This applies particularly to Institutional investors such as pension funds and insurance companies which represent thousands of individual shareholders, because of their power, are in a particular strong position to voice their concerns at company annual general meetings or indeed privately.

> **"Love is blind, and greed insatiable."**
>
> Chinese proverb

Auditors

- Audit committees should be appointed to oversee the financial reports and given appropriate powers.
- Auditors should be rotated every few years. This is one way of breaking up the cosy relationship that may develop between external auditors and companies.
- Trust but verify should be the motto. It is no longer enough to accept the mere word of a director or responsible official no matter how seemingly trustworthy. Auditors must independently verify and check things out for themselves.
- Where a company officer was previously employed by an audit firm, that firm should not be allowed to act as auditor to the company.
- Auditing and consulting services should be separately sourced to eliminate this potential source for a conflict of interest.
- An internal audit department should be appointed for the detection and prevention of fraud and the maintenance of ethics in the financial area. This should be independent of the finance function and liaise with the

audit committee, as otherwise it will only do the dictates of the finance director. Sometimes the internal audit function reports to the audit committee. Poor cash and stock control systems may provide opportunities for employees to steal. Therefore, both good ethics and good business require that internal controls and internal checks are necessary for the protection of the assets and staff of the company. The statutory audit provides a similar function for the annual accounts. (Note that internal audit is primarily designed to deter rather than detect fraud.)

♦ Complex balance sheets should be avoided, and particular care must be exercised regarding off-balance-sheet transactions, contingencies, and unconsolidated entities.

♦ Ethics training should be provided for all employees, but for accountants in particular. Most accounting degree programmes now have an ethics component. Accountants need to have an appreciation of the moral and ethical dimensions of accounting decisions.

Corporate Governance

♦ Companies should publish details of their corporate governance regime so that everyone, from managers and employees to potential investors, understands the rules under which the company is operating.

♦ Employees should be provided with a way to alert management and the board about potential misconduct, without fear of retribution. In other words there should be whistleblower protection for employees. Periodically conduct anonymous employee surveys to ascertain the standard of business ethics prevailing in the company. There should be zero tolerance for breaches of corporate ethics and strict disciplinary procedures in operation.

"A corporation cannot blush."

Howell Walsh

Six guiding principles for governance

Rezaee et al (2003) reports that the Business Roundtable, an association of chief executive officers of leading American corporations, has proposed six guiding principles of corporate governance:

1. The board of directors should select a chief executive officer (CEO) and oversee the CEO and other top executive activities.

2. Management is responsible for operating the company in an effective and ethical manner with the goal of creating shareholder value.
3. Management is responsible for preparing financial statements, under the oversight of the board of directors and its audit committee, that fairly present the financial condition and results of operations of the company.
4. The board of directors and its audit committee should engage an independent accounting firm to perform financial statement audits.
5. The independent accounting firm should maintain an independence in fact and in appearance, conduct the audit in accordance with generally accepted auditing standards (GAAS), inform the board through the audit committee of any concerns regarding the quality and integrity of the financial reporting process. In the UK and Ireland audits must comply with Statements of Standard Accounting Practice (SSAPs) and Financial Reporting Standards (FRPs).
6. Companies have responsibilities to deal with their employees in a fair and equitable manner.

Audits

Audits are not foolproof. They have many limitations. Audit committees are needed to oversee the process.

Limitations of audit

Firms of accountants who are supposed to bring probity and objectivity to the financial statements have often signed off on accounts, which have subsequently proved to be unreliable, misleading and even fraudulent. In practice the ability of auditors to detect fraud is limited. Obviously the auditors can't check everything. They only look at a sample of transactions to verify the internal controls are operating satisfactorily. They also only concern themselves with material transactions that have a significant effect on the financial statements.

> "Corporate bodies are more corrupt and profligate than individuals, because they have more power to do mischief, and are less amenable to disgrace and punishment."
>
> William Hazlitt

In large companies, external auditors rely on the expertise of the internal auditors and the financial executives in the finance department. They use

their discretion and judgement as to what to accept as genuine and valid and what to pursue with further investigations. The primary responsibility for the operation of the company's controls lies with the directors. Bearing all this in mind the auditors' report is not proof that the accounts are reliable.

Audit committees

Audit committees are expected to oversee corporate governance, financial reporting, internal controls, internal audit function, and external audit services. To carry out its role competently the audit committee should be independent, competent, financially literate, adequately resourced and properly compensated. Independence has been defined as not receiving, other than for service on the board, any consulting, advisory, or other compensatory fee from the company, and not being an affiliated person of the company, or any subsidiary thereof. Thus conflicts of interest are avoided.

The audit committee should consist of at least three members and meet about four times a year. Some experts maintain that these should be made up exclusively of non-executive directors. It is recommended that at least one member of the audit committee should have financial expertise. This expertise includes the ability to read and understand company accounts including the profit and loss account, balance sheet and cash flow statement. A written charter for the committee should be developed and approved, reviewed and revised by the board as necessary.

Key functions

Key functions of the audit committee include:

♦ Review of the quarterly, half-yearly and annual accounts with management and the external auditors before they are submitted to the board for approval. The report of the audit committee is to ensure that auditors have no conflict of interests affecting their objectivity, integrity and independence.
♦ Review with the external auditors the nature and scope of the audit.
♦ Review the internal audit function and any significant findings or internal investigations. Investigate any significant concerns of the internal audit function. Co-ordinate the work of the internal and external audits.
♦ Review of the external auditor's fee and appointment. Non-executive directors should be given sole responsibility for choosing the auditors.

- Require auditors to report to shareholders and the audit committee on instances of questionable accounting.
- Ensure that external auditors comply with the codes of ethics laid down by their professional accountancy bodies and that the accounting statements are in conformity with accounting standards.
- Engage the services of advisors as appropriate.
- Annually, review the programme that management establishes to monitor compliance with the company's code of ethics.
- Report annually to shareholders on how the audit committee have fulfilled their responsibility.

Remuneration committee

The general public has a reasonable ethical concern about the exorbitant remuneration packages often awarded to senior executives. In relation to the average wage, senior executives' salaries have grown enormously over the past ten years. Thus the setting of such remuneration packages should be seen to be above reproach. The remuneration committee should be made up of independent non-executive directors. Decisions on executive directors' remuneration packages should be delegated to the remuneration committee. Shareholder approval should be sought for new, long-term incentive plans.

Key tasks of the remuneration committee include:

- Recommendations for the remuneration of the chairman, chief executive officer and executive directors.
- Ideally directors' contracts should be for period of one year or less.
- Consideration of the board nominations, succession planning and senior management appointments.

Blue Ribbon Committee conclusions

The Blue Ribbon Committee (BRC 1999) revealed the following three conclusions regarding the oversight responsibility of corporate governance including the audit committee:

1. Quality financial reporting can only be achieved through open and candid communication and close working relationships among the corporation's board of directors audit committee, management, internal auditors, and external auditors.

2. Strengthening corporate governance oversight in the financial reporting process of public quoted companies will reduce instances of financial statement fraud.

3. Integrity, quality, and transparency of financial reports improve investors' confidence in the capital market while incidents of financial statement fraud diminish such confidence.

Summary

Corporate governance is how boards of directors oversee the running of a company by its managers, and how board members in turn are accountable to the shareholders and stakeholders of the company.

Best practices of corporate governance include control of stock options, design and publication of good governance guidelines, and ensuring that a majority of board members are non-executive directors. The position of chairman and chief executive should be kept separate.

Audit committees are expected to oversee corporate governance, financial reporting, internal controls, internal audit function, and external audit services. The need and importance of the audit committee and the internal audit function has been highlighted by recent corporate financial scandals which showed that financial statements certified by external auditors were later shown to be unreliable or even fraudulent.

Remuneration committees are needed to oversee the payment of the chief executive and directors and to ensure that they are paid on a fair basis and that there is no abuse of power. The lavish remuneration packages of senior executive has come in for a lot of criticism in recent times.

Remuneration committees are needed to oversee the payment of the chief executive and directors and to ensure that they are paid on a fair basis and that there is no abuse of power. The lavish remuneration packages of senior executive has come in for a lot of criticism in recent times.

Check Your Ethics Quotient

(circle the appropriate response)

1. Corporate governance tries to ensure that senior executives only act in the interests of shareholders.   True   False

2. Auditors only usually look at a sample of transactions to verify internal controls and systems are operating satisfactorily.   True   False

3. Stock options should not be accounted for in the financial statements.   True   False

4. A majority of the board of directors should be independent non-executive directors.   True   False

5. One person should hold the chairman and chief executive positions.   True   False

6. Audit committees should be appointed to oversee the financial reports.   True   False

7. The board of directors and chief financial officer should be held responsible for the financial reports.   True   False

8. Auditors should be rotated every few years.   True   False

9. A remuneration committee should monitor the salaries of directors.   True   False

10. The audit committee should consist of at least two members and should meet once a year.   True   False

Total the number of true and false responses and check Appendix 2 at the back of the book for the solution.

Case study: When corporate governance fails

The Australian retailer, Harris Scarfe had been in business for 150 years. On 2nd April 2001 it was placed into voluntary administration. Irregularities going back six years had been discovered. In their report to creditors, the administrators highlighted that the systematic overstatement of profit had been funded by increased debt, both by the bank and creditors.

Alan Hodgson, the chief financial officer, had altered the company's accounts to inflate profits. He had created a false picture that Harris Scarfe was in good financial health, permitting it to trade when it was virtually insolvent. In testimony given to the South Australian Supreme Court, Hodgson told the court that he had effectively authorised accounts to be changed at will, if a particular result was required by the company's managing director or the chairman. Hodgson was jailed for six years.

Apart from the fraudulent accounting by the chief financial officer, Alan Hodgson, it was also found that the audit committee lacked independence. The company had an audit committee of three, two of whom were from within the company including Alan Hodgson and only one independent and they only met twice a year. In addition, the auditors, Ernst and Young and PricewaterhouseCoopers, are being sued to recover at least A$70 million by the major creditor, ANZ bank, alleging negligence for not uncovering the discrepancies over a number of years.

Also, a shareholder has brought a class action against the directors. They allege that the directors engaged in false, deceptive and misleading conduct over a five-year period. The shareholder claims that as a result of the deceptive statements, investors paid more than the "true market value" of the shares and eventually lost the opportunity to sell their shares.*

Questions

◆ Identify clearly the corporate governance failures and how they could have been prevented?

- What was wrong with the way the audit committee was constituted and operating?
- Is it possible for external auditors to discover all discrepancies in the accounting system and financial statements?

(*Adapted from "The Mad Hatter's corporate tea party" by Philomena Leung and Barry J Cooper, Managerial Auditing Journal, Vol. 18, No.6/7 2003. Pp 505-516.)

12. Lessons for Ethical Compliance

- ♦ How can you create an ethical workplace?
- ♦ What are the lessons for the professions?
- ♦ What are the best compliance standards?
- ♦ What is the model for resolving ethical dilemmas?
- ♦ Why is regulation necessary?

"Anyone entrusted with power will abuse it if not also animated with the love of truth and virtue"

Jean de la Fontaine

In many professions self-regulation has not worked and the government has stepped in with appropriate legislation to protect the general public.

Ethical scandals have implications for managers, employees, politicians, medical practitioners, the church, and the judicial system. Those for directors, shareholders and auditors have been dealt with in the previous chapter. Recommendations for creating an ethical workplace are set down. A systematic problem solving approach is useful for dealing with ethical dilemmas.

Codes and compliance

The following are recommendations derived from previous chapters for creating an ethical workplace:

- ♦ Every company should have a code of business ethics including a section on frequently asked questions. All employees should get a copy and instruction in its use. An individual's capacity to rationalise unethical actions on the grounds of expediency or pragmatism or on the basis that everybody is doing it is unlimited and it is often surprising who will become involved in doubtful behaviour. It has been

found that when business executives are faced with an ethical dilemma, they tend to opt for the profitable and expedient course of action rather than the ethical one. Hence the need for a code of ethics to set standards and monitor compliance.

- In many companies, ethics and values are just for show and mere platitudes. Companies must widely publicise their code and get employees to sign annually that they have not breached the principles. But that doesn't mean that they are going to be actually put into practice and have real substance. Codes need to be actively managed and monitored to ensure compliance. Unless staff are constantly reminded about the need for ethics, standards tend to deteriorate.

- Not only should there be a corporate code but there should also be codes for each department. Functional codes will meet the particular needs and issues that arise in areas such as finance, marketing, purchasing and property where there are more temptations and opportunities than elsewhere for unethical behaviour.

- Multinationals should apply the same standard of ethics at home and abroad.

- The code should also apply to suppliers and contractors.

- Refresher training at all levels should be a feature of any serious ethics training initiative. Practical case studies, checklists, critical incidents and role-play related to organisational realities should be incorporated into the training process. These form the basis for syndicated discussion, analysis and problem solving.

- Boardroom training in ethics should be a feature of any programmes. It is essential that ethical awareness start at the top and cascades down to all levels. In addition, senior managers, middle managers, first line managers, supervisors and indeed work colleagues should be exemplars of ethical behaviour.

- A confidential phone line including an ethics office, ombudspersons and various monitoring and enforcement procedures should be in operation including disciplinary procedures for unethical behaviour.

- Hire and promote staff with good character and ethical standards. This is the foundation for good ethics in the company.

- Compliance programmes should be integrated into the operations of the company. The programme should prove the ancient maxim: An ounce of prevention is worth a pound of cure.

- Political contributions should be limited in size, controlled and made transparent to public scrutiny.

- There is a need to reward rather than punish whistleblowers. Their position should be protected in law. Many scandals would not have seen the light of day without the help of whistleblowers.
- Stakeholders should be given the same priority as shareholders.

Conclusion on ethics

Lewis (1985) summarises the conclusions of previous research done on business ethics as follows:

- Sound ethics are good business.
- Profit should not be the sole motive for business.
- Middle and lower levels of management feel the most pressure to compromise personal standards.
- Competition can cause persons to concentrate on the bottom line and ignore ethics.
- The person most likely to act ethically is one with a well-defined personal code of values.
- Persons with an ethical superior are likely to behave ethically.
- Ethics tend to be highest with the youngest employees and those in the final decade of their careers.
- Pressure from superiors to achieve results cause unethical behaviour.
- The more employees and managers are taught to identify with and be loyal to their companies the more they are encouraged to abdicate personal responsibility for their actions.
- Good interpersonal communication and interaction helps employees to emulate the good personal ethics of others.

Model for resolving ethical issues

Managers are expected to be as skilled in ethical and moral reasoning as they are in economic reasoning. The following problem solving model may be useful to managers for resolving ethical issues:

1. Define the problem and the ideal outcomes for the situation where ethical issues have been identified. One way to help you define an ethical problem is to look at the difference between the expected outcome and the actual outcome. The way you define the problem will determine what alternatives will be considered. Therefore, it is important to define the problem carefully.
2. Define the specific ethical issues or conflicts involved. Collect any facts relevant to the problem. How many people jump to conclusions without

first establishing the facts? Consider the legal situation, the company's code of business ethics, expressed key values and any other known guidelines such as company policy. If it is illegal, then don't do it. If you are unsure then get a legal expert to check it out. Remember something can be unethical but still legal. For example, in the case of a business gift ask yourself whether the gift is legal and reasonable or whether it would embarrass the company if it were disclosed publicly. Discuss the issue with other managers and professionals within the company. In particular, the HRM manager and the internal audit manager would be worth consulting. Get as many viewpoints as possible. Consider some of the philosophical approaches discussed in Chapter one to the solution of ethical problems such as deontology or utilitarianism for guidance. If you are a member of a professional body make sure that what you propose to do is within their code of professional practice.

3. Identify difficult obstacles to resolving the ethical issues and determine how to overcome them. Consider the issue from the various stakeholder perceptions.

4. Develop alternative solutions to the problem and prioritise each in relation to ethical standards. Legal but unethical options can still produce social sanctions such as loss of image and custom, and the public shunning of unethical management and their company.

5. Select the best solution having regard to known ethical principles including the company's code of business ethics, your professional body's code of ethics, the legal situation and personal values. Don't ignore your intuition. As a person of character and integrity how does it feel? Arthur Andersen's would still be in business if its auditors complied with the code of professional ethics of their accountancy body and operated in accordance with ordinary standards of decency.

6. Determine an action plan to implement your decision and consider the parties that will be affected by the decision. Use your empathy skills here to imagine what it feels like to be in their shoes.

7. Identify likely reactions and rewards, and determine how to sell the solution. To do this effectively you will have to take into account the concerns of various stakeholder groups including the media. Think through how you will justify your actions to the various groups. Consider whether you would be proud to see the reaction to your decision on the front page of the national newspaper or reported on prime time TV. Thomas Jefferson said: "Never suffer a thought to be harboured in your mind which you would not avow openly. When tempted to do anything in secret, ask yourself if you would do it in public. If you would not, be

sure it is wrong." Resolve the ethical issues by making the appropriate decision and justifying it.

8. Follow up to ensure that the solution worked. If not, what can you learn from the post-mortem? You may be able to apply lessons to future ethical issues.

This problem-solving approach will help managers to realise the situational nature of ethical problems and analyse and solve them logically. Although the model is presented in a linear format, in practice it may not be necessary or you may not have the time to go through all the steps or each step sequentially. One of the most common faults in ethical decision-making is to ignore the long-term consequences of the decision and not to take the wider effects of the decision on the various stakeholders into account. Managers may be tempted to choose the profitable and expedient course of action rather than the ethical.

Regulation

Regulation may be by law or through a code of professional conduct. In many instances self-regulation has proved to be unsatisfactory.

The law

The law now proscribes conduct that was previously considered acceptable if not ethical. Conduct that once only earned reprimand and embarrassment may now have more serious legal implications. The price for not adhering to the law includes massive fines, imprisonment, and even threats to the continued existence of the business. Thus executives who ignore the law run the risk of personal and corporate liability in today's increasingly tough legal environment as well as public humiliation.

The government will eventually fill the void with law if businesses don't adopt ethics voluntarily. For example, in the UK, advice on financial service products such as pensions is now highly regulated. Greater regulation was necessary because banks and insurance companies failed to implement measures to stop pensions from being mis-sold. An insurance representative may have recommended one pension over another to get better commission rather than having the best interests of the client at heart. Now representatives have to be qualified to sell products, complete more paperwork, and disclose commissions to customers.

Ethical issues often result in lawsuits and eventually lead to legislation protecting the public. The law is always a step behind due to rapid technological and social changes. For example, the law is still trying to

catch up with public concerns about the Internet, genetic engineering and cloning.

> "Like nuclear power, genetic engineering is not a neutral technology. It is by its very nature too powerful for our present state of social and scientific development, no matter whose hands are controlling it. Just as we would say, especially after Chernobyl, that a nuclear power plant is just as dangerous in a socialist nation as it is in a capitalist one, so I would say the same thing for genetic engineering. It is inherently Eugenic in that it always requires someone to decide what is good and a bad gene."
>
> Linda Bullard

Most businesses demand less rather than more regulation. Managers maintain that legislation exposes business to more potential lawsuits and discourages them from taking decisions involving risk, innovation, expansion and diversification. Regulation also means more bureaucracy in the form of paperwork and diverts the attention of business away from the core task of attending to business issues and making profits.

Governments have responded to the lobbying of entrepreneurs by deregulating business such as banking, telecommunications and transport. However some of the recent scandals have been in the deregulated sectors such as telecommunications and banking and consequently there is now more demand by the general public for even greater regulation. More laws have been passed to try to ensure that these scandals will not happen again. Tighter laws have made many unethical practices now illegal.

Laws enforcing business ethics

The consequence of all this is a comprehensive regulatory framework that companies must comply with when dealing with most ethical and related issues. Laws now exist covering every aspect of business including employment law, company law, and mercantile law. There are laws covering minimum wages. These were passed because some companies were paying hourly rates that were impossible to live on. Issues such as equality, discrimination, sexual harassment, health and safety, packaging, pricing, monopoly, competition, consumers, advertising and the environment are just some of the areas covered by law.

Laws protecting consumers require that companies provide accurate information about their products and services and that they follow safety standards. There are laws controlling the content of advertisements to

ensure that they are accurate, honest and moral rather than misleading. Environmental laws are very comprehensive and they try to protect the quality of our air, water and land. The harmful effects of toxic waste on our waterways and sea resorts have raised concerns about the proper disposal of these wastes. Health and safety legislation is aimed to protect the safety of workers and customers. Laws promoting equity in the workplace protect the rights of minorities, women, and the disabled. Other employment legislation addresses specific employment issues.

Laws regulating business activities are passed because society including customers, interest groups, competitors and the government, do not trust business to do what is right and equitable in certain areas such as health and safety and the environment. This concern has now been extended to the content of financial statements because the accounting profession seems to be unwilling or incapable of effectively regulating the process. Pro-competition laws are often passed to encourage competition and prevent activities that restrain trade and harm the interest of customers. Ethical businesses acknowledge obligations beyond the requirements of the law. If they don't, the law will eventually step in to close the gap.

Self-regulation by professions

Members of a profession have a fiduciary relationship with their clients. This is a relationship of trust so that any information that passes between them must remain confidential. Violating client trust or confidentiality can results in disciplinary action from your professional body. Medical doctors, managers, accountants, engineers, lawyers, HRM professionals, purchasing officers and marketing professionals all have their own codes of professional business ethics. These codes are voluntary but members in breach may be excluded from practising their profession.

Managers

The British Institute of Management (BIM) has drawn up a professional code of conduct for managers. It includes, among other things, the following stipulations:

♦ Managers when pursuing their personal interests should take account of the interests of others.
♦ They should never maliciously injure the professional reputation or career prospects of others.

- They should declare any personal interest conflicting with company interests.
- They should be concerned for the health, safety and welfare of all.
- They should respect confidentiality.
- They should neither offer nor accept any gift, favour or hospitality intended as, or having the effect of, bribery and corruption.
- They should ensure that all public communications are true and not misleading.

> "Integrity is not a conditional word. It doesn't blow in the wind or change with the weather. It is your inner image of yourself, and if you look in there and see a man who won't cheat, then you know he never will."
>
> John D. MacDonald

Accountants

There are ethical guidelines for accountants to follow when drawing up annual accounts. It seems that many accountants, including the accountants employed by Arthur Andersen in the scandals referred to in earlier chapters of this book, turned a blind eye to their own personal sense of values and professional code of ethics. These codes state among other things that auditors have a duty to act in the public interest, to be free of conflicts of interest and not to misrepresent facts. These codes are supported by Financial Reporting Standards (FRPs). Although they have only quasi-legal status, they are compulsory for members of the accountancy profession to follow.

Governments have passed laws regulating accountancy. For all practical purposes self-regulation no longer exists for the accountancy profession. The establishment of the Irish Auditing and Accountancy Supervisory Authority marks the end of self-regulation of the accountancy profession in Ireland. In the US the *Saranes-Oxley Act* of 2002 has a similar effect. The self-regulation of the legal profession has also come in for major criticism.

Medical

The body regulating the medical profession like the accountancy and legal professions has the power to strike off misbehaving members from their register. In practice this is rarely done and done only in the most extreme cases and after much investigation and public pressure over many years is brought to bear. In many cases the problem has to come into the public domain before anything is done about it. The British Royal Infirmary is a

case in point. Here many babies died during or after surgery because of a club culture operating in the hospital.

In the Harold Shipman case the UK's General Medical Council (GMC) were criticised for allowing Shipman to practice even when it was known that he had a criminal conviction for drug abuse. He had also been fined by the GMC for forging prescriptions. The GMC put the profession's interests ahead of patients. Also it failed to act when it became known about the large number of patients who were dying in Shipman's care.

In the case of Dr Michael Neary who allegedly performed unnecessary Caesarean hysterectomy operations the Irish Medical Council (IMC) were very slow to act. One wonders how this case happened and how it was allowed to go on for so long. Why didn't his nursing and medical colleagues blow the whistle? It was an outside UK consultant commissioned by the Health Board that finally reported that something was wrong. It seems consultants wield enormous power and their decisions are rarely questioned.

> "Power intoxicates men. When a man is intoxicated by alcohol he can recover, but when intoxicated by power he seldom recovers."
>
> James F. Byrnes

Lessons learnt

Dr Muiris Houston (2003), however, reports that lessons have been learnt from the case. The North Eastern Health Board has outlined measures to prevent a recurrence. All Caesarean sections are now reviewed weekly; staff are trained to operate in a multi-disciplinary way; team decision-making is encouraged and a forum for the open and confidential airing of professional concerns has been created. The sixth ethical guide published by the IMC in 2004 states that where a doctor feels the work of a colleague is impaired by ill health or substance abuse, detailed action is expected. This means that whistleblowing is now expected in certain circumstances.

Like the accountancy profession self-regulation by peers is not satisfactory and will always be subject to bias. In the past the police have always been criticised for investigating themselves. Nobody now trusts accountants, bankers or solicitors to police themselves. The Church too has behaved dismally in the regulation of its own members. Church law is no longer accepted as taking precedence over civil law.

Legal

The legal profession has defrauded clients. Some solicitors have been convicted and received jail sentences. They have been known to steal from client accounts to support a lavish lifestyle. The legal profession have also been accused of indulging in anti-competitive practice, of being outdated and being less than accountable and transparent. The distinction between barristers and solicitors is outmoded. Separate representational bodies like the Bar Council and Law Society are seen as duplication of resources and inefficient. Also, self-regulation of lawyers by other lawyers is not seen as satisfactory. Like all professions the priority is to protect their own interests rather than those of the clients.

"Either there are too few professions conducted honestly, or there are too few honest people in their professions".

Denis Diderot

Other Professions

Stockbrokers' and investment analysts' recommendations are often unreliable. They are inclined to forget their ethics in return for record fees and commissions. In addition, there may be a conflict of interest if they are connected to financial institutions selling products in the relevant fields.

Corporate communications and public relations are often no more than media spin. Some even engage in half-truths, deception and downright lying. People now expect spin as a matter of course rather than sincerity from their corporations, politicians, and churches.

"Of all the evil spirits abroad at this hour in the world, insincerity is the most dangerous."

J.A. Froude

Priests are just as capable as the general population to behave in an immoral and unethical way. Therefore they can no longer be trusted to behave morally with children. Third parties should be present when priests deal with children.

Regulations impose minimum standards. Progressive management should aim to surpass these. Remember that there are still many ethical issues not addressed by law. Hence the need for a business code of ethics.

Summary

There are many lessons to be drawn from the ethical scandals. Ethics and values are sometimes just for show and mere platitudes in many companies. Codes should be widely available and signed by employees annually to certify that they have not breached the code.

A systematic problem-solving model is suggested for handling ethical dilemmas. This will help managers to realise the situational nature of ethical problems and solve them logically.

Regulation may be by law or through a code of professional conduct. The law has stepped in where self-regulation has proved to be unsatisfactory.

Check Your Ethics Quotient

(circle the appropriate response)

1. Investment brokers' recommendations are reliable.   True   False

2. Public Relations communications can be relied upon.   True   False

3. It is often surprising who will become involved in unethical behaviour.   True   False

4. When business executives are faced with an ethical dilemma they tend to opt for the profitable and expedient solution.   True   False

5. Refresher training should be a feature of ethics training.   True   False

6. Persons with an ethical superior are just as likely to engage in unethical behaviour.   True   False

7. A problem solving model may be useful for solving ethical dilemmas.   True   False

8. Laws are passed to curb unethical excesses.   True   False

9. Most businesses want more regulations.   True   False

10. Self-regulation by the professions is unsatisfactory.   True   False

Total the number of true and false responses and check Appendix 2 at the back of the book for the solution.

Case study: Irish Financial Services Regulatory Authority (IFSRA)

Creaton (2004) reports that the Irish Financial Regulatory Authority (IFSRA) found that Ireland's biggest bank, AIB, deliberately hid the fact that it had overcharged thousands of customers on foreign exchange transactions more than €30 million for almost eight years. Staff and management who were aware of the overcharging for almost eight years failed to do anything about it. The bank claims that the overcharging was due to an error. A whistleblower brought the overcharging to the attention of the public by alerting IFSRA and RTE, the Irish national television broadcasting service. The IFSRA now intend to speed up the pace of regulation in the industry. The episode is expected to cost AIB more than €50 million in refunds to customers. Up to 10 senior executives in AIB are expected to face disciplinary action because of the revelations.

Speaking on the 7 December 2004, the IFSRA chief executive Liam O'Reilly said: "The failures within AIB uncovered by the investigations are completely unacceptable. We will not tolerate such practices within the financial services industry." In its final report into the scandal, IFSRA said at least seven opportunities arose to identify and disclose the overcharging at the bank between 1998 and 2004, but this had not been done.

The bank's procedures for raising matters "up the line" were found to be inadequate and IFSRA said this contributed to the overcharging persisting so long, along with the weak controls in relation to the monitoring of customer charges. The IFSRA report confirmed that AIB customers were overcharged by a total of €34.2 million, including interest, for a range of services. Around €13.5 million of this had been repaid.

Separately, the IFSRA also found that an offshore company that managed funds belonging to senior AIB executives benefited to the tune of €48,000 from artificial deals. The regulator said the company, Faldor Ltd, was managed by Allied Irish Investment Managers (now called AIBIM), and the €48,000 came out of AIBIM's own funds. IFSRA said it had ordered AIB to respond to the scandals by making all efforts to refund overcharged customers

and to consider and apply disciplinary action against individuals found to be responsible in both issues.

The IFSRA was established on the 1 May 2003. Before that date many cases of unethical behaviour in the financial services sector in Ireland came to light. The IFSRA has extensive powers to conduct formal inquiries where it suspects a contravention of designated legislation or of relevant codes of conduct. It covers bodies from major banks to small brokers. Significantly, it will also apply to "persons concerned in the management" of regulated firms, so that directors and employees may now face personal liability for regulatory breaches.

Sanctions that may be imposed include cautions; reprimands; settlements; directions; and fines of up to €5 million for corporate bodies and €500,000 for individuals. Findings and penalties may be published, thereby adding a reputation penalty. Individuals found to have committed serious breaches may be disqualified from management of regulated firms. There are safeguards including rights to fair procedures and legal representation, and rights of appeal to the Financial Services Appeals Tribunal and the High Court.

Questions

♦ Self-regulation does not work. Discuss.
♦ AIB has been in the headlines for all the wrong reasons. In relation to this and other scandals that have come to light in the banking sector how would you describe the culture operating in Irish banking?
♦ Generally, do you think banks operate in the interest of customers?
♦ If you were the chief executive of AIB what action would you take to improve the standard of business ethics operating in the bank?
♦ What impact do you think that IFSRA will have on the financial services sector in Ireland?

Appendix 1
Ethics Audit Checklist

Environmental issues

♦ Does the company pursue environmentally friendly policies?

♦ Does the company use renewable resources wherever feasible and conserve natural resources where renewable options are not available?

♦ Does the company first reduce; next reuse; then recycle; and finally as a last resort dispose of waste in the safest and most responsible manner?

♦ Is the company committed to the protection of the quality of the land, air and water on which it depends?

♦ Does the company ensure the safety and quality of its products and implement good neighbour policies in the communities in which it operates?

♦ Does the company have contingency plans in place to safeguard the general environment in which it operates and the specific environment within the workplace in the event of fires, floods or other natural disasters?

♦ Does the company observe legal requirements and regulations wherever it operates?

♦ Does the company ensure that environmental laws are complied with at all times and in the event of difficulties these will be reported to the appropriate regulatory authorities?

♦ Is the company committed to continuous education for staff on environmental issues affecting the business?

♦ Is the company open and transparent about the results of its environmental assessments?

Finance and accounting issues

♦ Does the company ensure the accuracy of its books and records and expense reports? In particular are company assets protected from misappropriation and abuse?

♦ Does the company disapprove of creative accounting?

- Does the company refrain from putting pressure on its accountants to compromise their ethics in any way?
- Is the pension fund independent and separate from the rest of the business?
- Does the company treat its suppliers in a fair and equitable manner? In particular does it pay its bill promptly?
- Has the company a policy in place regarding insider dealing?
- Does the company disallow loans to directors?
- Does the company protect the interests of its investors, give them a proper return on investment and communicate effectively with them?
- Has the company the best internal control procedures in place to prevent and detect fraud, false accounting and theft?
- Has the company an audit committee to oversee the audit process?
- Does the company refrain from employing its auditors as management consultants?
- Has the company a remuneration committee to regulate and control executive salaries?
- Has the company an accounting policy in place regarding the appropriate treatments of stock options?
- Has the company a policy in place regarding the use of tax havens?
- In the case of takeovers and mergers does the company undertake a due diligence exercise to ensure that the arrangement is good value for money?

HRM issues

- Does the company treat its employees in a fair and equitable manner? In particular, does the company have appropriate policies in place on recruitment, organisation, training and development, rewards, communication, working conditions, industrial relations, equal employment opportunity, sexual harassment, bullying, work-family balance, retirement, severance and redundancy?
- Does the company respect the human rights of employees?
- Does the company have a policy in place about moonlighting?
- Does the company have a policy in place regarding nepotism?
- Does the company recognise the right of employees to become members of a recognised trade union?
- Does the company have a formal business code of ethics?
- Does the company have a comprehensive ethics compliance programme in place including an ethics office and ethics training for all employees. Is this training ongoing?

- Has the code been given to all employees? Has it been widely publicised throughout the company? Do employees certify acceptance and compliance with the code on an annual basis?
- Does the company have a policy in place about whistleblowing?
- Does the company periodically rotate staff and ensure they take all their leave entitlements?
- Does the company have a disciplinary procedure in place to deal with breaches of ethics?
- Does the company have a policy in place regarding those who undertake research within the company?
- Does the company encourage staff to adopt the highest standards of honesty and integrity in all their dealings?
- Do all staff sign a declaration regarding the confidentiality of company information?

Marketing issues

- Does the company have a policy in place regarding price-fixing?
- Does the company treat its customers in a fair and equitable manner? In particular is priority given to customer needs, fair pricing and after-sales service?
- Does the company treat its competitors in a just and equitable manner? In particular does it comply with anti-trust legislation?
- Does the company have a policy in place to deal with the problem of bribery and corruption?
- Does the company have a corporate policy in place regarding supporting educational and charitable initiatives?
- Does the company disapprove of salespeople putting excessive psychological pressure on customers to buy unneeded or unaffordable products or services?
- Does the company disapprove of bait and switch operations?
- Does the company have a policy in place regarding genetically modified products?
- Does the company refrain from misleading advertising?
- Does the company have a policy in place regarding shoplifting?

Purchasing issues

- Does the company have strict regulations on tendering and purchasing procedures ensuring that they are fair, open and transparent?

- Does the company have a policy in place regarding the making and receiving of gifts, hospitality and entertainment?
- Does the company expect its suppliers and subcontractors to abide by its code of business ethics?
- Does the company conduct on-site ethical audits for subcontractors?

General business issues

- Do managers walk the talk and lead by example in matters relating to business ethics?
- Does the company carry out an annual ethics audit?
- Does the company have a policy in place about the use of animals in the testing of products or raw materials?
- Does the company have a policy in place regarding the making of political contributions?
- Does the company have a policy in place regarding conflicts of interest?
- Does the company have a policy in place regarding cyber crime?
- Does the company avoid spin in its public relations communications with the public?
- Does the company have a policy in place regarding industrial espionage?
- Does the company have appropriate checks and balances in place to prevent abuse of power by Board members and other senior executives?
- Does the company operate the best health and safety practices?
- Obviously the more yes responses to these questions the better the ethical standards of the company.

Appendix 2
Solutions to Ethics Quotient Quiz

Award yourself one point for each correct answer. A score of 8 points or more suggests that your ethical quotient is very good. A score of between 5 and 7 suggests that your ethical quotient is good. A score of 4 points or less suggests that you have plenty of room for improvement.

Chapter 1. 1. True. 2. True. Slavery was once legal but certainly never ethical. 3. True. 4. False. This is the oath followed by medical doctors. 5. True. 6. False. It should never be acceptable. 7. True. 8. True. 9. True. 10. False.

Chapter 2. 1. False. 2. True. 3. False. They are usually placed way down the list. 4. True. 5. False. 6. True. 7. False. 8. True. 9. True. For example, organic food. 10. True.

Chapter 3. 1. True. 2. False but the more ethical ones are doing it. 3. True. 4. True. 5. True. 6. True. 7. False. Bottom line considerations usually take precedence over ethics. 8. False. Some countries have non-existent or poor consumer protection laws. 9. False. Cigarettes cause disability and death but their sale is not illegal. 10. False. More progressive companies do it.

Chapter 4. 1. True. 2. True. 3. True. 4. False. The most important is regaining the public trust. 5. False. 6. True. Research shows most companies are poor at implementation. 7. True. 8. False. It now features on most business degree programmes. 9. True. Remember Enron. 10. True.

Chapter 5. 1. True. 2. True. Remember Arthur Andersen. 3. True. 4. True. 5. False. Best practice says they should. 6. True. 7. True. 8. True. 9. True. 10. True.

Chapter 6. 1. True. 2. False but it is unethical. 3. True according to one survey taken. 4. False. Frauds are usually detected through tips from employees, customers, suppliers and anonymous sources. 5. True. 6. False. You are stealing from your employer. 7. True. The FBI maintains that cyber crime represents the most fundamental challenge for law enforcement in the 21st century. 8. False. In fact it is more likely to be repeated. 9. True. A Management Today survey found that 40 per cent of managers wouldn't report fraud. 10. True.

Chapter 7. 1. False. It is both illegal and unethical. 2. True. 3. False but it may be unethical. 4. True. 5. True. 6. True. 7. True but it may be unethical. 8. False. Bribery is never acceptable. 9. True. 10. False.

Chapter 8. 1. True. 2. False. It is unethical and illegal. 3. True. 4. True. 5. False. But it may be unethical. 6. False. But it may be unethical. 7. True. 8. True. 9. False. Everybody should be responsible for ethical conduct in the company. 10. True. Ethical dilemmas are a feature of business life.

Chapter 9. 1. True. 2. True. 3. False. 4. False. 5. True. The jury is still out. 6. False. 7. True. 8. True. 9. True. The more progressive do. 10. True.

Chapter 10. 1. True. 2. True. 3. True. 4. False. 5. True. 6. True. However, some would maintain that it is no worse than other vocations. 7. False. The opposite was the case. 8. True. Many would consider the whole idea of cosmetic surgery exploits vanity, is unnecessary, and therefore unethical. 9. True. 10. False.

Chapter 11. 1. False. They should also act in the interests of stakeholders generally. 2. True. 3. False. Best practice suggests they should. 4. True. 5. False. Best practice is that they should be separate. 6. True. 7. True. This is now considered best practice. 8. True. 9. True. 10. False. It should consist of at least three members and meet about four times a year.

Chapter 12. 1. False. 2. False. They tend to practice spin. 3. True. 4. True. This is supported by research. 5. True. 6. False. 7. True. 8. True. 9. False. More regulation brings more paperwork. 10. True. Think about the accountancy profession and the banks.

References and Bibliography

Ahmed, Kamal. 2003. Airlines 'must clean up if they want to expand'. Observer, Sunday, December 14, 2003.

Agnew, Paddy. 2002. US Cardinals summoned to Rome over child abuse crisis, The Irish Times, 16/4/2002.

Akers, J.F. 1989. Ethics and competitiveness: Putting first things first. Sloan Management Review, Winter: 69-71

Armstrong, H.L. & Forde, P.J. 2003. Internet anonymity practices in computer crime, Information Management & Computer Security, Vol.11, No. 5, pp.209-215.

Arnold, Denis G. 2003. Exploitation And The Sweatshop Quandary, Business Ethics Quarterly, Vol. 13, Issue 2, pp.243-256.

Arnold, Denis G. & Bowie, Norman E. 2003. Sweatshops And Respect For Persons, Business Ethics Quarterly, Vol.13, Issue 2, pp.221-242.

Badaracco, J. 1992. Business ethics: Four spheres of executive responsibility. California Management Review, Vol.34, Part 3, pp.64-79.

Barnett, Antony. 2003. Revealed: how drug companies 'hoodwink' medical journals, Observer, Sunday, December 7, 2003.

Blair, Maria. 2004. The UN's role in corporate social responsibility, McKinsey Quarterly, Issue 4, p21.

Boseley, Sarah. 2003. Coroner calls for inquiry into Seroxat, Guardian, Thursday, March 13, 2003.

Boseley, Sarah. 2004. Doctor, no. Affairs between doctors and female patients are not uncommon but can be devastating, Guardian, Thursday, October 14, 2004.

BRC, 1999. Report and Recommendations of the Blue Ribbon Committee on improving the Effectiveness of Corporate Audit Committees., Blue Ribbon Committee, New York Stock Exchange and National Association of Securities Dealers, New York.

Brenner, Steven N & Melander, Earl A. January – February 1977. Is the Ethics of Business Changing? Harvard Business Review, Pages 57-71.

Brune, C. 2001. Managers Disregard Ethics, Internal Auditor, February 2001.

Carolan, Mary. 2003. Obstetrician critical of resources at hospital, The Irish Times, 4/9/2003.

Clark, Andrew. 2008. Browne speaks of Elton, elves and etiquette – but little of Texas City. The Guardian, Thursday, 24 June 2008

Clark, Andrew. 2008. Appeal courts say Black must remain in jail. The Guardian, Thursday, 26 June 2008

Clark, Dana L. (2002) The World Bank and Human Rights: The Need for Greater Accountability, Harvard Human Rights Journal, Vol. 15, Spring 2002.

Clarke, Margaret M. 2003. Corporate ethics programs make a difference, but not the only difference, HR Magazine, July 2003.

Connolly, John. 1998. An Irishman's Diary, The Irish Times, Friday, May 15, 1998.

Cooper, Neville. 1989. Whats All This About Business Ethics? The Institute of Business Ethics. London.

Corporate Reputation Watch 2004 survey. Brand strategy, Nov. 2004.

Coulter, Carol. 2004. Legislation on judges' conduct required. The Irish Times, 29/4/2004.

Creaton, Siobhain. 2004. AIB appears unscathed after recent scandal, The Irish Times, Friday, December 10, 2004.

De George, Richard T. 1990. Business Ethics, Macmillan Publishing Company. New York.

Dennis, Bryan, Neck, Christopher P & Goldsby, Michael. 1998. Body Shop International: an exploration of corporate social responsibility, Management Decision, Vol.36, No.10, pp.649-653.

Dhillon, Gurpreet, 1999. Managing and controlling computer misuse, Information Management & Computer Security, Vol.7, Number 4, pp. 171-175.

Doost, Roger K. 2003. Enron, Arthur Anderson and the Catholic Church: are these symptoms of a more chronic problem? Managerial Auditing Journal, Vol.18, No.8, pp.673-681,

Dravesky, Ray. 2004. Ethical Misconduct at Adelphia Requires New Leadership and Rebuilding, Communication World, Nov/Dec 2004, Vol.21, Issue 6, p38.

Dreher, Rod. 2002. Sins of the Fathers: Pedophile priests and the challenge to the American Church, National Review, Feb 11, 2002.

Emiliani, M. L. 2000. The oath of management, Management Decision, Vol.38, No. 4, pp.261-262.

Ferrell, O.C, Fraedrich, John, & Ferrell, Linda. 2002. Business Ethics Ethical Decision-making and Cases. Houghton Mifflin Company, Boston.

Foster, Malcolm. 2004. Reebok gets thumbs up from anti-sweatshop group, Associated Press, Friday, May 1, 2004.

Frankental, Peter, 2001. Corporate social responsibility – a PR invention? Corporate Communications: An International Journal, Vol.6, No.1, pp.18-23.

Friedman, Hershey H. 2004. Creating a Company Code of Ethics: Using the Bible as a Guide, Electronic Journal of Business Ethics and Organisation Studies. Vol. 9, No.2, 23/10/2004.

Gates, Jacquelyn, B. 2004. The Ethics Commitment Process: Sustainability Through Value-Based Ethics, Business and Strategy Review, 109:4 pp493-505.

Geller, Adam. 2003. Monitoring group backed by marketers find workplace abuses in overseas plants, Associated Press, June 4, 2003.

Gellerman, Saul, W. 1986. Why 'Good' Managers Make Bad Ethical Choices, Harvard Business Review, July/August 1986.

Gunther, Marc. 2004. Money and Morals at GE, Fortune (Europe), 11/5/2004, Vol.150, Issue 9, P64.

Hoffman, Michael W, Lange Anne E, & Fedo, David A. 1986. Ethics and the multinational purpose, Pages 306-307, University Press of America, Inc. Lanham.

Houston, Muiris Dr. 2004. Doctors and drug firms....an unhealthy alliance, Irish Times, 6/4/2004.

Houston, Muiris Dr. 2003. Power in the wrong hands? The Irish Times, 2/8/2003.

Johnson, Lewis D & Neave, Edwin, D. 2008. The subprime mortgage market: familiar lessons in a new context. Management Research News, Vol. 31, No.1.

Kaiser, Charles. 2002. Disturbing behaviour – last word – Catholic Church sex abuse scandal, The Advocate, May 28, 2002.

Keegan, Victor. 2004. Bitter taste to EU's sugar policy, Guardian, Friday, June 25, 2004.

Kelleher, Denis. 2000. Cracking down on the hack-pack, Irish Times, Monday, October 23, 2000.

King, Tim. 2004. Forgeries of euro notes and coins rising dramatically, The Irish Times, 23/1/2004

Kirkup, James. 2008. MPs face official probe into expenses. Telegraph.co.uk. 21 July 2008.

Kirkup, James. 2008. MPs banned from employing children but spouses still acceptable. Telegraph.co.uk. 5 August 2008.

Leung, Philomena, & Cooper, Barry J, 2003. The Mad Hatter's corporate tea party, Managerial Auditing Journal, Vol.18, No.6/7, pp.505-516

Lewis, Philip V. 1985. Defining 'Business Ethics: Like Nailing Jello to a Wall. Journal of Business Ethics, Volume 4, Pages 377-383.

Macalister, Terry. 2003. Minister tells BAT to quit Burma, Guardian, Thursday, July 3, 2003.

Macalister, Terry. 2004. Shell hit by US legal action, Guardian, Tuesday, January 27, 2004.

Maitland, Ian. 2002. Priceless Goods: How Should Life-Saving Drugs be Priced? Business Ethics Quarterly, Vol.12, Issue, 4, pp.451-480.

Maslow, A.H. 1970. Motivation and personality (2nd edition), New York, Harper and Row.

McCaffrey, Una. 2004. A history of ethical failure in Ireland's banking system, The Irish Times, 7/5/2004.

McDougall, Dan. 2008. The hidden face of Primark fashion. The Observer, Sunday, 22 June 2008.

Moon, Chris. 1989. Green Bills or Proud Coins – Can Business Ethics Resolve the Dilemma? Management Education & Development, Volume 20, Part 3, Pages 143-152.

Moorhead, Gregory & Griffin, Ricky W. 1998. Organisational Behaviour, Houghton Mifflin Company, Boston.

Near, Janet P., Rehag, Michael T., Van Scotter, James R., & Miceli, Marcia P. 2004. Does Type Of Wrongdoing Affect The Whisteblowing Process, Business Ethics Quarterly, Vol. 14, Issue 2, pp.219-242.

Omestad, Thomas. 2004. A Spotlight On The Consummate Insider, U.S. News & World Report, 13/9/2004, Vol. 137, Issue 8, p44

O'Clery, Conor. 2002. Abuse scandals put Catholic Church in US in cash and manpower crisis, The Irish Times, 13/4/2002

O'Halloran, Barry. 2005. Corporate crime costing €2.5bn. Irish Times, 17/6/2005

O'Rourke, Morgan. 2004. Fighting Fakes, Risk Management, Nov. 2004, Vol.51, Issue 11, p9.

O'Toole, Fintan. 2004. A culture of total impunity. The Irish Times, 1/6/2004.

Pace, Larry, A. 2004. The Ethical Implications of Quality, Electronic Journal of Business Ethics and Organisational Studies, Vol. 9, No. 2. 24/10/2004

Paine, Lynn, Sharp. 1994. Managing for Organisational Integrity, Harvard Business Review, March/April 1994.

Pallister, David. 2007. 500,000 Chinese-made toys recalled over date-rape drug link. The Guardian, Saturday 10 November 2007.

Personnel Today, 2002. Graduates drawn to ethically sound companies.

Peters, C., Branch, T. 1972. Whistleblowing: Dissent in the Public Interest, Praeger, New York.

Pilhofer, Aron & Williams, Bob. 2004. Big Oil Protects its Interests, Industry spends hundreds of millions on lobbying, elections, Washington, July 15, 2004, The Centre for Public Integrity. Special Report.

Pomeroy, Ann. 2004. Tarnished Employment Brands Affect Recruiting, HR Magazine, Nov. 2004, Vol.49, Issue 11, p16.

PwC (PricewaterhouseCooper) European Economic Crime Survey 2001. www.pwcglobal.com

Radin, Tara J. 2004. The Effectiveness of Global Codes of Conduct: Role Models That Make Sense, Business and Society Review, 109: 4, pp.415-447.

Raftery, Mary. 2005. Time to reassess Prozac use, The Irish Times, 6/1/05.

Raftery, Mary. 2004. Time to come clean with MRSA, The Irish Times, 2/12/2004.

Rezaee, Zabihollah, Olibe, Kingsley O. & Minmier, George. 2003. Improving corporate governance: the role of audit committee disclosures, Managerial Auditing Journal, Vol.18, No.6/7, pp.530-537.

Reville, Dr William. 1996. Piltdown Man hoax a sorry saga of science, The Irish Times, Monday, June 17, 1996.

Reville, Prof. William. 2003. Ways of detecting the art of forgery Under the Microscope, The Irish Times, 16/10/2003.

Romm, Joseph. 2008. Ignoring the climate change alarm. Guardian.co.uk. Wednesday, 9 July 2008.

Salierno, D. 2004. Ethics survey offers mixed messages, Internal Auditor, June 2004.

Sample, Ian. 2004. Why GM-free UK is popular but unfeasible, Guardian, Thursday, Febuary, 19, 2004.

Scally, Derek. 2003. The secret diaries of a Nazi dictator, aged 511/2, The Irish Times, 26/4/2003

Schlegelmilch, Bodo B. 2001. Marketing Ethics: An International Perspective, Thomsom Learning, London.

Scott, Elizabeth, D. 2002. Organisational Moral Values, Business Ethics Quarterly, Vol.12, Issue 1.

Seymour, Dan. 2008. America's Rogue Trader Scandal. ABC News, 29 February 2008.

Shea, Gordon T. 1988. Practical Ethics, American Management Association. New York.

Sherwin, Nuland, B. 2004. The Death of Hippocrates, New Republic, Vol.231, Issue 11/12, p.31. 13/9/2004

Smith, Ian. 2004. Why GM-free UK is popular but unfeasible, Guardian, Thursday, February, 19, 2004.

Spooner, Peter. 1992. The Changing Face of Corporate Responsibility, Annual Review of International Management Practice, Pages 400-402, Management Centre, Brussels, Europe.

Stainer, Alan & Stainer, Lorice. 1999. Ethical dimensions of environmental management, European Business Review, Vol.97, No.5, pp.224-230

Steiner, George A. 1971. Business & Society, Random House Inc., Toronto.

Stewart, Elizabeth. 2008. Remains of five children found at Jersey care home. Guardian.co.uk. Thursday, 31 July 2008.

Suiter, Jane. 1999. Churning report urges vigilance, The Irish Times, Friday, February 5, 1999.

Traynor, Ian. 2004. Austrian Church in further sex scandal, The Irish Times, 13/7/2004.

Treanor, Jill. 2003. BCCI settlement costs top $1.2 billion, Guardian, Thursday, May 15, 2003.

Trevino, Linda K & Nelson, Katherine A. 2004. Managing Business Ethics Straight Talk About How To Do It Right, John Wiley & Sons Inc. USA

Verschoor, Curtis C. 2004. CEOs Set Ethics Priorities; Ordinary Citizens Define Ethics Broadly, Strategic Finance, Nov.2004, Vol.86, Issue 5, p17.

Vinten, Gerald. 2000. Whisteblowing towards disaster prevention and management. Disaster Prevention and Management, Vol. 9, No.1, pp.18-28.

Vinten, Gerald. 2004. Whisteblowing: the UK experience. Part 2. Management Decision, Vol. 42, No. 1, pp.139-151.

Vogel, David. 1992. The Globalisation of business ethics, California Management Review, Vol.35, Part, 1, pp.30-49.

Walton, Mary. 1986. The Deming Management Method, Putnam, New York.

Waterfield, Bruno. 2008. Second Tory MEP Den Dover loses position over expenses. Telegraph.co.uk. 7 June 2008.

Weber, James. 1990. Measuring the Impact of Teaching Ethics to Future Managers: A Review, Assessment and Recommendations, Journal of Business Ethics, Vol.9, Pages 183-190.

Weber, James & Getz, Kathleen. 2004. Buy Bribes Or Bye-Bye Bribes: The Future Status Of Bribery In International Commerce, Business Ethics Quarterly, Vol.14, Issue 4, pp.695-711.

Weber, Leonard J. 2002. Protecting Public Health And The Environment: Business Ethics And Responsibility, Business Ethics Quarterly, Vol. 12, Issue 3, pp. 547-554.

Webley, Simon. 1988. Company Philosophies and Codes of Business Ethics, Institute of Business Ethics. London

Westhead, Rick. 2004. Hollinger board amends ethics code, Toronto Star, December 4, 2004.

Winstanley, D & Stuart-Smith, K. 1996. Policing performance: the ethics of performance management, Personnel Review, Summer, pp.66-84

Useful Internet Sites for Business Ethics

www.corporatewatch.org.uk
www.ethicalconsumer.org
www.guardian.co.uk
www.cbgnet.org
www.business-ethics.org
www.oecd.org
www.scu.edu
www.transparency.org
www.globalchange.com
www.stopesso.com
www.eia-international.org
www.environment-agency.gov.uk
www.tridos.co.uk
www.findarticles.com
www.gallup.com
www.ethicaltrade.org
www.ireland.com
www.publicintegrity.org
www.fairlabor.org
www.cepaa.org
www.law.harvard.edu
www.cauxroundtable.org
www.ethics.org

Index

Accounting, 175
Adelphi Communications, 117
Adidas, 227
Advance Pitstop, 183
Advertising, misleading, 147
Agnew, Paddy, 218
Agriculture, 134
Ahmed, Kamal, 189
Air pollution, 189
Airline industry, 109
Akers, John, 18
Alcoa, 225
Allen, Timothy, 127
Allfirst, 151
Allied Irish Bank (AIB), 103, 151,
    154, 259
Amnesty International, 167
Anderson, Warren, 202
Animal rights, 42
Ansbacher scandal, 102
Archer, Jeffrey, 206
Argos, 133
Armstrong, H.L., 125
Arnold, Denis, 226
Arnold, Denis et al, 61, 157, 168,
    177, 224, 225
Art scams, 113
Arthur Andersen, 107, 110, 128
Asbestos, 66
Association of Certified Fraud
    Examiners (ACFE), 122
Auditors, 237
Audits, 239

Bacardi, 133
Badaracco, J., 40
Bait and switch, 139
Bank of Credit and Commerce
    International (BCCI), 164
Banking, 135
Barings, 150
Barnett, Antony, 213
BASF, 89
Bayer, 43, 143, 187
Beech-Nut Nutrition Corporation,
    148
Beef Tribunal, 103
Ben & Jerry, 57
Bevan, Dr Keith, 212

Bhopal, 202
Bildman, Lars, 92
Black, Conrad, 92
Blair, Maria, 54
Blodget, Henry, 155
Blue Ribbon Committee, 241
Blunkett, David, 206
Body Shop, 42, 57
Bollard, John, 217
Bord na Mona, 197
Boseley, Sarah, 143, 212
Boycotts, 44
BPB, 133
Brenner, Steven, 179
Brent Spar, 56
Bribery, 159
Bristol Royal Infirmary, 85, 211
British American Tobacco (BAT), 58,
    106
British Biotech, 85
British Nuclear Fuels (BNF), 192
British Telecom, 197
Brown & Williamson Tobacco
    Company, 83
Browne, Lord, 110
Brune, C., 123
Burke, Ray, 104
Business Roundtable Institute for
    Corporate Ethics, 75
Buy one, get one free, 139

Cadbury report, 235
Capitalising expenses, 39
Carolan, Mary, 209
Casey, Bishop Eamonn, 218
Challenger disaster, 86
Chaudron, Yves, 114
Cheating, exams, 108
Chemical industry, 59
Chichester, Giles, 169
Child labour, 226
Chinese Wall, 155
Chiquita, 55
Church scandals, 216
Churning, 156
Clark, Andrew, 93, 110
Clark, Dana, 198
Clarke, Margaret, 77
Cleary, Father Michael, 219